A LONG RETREAT

A LONG RETREAT

In Search of a Religious Life

ANDREW KRIVAK

Farrar, Straus and Giroux / New York

Farrar, Straus and Giroux
18 West 18th Street, New York 10011

Distributed in Canada by Douglas & McIntyre Ltd.
Printed in the United States of America
First edition, 2008

Library of Congress Cataloging-in-Publication Data
Krivak, Andrew.
    A long retreat : in search of a religious life / Andrew Krivak.
        p.   cm.
    ISBN-13: 978-0-374-16606-9 (hardcover : alk. paper)
    ISBN-10: 0-374-16606-4 (hardcover : alk. paper)
    1. Krivak, Andrew.   2. Catholics—Biography.   3. Jesuits—Biography.
4. Spirituality—Catholic Church.   I. Title.

BX4705.K75115A3 2008
271'.5302—dc22
[B]

                                                            2007005102

Designed by Jonathan D. Lippincott

www.fsgbooks.com

1   3   5   7   9   10   8   6   4   2
3 8835 1001 6822 3

To Amelia and Cole

Late have I loved you, beauty so old and so new:
late have I loved you.

—St. Augustine, *Confessions*

It will be neither a return nor a departure but a continuing.

—John McGahern, *The Leavetaking*

AUTHOR'S NOTE

This is a work of nonfiction. Some names and details of places have been changed to protect the privacy of certain persons, but I have otherwise sought to describe characters and events as they were. For these I've relied on letters, journals I kept as a Jesuit, and memory. When I had to question one or all three of these, I went back to my brothers, blood and spiritual both. Apart from who watched a fast creek and cheap raft collide one Saturday of Easter weekend a long time ago, and whether or not it really did snow in Syracuse on Christmas Eve 1990 (it always seemed to be snowing), those I've asked for corroboration have corrected or otherwise found little fault with this retelling. What mistakes remain are mine.

A LONG RETREAT

PROLOGUE

L et me begin with an ending not yet my own.

The two or so December days during which my family waked and buried my father after his sudden death at the age of eighty moved in a kind of brume that shortened sight and left memory behind. But after the prayer of committal, as we and an entire community of mourners were all about to leave the church, I heard the few spoken words that gave me some peace in the last quiet moments of that Mass for the dead. Father Peter Crynes, the priest my father in his old age had come to know and trust, one in a long line of priests who labored as good pastors in the vineyard we knew as St. Therese's, rested his fingertips on the coffin's lacquered pine surface and whispered as though only the departed should hear: "Well done, good and faithful servant."

Rain held off until the interment. Then, while we were gathered for lunch inside a windowless dining room of an American Legion hall in the old mining town of Luzerne (the only venue unoccupied on such short notice in the Christmas season), the skies let loose in a torrent that pounded like fists on the roof.

My wife Amelia and I rode back to my mother's house with my younger brother Matthew, and as we drove through the downpour and into the Back Mountain toward the town of Dallas, Pennsylvania, where we grew up, he broke the silence, wondering out loud in a moment more of anger than of introspection if in fact there *was* a Heaven, some life after death. Or if there was, in spite of what our father and mother had taught us and believed in themselves, nothing.

Of my three brothers and three sisters, he lived the closest to my parents, after having moved back to "the Area," as everyone called this part of Northeastern Pennsylvania, from Iowa a few years earlier. The two fathers of sons seemed to hit it off all over again, and I think that when the old boy died, my younger brother lost a friend. So I considered what arguments I could and could not give from philosophers and theologians Matthew had never read, but to whom I had turned when it was my time to leave home. I remembered that in years past he used to smile, clasp my shoulder, and say "Hey, Padre!" whenever we met. I believed on that day, as St. Paul told the earliest Christians, that our homeland is in heaven and our lives are a kind of waiting, our death only the appearance of an end. *Behold, I tell you a mystery. We will not all sleep, but we will all be changed.*

I said, "Is there a Heaven? I hope so. More than that I just don't know."

He nodded, disappointed with my answer, I thought; then realized that this was what he expected from the brother who had read and traveled more than he but who had no house, or car, or occupation that he could point to. What did he want me to say? *("This I know!")* "Well, I think there's nothing," he said, accelerated around the slower traffic, and put an end to the conversation.

Absence is an equable and yet vertiginous state. Sit calmly at a distance and it appears yet another fact of existence, a thing to touch and say, "Yes, this is so." But stand to approach, or rather to face it approaching, and the calm shatters into dizziness, weakness, and tears so unexpected that you cannot be certain you won't somehow drop or fall inexplicably if you take a single step—the characteristics, not coincidentally, of a deep, if not unshakable, faith. We did the best we could that day as a family in name to cohere around the edges of what my father had occupied with his blithe yet booming presence and then so uncharacteristically left. Until it was time for each of us to leave. After three days, in spite of the chasm between what one might and what one might not discover beyond, we had to get on with our lives. We had to continue with our work, wives, husbands, children for some, and now the one thing we all held in common: loss.

My mother sat me down as I was packing and asked me if there was anything of my father's that I might like to have as a remembrance. My brothers owned property and worked with their hands for a living, so they took the tools and saws and machinery that were scattered about the basement workshop of the small, three-bedroom ranch my parents had lived in for fifty years. There was a plane to catch and an ocean to cross. A tiny, pearl-handled pocketknife gleamed among the effects she had spread out before me. I remember seeing it and wanting it as a boy when I became aware one day that I had grown tall enough to peer into that seemingly gigantic man's high, wooden dresser. I plucked the knife from the offering of watch, fountain pen, religious medals, and cuff links. "Yes, take that," she said, understanding, I believed, the significance of such an insignificant piece. What else was there that my father hadn't already given to me? When I wanted to drop out of college, work on boats, and travel around the world (my first vague notion of retreat), he said, "There won't be anything when I'm gone. So take the education I'm offering now, will ya?" And I did.

Amelia and I were returning to London on an open jaw out of Boston. It would be a long shot through the Poconos, across the Delaware, and into New England, so I suggested we drive to Syracuse for the evening, stay at an inn on Lake Cazenovia, and take the Thruway to Massachusetts the next day. I wasn't being romantic. Snow was forecast for the entire East, and the emotional weight that came with death had ground me down to exhaustion. I felt as though I had been awake for three days. That lake—a place I used to go to rest in another life—was the only place I knew where I could stop, lie down, and sleep. Maybe, though, in the back of my mind, I knew what I was doing coming this way one more time.

When we got to Syracuse, I recognized immediately our proximity to the Jesuit novitiate of St. Andrew's, a house in which I lived for two of the eight years I spent in training for the Catholic priesthood with the Society of Jesus. Its presence was compelling. Unavoidable, I have to say, as unavoidable as on the day my mother and father drove me there in August 1990—after I had graduated from college and graduate school, and worked for two years—to begin the life they thought I would live to its natural conclusion.

I said to Amelia, "Let's go up the hill to St. Andrew's." She looked puzzled, but not because she didn't know this was, in a sense, where it all began. She knew my story better than anyone and had witnessed the final few chapters in a different place, from her own vantage point in my life. No, she was puzzled because she was worried about me, not knowing if this return was the direction in which I should now go. But I insisted. "I want to see if anything's changed."

From Salt Springs Road and across the field by St. Mary's dormitory of Le Moyne College, I saw again in complete detail the house I once associated with the entrance into religious life. A redbrick and sandstone manse built in the 1950s with a gabled front and boxy sides, it looked more like the home of some austere and eccentric businessman from Upstate New York who made his fortune in ball bearings or the disposable razor than like a Jesuit novitiate. Tucked into a sloping hill that seemed unsteady while remaining intact, the house had nothing overtly religious about it unless you knew what the barely discernible "IHS" symbol over the door meant.

The driveway was lined with cars. Priests or parents visiting, I thought, but dismissed the possibility. In December this should be no more than a house of young Jesuits with their minds and hearts set on where they would be going come January, when half would be sent into silence, the other half out into the world but not to be of it. I parked in an open space. Through the glass I could see someone whose face bore the look of the earnest walking toward us. He opened the side door by the kitchen, which I knew was the proper entrance; its metallic screech invited me in as a once-welcomed visitor, whose absence former inhabitants often wondered about on days when the weather made hot drinks and conversation the only possible, if not desirable, activities.

Amelia and I walked together through a short, darkened hall that led into the open house refectory. We shook hands with three curious yet hesitant young men who, after they heard why I was driving through Syracuse, expressed their deepest sympathies for my father and gratitude for my visit. I asked all of the appropriate questions: Is the novice master around? Are we disturbing a day of quiet? Are you busy getting ready for Christmas? They assured us that we had only caught them having coffee. We were welcome to join them for a cup.

"I think we'd like to go up to the chapel, sit for a short prayer, and then we'll leave you to your Saturday," I said finally.

"You won't be leaving us to much," the one who had answered the door said. The *secundi* (novices in their second year) were in a special conference. The *primi* (first-years, as these men were) had just finished their assigned housecleaning and were enjoying the quotidian lull.

In the small chapel—a tenebrous space we used to call "the womb"—I sat quietly and tried to summon words from prayers that had issued easily from my lips and heart the last time I sat here, almost fifteen years ago: prayers of the Divine Office, a Jesuit's Examination of Conscience, or sometimes the holy sigh of "Christ, what am I going to do?" uttered not in vain but in times of spiritual exhaustion. I looked up and watched Amelia circle the altar as though she had come to perform a reverential dance, and I fell in love with her all over again seeing her move with such grace in that place. Wanting to leave me to my own meditation, she walked to the back of the room to see the stained-glass-window portraits of the North American martyrs that let in what little light there was: Isaac Jogues, René Goupil, John de Lalande, and the young Mohawk woman, Kateri Tekakwitha. The three men were Jesuits who died far from their homelands and, as a result, were remembered for this. The Native American was proof that some of their labor paid off. "Saints," Amelia said, then with a sheepish smile whispered, "Sorry." But I smiled back, because it occurred to me that no one in that room, man or woman, living or dead, had anything to be sorry for.

After a few minutes I brought my short prayer for the peace of lives past and lives yet lived to a close and wanted to leave that house as decidedly as I had wanted to come. The *secundi* would be done with their meeting soon, priests I no doubt knew would be wandering into the kitchen for their own cups of coffee, and my short visit would turn into a long story, one I wasn't sure I wanted to tell that afternoon. Besides, I suspect those well-meaning first-year novices had given us the run of the place too quickly. Visitors to the novitiate weren't allowed upstairs unaccompanied in my day, regardless of whether or not they were former Jesuits who'd returned with their wives to say a prayer in the wake of a loved one's passing.

I remember sleeping well that night in our suite on the lake. Just before sunrise I stirred and took in the surroundings of the room: half-unpacked suitcases at the foot of the bed; yesterday's clothes draped over a chair; curtains drawn back and the window opened a crack for air; outside the black surface of water. In the half-light I had to remind myself of where I was, and then watched a familiar snowfall drift against the window and accumulate in tiny piles on the ledge. Slowly, the predawn silver began to distinguish itself from the white cover that lay everywhere around, and I thought, How beautiful it all is. Beauty so old and so new. Amelia, almost seven years my traveling companion and five years my wife, rolled in to me, heat and the hint of brine rising from beneath our comforter, and asked if anything was wrong. "No, nothing. Nothing at all." I kissed her and said, "Go back to sleep."

We went to Mass at St. James's in Cazenovia among a thin crowd of locals that morning. I prayed for my father and asked him to pray for us, because I believe that the communion of saints is capable of such a thing. Afterward we ate a breakfast of French toast and eggs at a diner on Albany Street. And there I thought of the novices at St. Andrew's, who I knew would be shoveling snow and then going to Mass themselves. I had done as much in the work and prayer of Jesuit life, a life that each man who entered by that door began out of some unspoken desire to search for God and the self, regardless of how early or late he had come to that desire. I didn't wonder which novice's story would be like mine. Each one's and no one's. That day, I just hoped that the men we met would sooner or later find themselves changed.

Outside, the squall tapering, skies clearing, Amelia and I got into our rental car and continued east on the next leg of our journey.

PART I

By experience we have learned that the path has many and great difficulties connected with it. Consequently we have judged it opportune to decree that no one should be permitted to pronounce his profession in this Society unless his life and doctrine have been probed by long and exacting tests.

—from *The Formula of the Institute of the Society of Jesus*

ven now my memory is never far from a composition of that time and place. Saturday, the twenty-fifth of August, the skies—at least for an hour or two—a rare blue, with a nudging breeze on which wafts the brewed-tea smell of an early autumn. The sun feels warm but weakening. Inside a high-ceilinged, stained-glass-lit modern sanctum of the Jesuit Residence on the campus of Le Moyne College in Syracuse (the chapel of St. Andrew's novitiate too small to host everyone), the air is conditioned slightly toward a chill. A staggered collection of thirteen young men dressed in khakis, polo shirts, and button-downs sit in a semicircle of chairs in front of the simple altar adorned with a white cloth. To five of the men belongs a smaller cadre of parents. A few middle-aged priests dressed in their own street clothes sweep into the room through swinging doors and join the company of worshipers. Another priest, wearing on this day a white stole of the liturgical celebrant, sits in a larger chair facing this congregation and stands when everyone has settled. "Welcome," he says.

An entrance hymn is held up on the confident voices of those who are at home here. The penitential rite at the beginning of the Mass feels, as it should, consoling. The readings are taken not from Sunday but from Saturday, the twentieth week in Ordinary Time, the Gospel for which is Matthew 23:1–12: "Whoever exalts himself will be humbled. Whoever humbles himself will be exalted." And then, Father Don Gannon, SJ, Master of Novices in the New York Province of the Society of Jesus, waits as we all sit back down again to begin speaking to us as a tribal father might to his many sons, we who have gathered to begin religious life as Jesuits at a time when a first-year class of five is considered a respectable number of vocations (the eight remaining in the second year suggests something of a boon). Having seen them come and having seen them go for nearly six years as superior of a house of formation, Father Gannon—in the unshakable attitude of the forgiven—says, "Some of you will leave this community after having joined it today."

He means this to be neither insight into a betrayal nor a taunt, but a fact of religious life, in the present and of the past, for the earliest Jesuits knew this, too, in sixteenth-century Spain, France, and Portugal. I watch some of the mothers shift in their seats and fidget slightly, perhaps conscious for the first time that the odds are against their sons ever being ordained priests, regardless of how hard they have prayed. And I realize myself that, after having arrived in Syracuse this morning on emotional autopilot, not knowing how to respond to the enormity of this day, I suddenly feel as though a challenge has been thrown down before me. "One year ago, odds were I wouldn't have made it this far," an internal voice responds, as though wanting to vent its own tough, screw-the-odds-I'm-staying attempt to pray. Then, as if he can hear a fuguelike variation of that same prayer in each one of our heads, Father Gannon goes on to insist that the work of the Jesuit novitiate is to allow both the novice and the Society of Jesus to make a deeper discernment about the man and the men who surround him. Should the novice stay and take vows to remain in the Order, it doesn't indicate spiritual success, for the journey that is religious life then becomes the journey of a lifetime, bringing with it failures beyond the imagination, yet those to which each one of us has been called by God. Should the novice leave and go back out into the world, it doesn't mean he has failed. A lifetime of journeys remains there, too. "He's still called to discernment and discipleship," Father Gannon says. "And who knows? That may mean a more difficult path."

"He." Not "you." Not me. But surely one—if not all—of us. Who then? I wondered, as I looked around at the other men who had traveled from New York, Pennsylvania, and New Jersey to gather in that place on that morning. If not me, who?

Chris Bellito was the most energetic and talkative of our class. He was from the Bronx, the North Bronx, and had been teaching history at a Catholic high school there. He was short, with dark, tufty hair and a beard. He wore wire-rimmed glasses and drew attention to the obvious fact that he was Italian, at times dropping into a *Goodfellas* accent for humor, appearing sure of himself, almost fearless.

"So you're Andrew," he'd said to me as we lingered in the novitiate refectory that morning, before we walked over to Le Moyne for Mass. "I read your bio. You spent the entire summer sailing?"

I had forgotten about the short personal blurbs that had been printed in the Jesuits' *Company* magazine along with the photographs of all the new novices in the American Assistancy. I'd read the ones on the guys from New York, but I resisted memorization. "I was helping out on a boat delivery from the Bahamas to Cape Cod."

"Delivering, like, on what? The ocean or a tractor trailer?"

"On the ocean. Eight days, sometimes a hundred miles out."

"Whoa! I'd get sick or go crazy."

I smiled. "Or both." I admired him, but there was something as well that made me resentful of his ease. You could be fearless and still be scared, like Faulkner's young man in *The Bear*.

When at some point I broke off from that conversation, Frank Evans stepped away from the group he was in, walked up to me, and said in a conspirational tone, "I don't know about you, but I can only take so much of these family gatherings before I'll do anything for a beer. *Jee*-zus *Christ!*" He started laughing as though both of us had been watching the entire day from a separate vantage point, and I started laughing with him from sheer relief—and disbelief—at his lack of piety.

Frank was a tough, barrel-chested guy from Upper Montclair, New Jersey, who had that rare quality of always being able to summon respectful satire. It wasn't a mask so much as a criterion, for behind the humor and the healthy irreverence (I would discover in time), he maintained a deep faith and a desire to express it. He had gone to

Boston College and worked as a consultant in Manhattan, giving up a real career to join the Jesuits. His father had driven him to the novitiate that morning; his mother had died sometime in the recent past.

"All right," he said. "I'll be good. Let's go see what the guy who won't shut up is all about."

Frank meant Billy McGuinness, another one of us who stood close by our more sociable parents as though protecting them, or they us. Billy was an elevator repairman from Oceanside, Long Island. He had entered not to become a priest but to be a brother, a man who takes vows in the Society of Jesus but chooses not to get ordained. A Jesuit brother's vocation is described as sharing "in the same religious commitment" as the priest's, one complementing the other, each serving the Church. In the past that meant they took their vows and got to work without any further education. These days they were artists and physicists with Ph.D.'s. They taught in schools, *after* they built them. At the time, though—brother or priest—it all seemed the same to me. I had heard that Billy was next to the youngest in our class, and that he had chosen not to go to college. At twenty-one, he had the stolid look of a man who knew physical work more intimately than he knew books or leisure.

David McCallum, the youngest by a few months, was mingling with the second-year novices, whom he clearly already knew. David was from Rochester and had just graduated from Le Moyne. Two priests teaching in the English Department there had inspired him to think about life in the Order, and so he'd made his way across the street enough times in his last two years of college to see what went on at St. Andrew's. It was clear from the start that the spiritual knight-errantry of St. Ignatius of Loyola, and all of his followers since, appealed to David's romantic and literary side. But he entered, he told me later, out of a desire for a spiritual freedom he couldn't define. David was on the universal path of that ancient struggle to "Know Thyself." We all were, I suppose, but David's path was being paved by adversity. His decision to enter the Jesuits had not gone over well with his parents. He and his sister were their only children. Priesthood meant the family name would stop with their son—outgoing, intelligent, attractive with his Roman nose and slate eyes . . . and celibate.

They loved the Jesuits they had met at Le Moyne, but you could see the awkwardness and disappointment on their faces that day. It said enough: let some other mother's son do it.

How can you place odds on a first impression of lives like these? And was I so sure I wouldn't be the first one to come and go from here, once the reality of this adventure emerged and the ideal I had fomented in my imagination wore off? In some ways it was a move lucid and right, as though I had returned home after a long time away. And yet, I also couldn't shake the sense of being disoriented because I had decided to give up the idea of *home* for the rest of my life. Maybe the two were the same. I thought of my own drive here with my parents that morning, through Wilkes-Barre and Scranton and up into the Endless Mountains region, passing the sign on Interstate 81 for the town of Great Bend, where the Susquehanna River makes a full 180-degree turn, retreats north, wanders west toward its confluence with the Chemung, then threads its way south and east again through a labyrinth of dense and reclusive forest until it arrives at the exact point to which it would have been drawn had it not been sent out into a wilderness. I could cross that bridge a hundred times in one day and still feel as though the river had tricked me into believing I was suddenly moving in a new direction while I traveled steadily in the same.

I wasn't driving, though. My father was. It's what he always did when we needed him, drive us from place to place, as though his vocation was to ferry others from one shore to another, then let them get on their way. At sixty-six, he was still a tall, handsome man with a sharp profile and a full shock of gray hair that over the years had passed from the look and texture of steel to cotton wool. Everybody loved Tom Krivak. Strong and exacting with his children, he was an ebullient and generous man toward anyone who considered him a friend. His father had died in a Wilkes-Barre coal mine at the age of thirty. He was three and so never knew what it was like to *feel* a father's commanding presence, a presence every single one of his seven children spent a lifetime under the aegis of. I loved him, too.

My mother, Irene, a petite woman with black hair and olive skin (perhaps giving away the presence of a distant outsider in the family

15

generations ago), began her habitual rosary as my father drove and I pondered my future that Saturday. She prayed not out of timidness or dread, and not because I was being delivered to a Catholic seminary, but out of her lifelong desire to transform everything she did into worship. No distractions, no noise, she craved a contemplative life that, like those of the desert saints, would never falter or cease. I often wondered how the ferryman and this mystic were partnered so well, but in the Greek of the Church Fathers, *eirene* means "peace," that thing for which every traveler and anchorite longs.

My mother's Marian devotion wasn't thoughtless piety. It was an invitation, as though a call or reminder all its own of what remained important in our family, in our world. Anyone present was expected to respond. I can hear the rising and falling recitation that my parents and I uttered together as we crossed the border into New York State at a steady sixty-five miles per hour. I had heard it moving along glass, wood, and stone beads my entire Catholic life: before daily Mass in the mornings; after dinner in the months of October and May; at penitential intervals during Lent; and on the lips of great-aunts and -uncles sitting in their sorrow at a loved one's wake. It's an atonal but heavily accented dactyl-like profession of faith in Christ and the Virgin, as Hail Marys and Our Fathers stress one word over the elision or silence of others—". . . who ART in heaven, HALLOWED be thy NAME . . ."—an articulation and silence that would keep this man and woman bound to each other, in the end, for fifty-three years. At the age of twenty-seven, though, I turned elsewhere for my vows, my own sacred union.

In 1986, after I graduated from the close and lettered world of St. John's College, Annapolis, I spent time as an ocean lifeguard, worked in boatyards, chipped away at a collection of poems, got accepted into a good graduate writing program, and went. I dated some interesting and attractive women and told them that I dreamed of sailing across the Atlantic and buying a house by the ocean. But a more fervid corner of my heart lay hidden, biding its time. I knew what I wanted to do. What I didn't know was how to go about it, whom to approach or where, though I trusted that these details would take care of themselves. Meanwhile, friends and classmates became bankers, lawyers, mathematicians, carpenters' wives.

Eventually the details fell into place and the path appeared as I had pictured it: a disciplined, prayerful, and intellectually engaging community that wanted me to be a part of it.

But once I began to say that I was going to become a priest, it came as a shock—sometimes humorous, sometimes cautious—to everyone I knew, even those who were Catholic. "A priest?" they'd say. "My God, what for!" "Father What-a-waste." "I thought you were smart." As we sat at the bar of old Cannon's Pub after a poetry workshop in our last semester as graduate students at Columbia, my friend Greg slid *Narcissus and Goldmund* across to me. "Read this," he said, in his habit of using as few words as possible (the book now among my favorites). The idea of becoming a priest—once as common-sounding to me growing up a Catholic in rural Pennsylvania as the idea of becoming a fireman or a truck driver—suddenly sounded more uncommon than I realized. Only from my family was there no resistance. What seemed initially like indifference among my brothers and sisters I realized later was their own insight into what kind of life I'd probably lead. "I'm not surprised" was the answer I received from each of them, not because they considered me a freak or a misfit but because they sensed that I had been searching for this the whole time. My parents, visibly pleased and yet respectful of my decision when I told them, seemed most of all to believe that I had chosen a path deserving and lasting. More important, I was doing something they could point to and be proud of, something that proved my intelligence and in some way offered more than I took from the world. "He's a *doer*" was the highest compliment my parents could pay a person. And I had finally decided what it was I wanted to do.

For my part, I believed that I had, after years of running, stopped resisting the Hound of Heaven and turned in a direction that was meant for me. It's hard to explain what goes through the mind of a young man when he feels as though he's being "called"—the prophetic voice that's supposed to single out God's ordained—to serve in this way, a Catholic male brought up to believe that priesthood is the noblest path a man can walk. *Poverty, chastity, and obedience?* So be it. Every life demands sacrifice. *What about freedom, or a sense of adventure for the sailor and ex-lifeguard?* What an adventure, a kind of exploratory team or Foreign Service for Christ. *Something countercultural, then, from the boy who wanted and yet refused to belong?* Could anyone have moved any further counterculturally in the late 1980s, when priests were being assassinated in El Salvador, monks decapitated in North Africa, and most Catholics had yet to line up politically with conservative Evangelicals? And of all the orders, I had chosen to join the Jesuits. Perhaps I should say that they chose me, but like the brag of the English martyr Edmund Campion before he was hung, drawn, and quartered during the reign of Queen Elizabeth I, I wanted to walk this path no matter what was required. Life—and death, should it come to that—would mean something for me and thereby, I hoped, for others. "The expense is reckoned," Campion said, "the enterprise is begun. It is of God; it cannot be withstood."

Does all this sound strange to you? Is it because the very mention of *priest* now evokes as much suspicion as respect? Someone might say about my Catholic boyhood's innocence, my love for the Church I grew up in, the priest I knew, "You got lucky." But I would call it grace, something given that I never deserved. From the time I made my First Holy Communion at the age of seven until I went away to college, I knew one man who wore the black cassock and white collar, and who guided the souls of both professional and working-class parishioners from within the graceful stone outline of St. Therese's: Father Joseph Sammons. I never thought about it then, but it gradually became clear to me that he held our parish together with something more than duty, something that strengthens faith and proves love, something that he alone understood and desired: the search for God every waking hour of the day through the holy dialectic of prayer and work. Once I could see this and understand it, I stopped wandering about and got started on that search for myself.

And so I have to confess that the mental game of *Who won't make it?* faded from my mind as quickly as it had risen on that first day of my life as a Jesuit and was replaced by this one, all-consuming virtue: Hope. Sure, there were other feelings and emotions swirling in my belly and behind my eyes in the heady and disorienting rush of the day, just as there were stretches when I never felt a thing (blank-masked-as-introspection an equally powerful defense against the fear of first days), but I remember *hope* most of all because I held out the hope that maybe we'd all stay. My entire class of five, that is. This was strongest in Mass at the sign of peace, when I embraced both my parents, and then went around the chapel to grasp the hands of Chris, Frank, Billy, and David. Then we all bowed our heads, regardless of what doubts or convictions remained inside, and prepared to receive the body of Christ, this mystical union that drew us now as companions toward a common purpose.

After Mass we walked back to St. Andrew's Hall along a path down the center of campus and across the field that led to Demong, up the driveway, and in through the kitchen door at the side of the house. There was a lunch set up in the sheltered backyard—burgers, hot dogs, plates of potato salad—and when it was over, Father Gerry Blaszczak, the august and gregarious assistant novice master who instilled trust in every mother there, told our parents it was time to go. Lingering by the cars, before announcing his own departure with a signature "Okay, Irene," my father grinned and put his arm around me. We were the same leggy six foot three, though he held more power in his chest and shoulders. Now I could feel in our embrace that he was getting old, not as strong as I would always remember him. He said, "Take care, Age," his name for me since I was a boy, from my initials, A.J. I told him that I would. My mother dissembled with a smile, and I saw the tears well in her eyes. "You're in our prayers," she said, something I would never doubt. Then they drove away, back to a place that I once called home and never would again.

W e called it "faith sharing." And for the first three days of novitiate, it was all we did.

There is a tradition for this kind of spiritual accounting within the Jesuits. Ignatius Loyola dictated his autobiography to Luis Gonçalves da Câmara when Jerónimo Nadal requested from the aging Ignatius "some admonition as a testament" that would show other Jesuits "the way to virtue." It was meant to be an exercise for the benefit of the teller and the listener, for both should come away asking, "What have I done? What ought I now to do?"

I was a voracious reader as a boy, so much so that I was often taunted at school with shouts of "Hey, bookworm!" I didn't care. Books were my map out of that small Pennsylvania town. I say this because, when my mother thrust a copy of Thomas Merton's *The Seven Storey Mountain* in front of me one day (I couldn't have been more than fourteen), I devoured it. And *that* life—a wanderer, a bad boy with a brain who in the end finds his place of belonging—became for me the ideal of what it meant to have a religious "calling." So I set my heart on becoming a monk.

That's no surprise to anyone who has read Merton. What young man who has come to the Trappist's final *Meditatio Pauperis in Solitudine* hasn't wished that he might find himself among those at Gethsemani "who have a thousand things to do. Some are busy with food, some with clothing, some with fixing the pipes, some with fixing the roof . . . One goes to the bees with a mask on and takes away their honey." The starkest and holiest work of the day and work of the hands there in the hills of Kentucky, until "the bell rings in the steeple," the work stops, and "all go to choir," where one thing makes the difference of their lives: prayer. "On the altar will be offered to God the eternal Sacrifice of the Christ to Whom we belong, and Who has brought us here together." This notion of a community in solitude, men stoking a silent yet ardent furnace of prayer and believing that their work could make a difference in the world, was what I yearned to find. What did I know of vocation directors, retreats, discernment, or grace? "Pray and you'll get there," my mother said to me after I had finished that big and unsettling book and expressed the practical and frustrating question of how one goes about becoming a monk.

Well, my mother was right, of course. But rarely, it seems, does the *why* of any prayer become the *how* we envision as an answer. The Novitiate of St. Andrew's, in which I now awoke and went to sleep as a religious, wasn't a monastery. We said Morning Prayer and Night Prayer as novices, but Jesuits aren't monks. The same Nadal who knew the mind of Ignatius, as John O'Malley writes in *The First Je-suits*, was clear about this from the start: " 'The world is our house.' Again and again Nadal reiterated the point. 'We are not monks . . . The world is our house.' " That truth was what turned me, so unexpectedly, from the search for an order of monks whose solitude would be mine to the work of the contemplative in action, as the Jesuits are known. But I'm getting ahead of myself. All of this belongs to the story I told my brothers of how I had come to be among them, and not left out in the desert. It was a story that had already taken on, in my mind at least (as I rehearsed over the few days I waited before it was my turn to "share"), the outlines of a conversion narrative. And by that I mean the unexpected directions in which we are thrust by grace.

Christmas Eve 1984, I was living in Santa Fe, New Mexico. It was my third year at St. John's College, a school steeped in the tradition of the Great Books, where we read Plato and Homer in Greek, translated line by line the French of Racine and Baudelaire, compared the

God of Kierkegaard and the God of Nietzsche, and puzzled over the faith of characters in Joyce and Dostoyevsky. Santa Fe was my year away from the school's eastern campus in Annapolis, and so, never having lived out West before, I decided to stay in town over the winter break, skiing in the daytime, busing tables at night, reading Willa Cather, Paul Bowles, and more Merton whenever I could. That evening the sun had just disappeared behind the Jemez Mountains when I left the house on Garcia Street for work at a restaurant called Fresco on the plaza. As I walked down Old Santa Fe Trail, I looked back out of habit at snow-covered Atalaya to the east and the rest of the Sangre de Christo Mountains, the last bit of light turning them a red that deepened slowly but visibly from scarlet into perse as they reflected the alpenglow.

On Sunday mornings in Santa Fe, I would hike down the empty arroyo that ran along the edge of the St. John's campus and go to Mass at the Carmelite monastery that sat in its own world of desert brush below the college. The sisters at St. Michael's were discalced and cloistered, praying in their choir stalls, where they remained hidden behind a wooden screen. An old priest from Missouri, Father Bakewell (a Jesuit, they said, which meant nothing to me at the time), said Mass for the sisters and those of us who entered the chapel from the outside. While the philosophical education with which I had been engaged for the past three years had challenged my adolescent understanding of faith and belief, it had also challenged me to seek deeper reasons to believe. We had read Augustine's *Confessions* as sophomores (along with the *Enneads* of Plotinus, Aquinas's *Summa Theologica,* the Old and New Testaments, and St. Paul's epistles, all as works essential to Western thought), and his own conversion narrative stood at a crossroads with me when I wondered what direction I should take as a Catholic. It was he, Augustine, who spoke this time: "With what end in view do you again and again walk along difficult and laborious paths?" Catholicism seemed more unexplored and unknown to me than unredeemable. And so I clung—yes, I will use that word *clung* because I don't believe weakness is a thing to be ashamed of when it is a matter of faith—to the Church in which I was raised, heard the voice of both mothers, "Pray and you'll get there," and continued in my own awkward and adolescent way to go to Mass out of a desire for those two competing Catholic needs: solitude and communion.

That's why when I was feeling more like I wanted to be a part of the kind of parish in which I grew up, I biked down Camino de la Luz to the Church of Cristo Rey, a traditional New Mexican parish on Upper Canyon Road. Even in that area of Santa Fe—art galleries, prime real estate, views of the Sangres—the look and feel of the church was working class. The congregation was predominantly Hispanic. The homilies of the old Castilian priest were never overtly philosophical or theological but rather plaintive. Act with love toward your neighbor, he or she is the person of Christ. If the choice to be a Christian is at heart a desire to live in peace, do so. It seemed to me an intensely private and insular community, but not from a lack of hospitality. That was the spirituality of the New Mexicans. Simply practical, deeply prayerful. They could swing from rifts over money and education to an intense and almost mystical expression of love and single-mindedness in their belief. Which made it seem to me like just another Catholic church. But rather than repel or at least stifle my newly sharpened sense of faith, it quickened me, and I began to go there for Mass on Sundays more often than the Carmelite cloister.

The week before Christmas in Santa Fe, work at the restaurant was busy. In one night I made my rent, in another enough to pay for a semester's worth of books. And I wasn't waitstaff. December 24, though, the tourists and the locals all seemed to have stayed inside. By 11:00 that night we were nearly empty. I reset the tables, stocked what they'd need for the next day, and asked the manager if I could leave for Midnight Mass. He looked at me as though I had asked him in Arabic if he knew the way through the Empty Quarter. Then he shrugged and said, "Make sure you punch out."

One of the waiters gave me a ride up Canyon Road. The surrounding neighborhood and the grounds of Cristo Rey were outlined in and lit up with low, ghostly columns of *farolitos*, candles burning in white bags weighted down with sand. The smell of piñon smoke was stronger here, and with that scent came the feeling of being welcomed by this community to celebrate with them God among us.

Inside the church, lights blazed and the pews overflowed with parents, children, aunts, uncles, grandparents. The men wore dark suits and shirts drawn closed at the neck with turquoise bolo ties. Younger women wore plain, linen dresses, not wanting to draw attention away from the pair of earrings, bracelet, or new necklace they had been given to wear that evening. Mothers were dressed nearly identically, blouses bleached white, embroidered with varicolored patterns or dyed a scarlet red, their skirts black or something close to the colors of the sunset. Some wore as veils the traditional *rebozos*. My head swirled. I felt barely presentable at this feast wearing the sweaty white shirt and food-stained pants I had worked in all night, but the sense and then knowledge that I was among family here, two thousand miles away from where the good people of St. Therese's were celebrating Christmas, prevailed, and my brief desire to flee dissipated.

As I stood at the back of the church one minute before twelve, an old woman moved to make room for me in the last pew. The music began and readers, altar boys, and priests proceeded past us down the aisle. She smiled, and I whispered *"Gracias."*

We sat down for the first reading. I slumped a bit out of exhaustion. She patted me on the knee as if to say, "I know, I know." Then the lector pronounced, "A reading from the Book of Isaiah . . ."

When I awoke, the old woman, against whose shoulder I had fallen asleep, was rising to go up for Communion. There were almost as many people standing now as there were sitting, everyone singing along with the *guitarristas* . . . *"Junto a ti, buscaré otro mar . . . ,"* moving in the old wood and adobe church like a single body as they walked forward, bowed their heads, ate, crossed themselves, walked back, and prayed in ways visible and invisible, one after another. *"Ven, hijo,"* the *abuela* said to me. *"Ya es hora."* Dazed, self-conscious, and a little embarrassed that I had fallen asleep like a child, I stood and followed her into line.

But it wasn't time to go. Not there, not then. At least not yet.

A few months later, in the spring of that year, I went to the Monastery of Christ in the Desert in Abiquiu, New Mexico, with a group of students for the Easter Vigil Mass at sunrise. I had heard of this pilgrimage. Every year a busload of "Johnnies" made it, and I didn't want to leave Santa Fe without having seen something of this Christ in the Desert. I believed that the monastic life was a pinnacle to which I might be led.

After driving for hours through northwestern New Mexico in the dark, our bus made a left onto a dirt road and inched thirteen miles along the edge of the Chama Canyon to where a small community of Benedictine monks worked and prayed in the spirit of the earliest Christians who had retreated from the cities into the Egyptian desert. When the bus driver came to a stop, killed the lights, and shut off the engine, it was impossible to say if we were anywhere other than on the side of a road in the dark. There was no moon. We filed out and walked on. I could see against the starlit sky outlines of flat roofs in the distance and one large discernible cross on a slight steeple. I felt as though there were other buildings around us, but I had no way of knowing. The dark night. Get through it and God is in the rising of the sun. Tall, hooded figures wearing robes of black came and went noiselessly. We were intercepted by someone who merely said, "This way" and led us into the large wood and adobe structure on the top of which rose the cross.

We emerged in an open space of chairs in a semicircle around an altar, illuminated by a necessary candle here or there against the night's thick pitch. Now the entire community of hooded worshipers entered the chapel, the abbot wearing a white stole of the priest who presides at Mass. "Brothers and sisters in Christ, on this most holy night," he began, and I knew exactly where I was. Any altar boy who has served Easter Mass year after year, as I had with Father Sammons, would know. I lifted my head as the abbot intoned, "Christ our light . . . our light . . . our light."

When the light came, it wasn't only from the candles and tapers spread out among us, lit from the Paschal flame. The lofting eastern wall of the chapel was made almost entirely of glass. As the sky's hue softened and the sun breached the lip of the canyon, a New Mexican dawn poured in like a flash flood down an arroyo. Christ is indeed risen, I thought to myself, and the frozen, sleepless tension of an alien night became the comfort of morning after a long rest.

St. John Chrysostom wrote in the fourth century, "If you want to see heaven on earth, go into the desert of Egypt." As deserts go, Chama is not the inhospitable Sinai. But it may be heaven, if the salvation of simplicity is what one is searching for in this life. There the monks grow legumes and potatoes in the fields along the banks of the snow-fed river. Less hearty vegetables, like tomatoes and peppers, they cultivate year-round in greenhouses. They sell their own hand-made crafts—rosaries, icons, earthenware, blankets—in a small gift shop. And they allow guests, who are also welcome to work and pray with the community, to stay in the tiny adobe houses we had passed in the dark, unseen. "Let all guests be received as Christ," St. Benedict said.

After the liturgy and a breakfast of eggs, homemade bread, and black coffee, those of us who had come for the Easter service were given a tour of the grounds by one of the monks. There wasn't much more to see, though, than what we had already found. Beyond the chapel and other few buildings that made up the monastery compound, the desert opened out like a vast canvas everywhere you looked: jagged red-rock cliffs lining the canyon; chamisa and piñon a dusty silver and green against a similarly shaded ground; the river flowing flat and glassy, but fast from the melting snows; the morning sun giving everything a glint of silver that slowly faded as it rose. What must it take to remain here? I wondered, when the bus driver signaled it was time to go. What if, when I finished the semester in Santa Fe, I never went back East? What if I worked in town and visited this desert place until they asked me if I wanted to stay? Did I want to do this badly enough to risk my college education on the *ora et labora* of the Benedictines?

They say the desert itself asks you to stay or leave in Santa Fe. I moved back to an apartment on Prince George Street in Annapolis. The winter after I graduated from St. John's, I took a job at a boatyard on the slow and coppery Waccamaw River near Myrtle Beach, South Carolina. It wasn't the trade of shipwright I was hoping to turn to. For the past four years, in addition to the classics I had studied, I had been trying my hand at writing poetry. It was the language of Homer in the original Greek that made me look up from the page one day (translating for tutorial the passage of Scylla and Charybdis in the

Odyssey) in a realization of how form and language melded together and became song. *Prosody*. In my sophomore year I had received an honorable mention for a poem and was given the award by Robert Fitzgerald just months before he died. Then, in my senior year, I received the Baird Award for a short collection of poems I had been honing ever since Santa Fe. They were based loosely on the landscape of Pennsylvania from which I felt I had escaped. (In these two ways only did I distinguish myself at St. John's College.) With no loans to pay off, and no desire to get a job on Wall Street (this was 1986), I found the work at the boatyard gave me time to write, which I began to think, after the temptation in the desert faded, might be a life I could lead. And I liked the South for the sheer feel and fecundity of the place, imagining the beginnings of William Faulkner, James Dickey, and Breece D'J Pancake, though I was neither alcoholic nor suicidal. Just naïve. I believed that time was more important than money, and if I kept praying I'd get there, though I confess to not knowing at this point in my life where *there* was.

When I shook off at least a bit of my naïveté, enough to see that I was engaged in drudgery more than redemptive labor, I packed up my things and moved north to Massachusetts, where my oldest brother, John, helped me get a job in the rigging loft at MacDougalls' Cape Cod Marine.

You might wonder what the Catholic parents of a young man they had sent through four years of college to study philosophy and classics were thinking when I told them in April 1987 that I was working in another boatyard. The truth is, as I look back on the many frank and at times strained conversations I had with my parents in those days, they never said, "Oh, Andrew, *do* something useful with your life." I don't know why they should have been so believing, if that's the word. Maybe they had more faith than I, or anyone I knew of. In any case, they said nothing. When I tried to probe my father for some indication of how I was using his investment, he said (and I remember this well), "I sent you to school for an education, Age. What you do with it is up to you." And that was the end of it. So, I kept doing what I was doing, however much it seemed as though I was setting out across an ocean with thread for sheets and muslin for a sail.

I was poor, for a college graduate, but I didn't need much. My rent was cheap. A sailboard was my one expensive habit. I drove a used pickup truck that I financed through a bank in South Carolina for $125 a month. The most important thing about what I was doing was that this new work felt satisfying and meaningful. The yard manager at MacDougalls' was fair. The men in the other shops—painting, hauling, carpentry, machine—were fraternal in that cold New England way of theirs. And my job became more of an apprenticeship to the rigger, a bearded and brilliant artisan of a sailor from the North Shore of Boston named Mark Tremblay, one of the best teachers I've ever had. "Books and a balance," the seal of St. John's College says, leaving us to discover the latter on our own.

It was on Cape Cod, too, that I got closer to the brother who was long gone from home by the time I was old enough to know him better. We were a pretty diffuse bunch, my brothers and sisters and I (you'll not hear much about them in this story), spread out around the country, some of us with little more than a surname in common. John and I, though, were like the bookends. We happened to end up living on a spit of sand together, laboring away at life and searching for what that labor might mean. "A comfortable rut," John would always say, happy, but with a kind of growing resignation. In the early seventies, he'd just missed being drafted for a tour in Vietnam; then he went to college in Massachusetts to study marine biology, didn't finish, joined the Coast Guard, moved up to third-class petty officer but never got on well enough to make a life out of it, and stayed on the Cape when he got out because there was nothing better than water and boats.

I worked and kept writing. And through all of this I kept going to Mass. My Catholicism remained, in a sense, the anchor to which I weekly tied the rode, from which swung my own as yet unharbored craft. Perhaps the maintenance of this exercise, though, is why, beneath the travels, the work, the writing, there smoldered the old desire to find something else, some place of silence, like the lingering whiff of candle smoke in an empty church after everyone has gone. That's why I called St. Joseph's Abbey, the Trappist monastery in Spencer, Massachusetts, in the winter of 1988. And it seemed providential to me that a room in their guesthouse should open up for the weekend of Palm Sunday, after I had been on the waiting list for only two days. When I saw John after work that evening at Paul's in Falmouth for a beer, I said, "Remember when I told you I had called the monks about a visit to Spencer?"

"Yeah, and they laughed and said they were all booked up."

"Well, someone canceled. I'm going up there next weekend. Can't wait."

I studied his hands as he raised his glass to his lips. Cold-cracked, bleeding in places, and windburned. Mine had become the same. He ordered another round for the two of us and started nodding as though he had finally found the words for what he wanted to say. "I always loved that passage in *The Seven Storey Mountain,* toward the end. Remember? Where Merton greets the porter at the gates and he asks, 'Have you come here to stay?' "

"I remember." It turns out that my mother had given him the book to read when he was a teenager, too, which I hadn't known, but which that day made some sense to me.

I slept in a small, restful room (not the cell I had envisioned) in the guesthouse at St. Joseph's Abbey that weekend, prayed Matins, Vespers, and went to Mass with the silent and seemingly forbidding Trappists, and listened to a talk given by one of the monks on the virtue of forgiving as an act of complete forgetting. Most memorable, though, was my own conversation with a Brother Aelred, who was acting director of vocations. I had asked to speak to someone about the possibility of becoming a Trappist, and so was scheduled to sit down with this shorn and severe young man (not much older than my own twenty-five years at the time) the day before I left. When I told him I had been wondering lately if I had a vocation to the priesthood, he asked, "Priesthood, or monasticism?" I said I hadn't gotten far enough to sort out the difference, and he informed me that the men at Spencer were called to be monks, not priests. "We are a community called to prayer," he said, already closing the folder of information he had brought with him, as though divining that it was not these gates to which I'd be returning. "Only if the monastery needs a priest and there is someone within who is called to the work is he sent away to study so that he can return to serve the others in that capacity."

"Oh," I said, "I see." But I didn't. Instead I decided that what I wanted to do now was get back to my applications for graduate school and find out if anyone believed I had what it took to become not a monk but a writer. I had a new stack of poems on my desk in my upstairs room at 32 Ranch Road in Hatchville, next to the bottle of rum John had given me, "For when you're finished . . . or can't get started." And I had my heart set on going to Columbia, not because of Thomas Merton but because it was in New York City. I feared the idea of moving to New York after the ocean pastoral of Cape Cod, but I also suspected that the kind of life to which I might be called probably wasn't in those places—small towns, deserts, islands, woods—to which I had always felt drawn and then ultimately left when I faced the realization of my ever-growing restlessness. Restless to know what it was I ought yet to do. At least it was becoming clear to me—as another Easter swung around on the liturgical calendar, an Easter I celebrated with little solemnity at a parish church in Falmouth—that for all of the reading and dreaming about the life I had done, I was feeling less and less called to be a monk. Four months later I traded the Cape for the Upper West Side.

Hunts Point, a once thriving South Bronx neighborhood with a coast on Long Island Sound, died a slow death when it was cut off from the rest of the borough by the Bruckner Expressway and beaten down by the rising noise and air traffic from La Guardia Airport. In the late 1980s it was one of the neighborhoods in New York most devastated by crack. Dealers set up in the cinder-block hollows of abandoned apartment buildings, addicts lining up outside all day long for a vial of "rock," as though they were at the drive-in window of a fast-food restaurant. The clientele weren't only prostitutes and bums who had scraped up five bucks. Men in suits and college kids who looked like me waited impatiently on line in weed-choked lots.

On Manida Street, though, every residence looked occupied, lived in, maintained. Three doors down and I stopped in front of a brown-shingled duplex. I could see "Jesuit Community" written next to

"2nd floor." I opened the latch of the metal gate, closed it behind me, pressed the buzzer, and heard footsteps coming down the stairs.

"You're a little early," the man said, stepping out onto the walk. "Joe Towle." We shook hands. His grip was viselike. "Welcome to the neighborhood." He looked like a merchant seaman in his peacoat and watch cap, blue jeans and work boots, but with an impish grin and sad eyes. He was a well-worn fifty-five, I guessed, his Irish features more creased with the elements of prayer and work than those of any monk I had seen in New Mexico or Massachusetts. I liked him instantly. "I see you didn't get lost."

"I stuck to the directions," I said. "Once I got out at Simpson Street, it seemed the best thing to do."

"Good. Come on, we can talk inside later. I want to show you around the neighborhood before it gets too late."

In the fall of 1988 I had enrolled in the MFA program at Columbia to write poetry. I lived on West 100th Street in a small two-bedroom apartment that I shared with a serene young black woman who worked as a flight attendant and was training to be an opera singer. Beverly's voice and manner both were canorous and seductive. I wish that I could say she was my lover (I was so taken with the fact that I got to live with a woman this beautiful), but our arrangement for sharing the flat was strictly business. It's just as well. She could act sisterly to me when I went out on dates ("Now, AJ, you don't *ever* want to wear jeans with that shirt," she'd say. Or, "Home by two, and if you can't be good, be careful"). And I'm sure that due to our close proximity, any relationship other than a friendly one would have meant a conflagration—first exciting, and then disastrous—in no time.

In New York, too, my restless nudging toward a desire for religious life persisted. It had seemed erased entirely once I got there. I thought I would be free from it in the city, surrounded by so many opportunities to satisfy the body as well as the soul, now that I had grown up, in a sense. Which is to say, I had, almost without realizing it, stepped away from the longing for some idyllic landscape I romanticized in my youth.

But before I moved from Cape Cod to Manhattan, I had the

chance to talk to a cousin of mine who had become a diocesan priest when I was in college, and who was curious when I mentioned offhandedly that I had been wondering recently if I had a vocation to religious life. "The problem is," I said, "I don't know what kind of *life* that would be." And he said, almost as a matter of fact, that I should go talk to the Jesuits. They were best at what he called "spiritual direction." So, after a few months of school—writing now, constantly, and (when I wasn't writing) exploring the city—I found the number for the provincial's office of the New York Province of the Society of Jesus in the phone book and gave them a call. I don't know what put my mind to it, a confluence of practicality and grace no doubt (having been told "They're in the book," and seeing the book that day right there within reach). I spoke with the vocations director, Father Vincent Biagi, SJ, and he agreed to meet with me for an interview.

I won't tell you all of what unfolded between November 1988 and February 1989, when I found myself on the steps of the Jesuit Community in Hunts Point. When I saw Father Biagi—or Vin, as I was instructed to call him—for the first time at Xavier High School on Sixteenth Street, he asked me about my life, spiritual and otherwise. Did I go to Mass regularly? (Holy Name on Ninety-sixth and Amsterdam every Sunday. No Corpus Christi—the church where Merton was baptized—for me.) What kind of student was I, and what poets did I like? (Hardworking, and a reader of the mid-century Americans, like Lowell and Berryman.) Sex, drugs, and rock 'n' roll? I told him that I wasn't a virgin when it came to either of these, nor was I obsessed with or addicted to anyone or anything. I seemed to pass whatever test he was administering to this would-be Jesuit that day, and he began telling me about what I had come to hear.

"If you feel as though you want to move forward with this," he said, "you need to begin to think seriously about cultivating a life of prayer. That won't be easy, being a student and a young man in New York, but that work is itself a test of your seriousness. I can recommend a spiritual director for you, and he can help you with your progress. What do you say? Is it something you'd like to pursue?"

I said, "It sounds like what I need." And so I began traveling one Saturday a month to Fordham University, where I spent the afternoon in spiritual direction with the same Father Gerry Blaszczak who would later become the assistant novice master at the novitiate of St. Andrew's.

In that earliest stage, spiritual direction meant getting used to a regular practice of prayer—usually one half hour a day of meditating on a passage of Scripture—then recording how this kind of exercise felt within me, how it moved me once it became habitual. Was it something that gave me joy or consolation, or did it disturb me and make me want to turn away? The answer was that it did both, and that was telling to my director. The disturbance came when, in those complex ways that pride works on us, I believed I would in no time discover myself admitted into some New York literary scene: poet, professor, example of the erudite. The further my mind reached, the thinner my life felt. Surely there had to be some good in an ambition such as this, if it came of hard work and study? But it wasn't the work as means. It was the man I should become in the end. And the joy? That came, at times, when I went to receive communion at Holy Name among the mix of Cubans, Dominicans, Haitians, and Columbia graduate students—believers all, in ways perfect and imperfect. Or, when I had the apartment to myself, my writing done for the day, and I sat with a passage from Scripture, like this one from the Gospel of St. Mark: "I have faith. Help my lack of faith." To live and work, somehow, with that kind of faith, even as I could not deny my own lack of it—that, oddly enough, was a great joy and consolation to me.

It was in the new year, two months into spiritual direction, when Gerry asked me if I'd like to live in a Jesuit community for the summer to get a feel for the "real Society." That sounded as intriguing as it was daunting to me. "Go talk to Joe Towle in Hunts Point," he pushed gently. "He'll need some help with his summer school program." If this all sounds so undramatic at a time when you know precisely where it leads, I should tell you that the Jesuits seemed to proceed with very little drama in these sorts of things. Like the Benedictines, who are instructed to turn away any aspirant at least three times when he comes knocking at the door, the Jesuits practiced their own brand of all-seeing indifference. God, not they, should do the work of turning men's heart to new paths in life, be those turns dramatic or mundane. And so I followed their lead, said "Okay," and got on the 2 train one day heading into that wilderness they called the Bronx.

It struck me that you didn't really *talk* to Joe Towle. You followed him, which it became clear wasn't going to be easy. At 5:30 p.m. in February, the city was already dark. Under the sodium glare of streetlamps, the man and I walked down Manida, back onto Garrison, then turned and moved up Hunts Point Avenue.

We approached a scene that I can only describe as stygian. Abandoned buildings, lifeless streets, echoes of disembodied voices, and the quick, shadowy moves of men and women flitting across the field like tracers, not one of them seeming like an actual, physical person. And this priest they called "Father Joe" moved among it with an odd mixture of singularity and sorrow, a shepherd with his sheep irrecoverably scattered. He pointed to one building that was scheduled to be demolished, another that was going to be rebuilt for housing, shaking his head when he saw someone he knew scurry from a crack den.

On the sidewalk between Faile Street and Bryant Avenue, Joe saw a woman who, he whispered to me quickly, came to the parish from time to time.

"Marie Elise?" he said, feigning surprise and disarming concern. She looked over at us and suddenly seemed embarrassed. The man who was with her took off with the same head-down walk that everyone in the neighborhood seemed to move with. "I thought we'd gotten you out of here," he said to her. "What happened?"

"Oh, Padre," she crooned, pretending to inspect a button on her flimsy coat. "Don't look at me like this. I tried, I tried, I tried . . ." Her voice dissolved into a whimper.

I was staring at her, mesmerized by the way she seemed to look at and yet see nothing, when a man came up from behind us and said, "Yo! You want a piece of that little number and some rock to smoke it with?"

Joe turned around fast and looked right at the guy without any trace of a smile, happy or otherwise. "Who are you?" he said.

"Who am *I*?" the pimp shot back. "Wrong question, Grampa. Who the fuck are you?"

Joe squared himself, a former boxer no doubt. Cocky flyweight. So this is it, I thought. This is where it's going to end for me. "You have something to do with this?" he said to the pimp flatly and pointed at Marie Elise. I watched and waited. Where could I run, or hide?

Just then, another voice came from around the corner and out of the dark.

"No, Rufus!" he shouted. "That's the *priest*, man. Don't give him no shit!"

"What priest?" Rufus said, his voice full of disdain and attitude. "Ain't no fuckin' priests around here! This dead man's gonna need one, though."

"The kids, man, the school. Don't mess with this guy." The unexpected emissary had Rufus's right arm locked in his, pushing whatever Rufus had in his pocket back down into it and pulling him into the shadows, Rufus all the while putting up a defiant front.

"Don't worry about him," Joe said to me. "He's got no say over who comes and goes around here." Marie Elise looked out into the street at whatever it was she saw. Joe turned back to her. "When you get clean," he said, "come and see me and we'll get you some work." She then seemed to remember the conversation.

"Oh, Padre, I will, I will. Don't look at me like this." She dropped her head and toed a cigarette butt. Then she shuffled off in the direction of Bryant Avenue, mumbling something neither of us could hear.

"The odd thing is," Joe said when we turned the corner back onto Manida, as though we had been talking the whole time instead of walking in silence, "it's the kids who save them. They're so proud of their kids when they're at school, or in sports, or doing anything that will get them out of here. We need to get the kids themselves to see that. And that's why I need you to come up here for the summer." I nodded as though I understood and would certainly accept his offer to come work with him, but in my heart not knowing how in hell I could ever make a difference in this neighborhood in the space of seven weeks.

For the last half of June, all of July, and the first week of August, I lived in the back room of the house at 360 Manida, a kind of coop that had been added onto the flat black tar roof as an afterthought, most likely an illegal one at that. One door, no windows, all heat. It was the chapel in the winter. When I moved in, they replaced the altar with a cot, and Mass was moved to the coffee table in the living room, where we—five of us, four Jesuits and me—would gather every morning at 7:00. This was like no monastery I could have ever imagined spending a weekend in, and yet it felt like a deeply prayerful place, this upper-room apartment in the Bronx. *Laborare est orare*, the monks say. Here it was, finally, clear to me what it all meant.

In the neighborhood, we commandeered the ground floor of PS 75 and went from 8:00 until 12:00, kids begging to be allowed in, even when they became undisciplined and disruptive in what seemed like a few short minutes. I taught reading for the first hour, mathematics for the next, then managed to do something to keep us all occupied and noncombative (lots of breaks and disgressions about everything from life in the neighborhood to the erratic play of the Yankees that year) until noon.

"No," Joe said when I wanted to dismiss a girl in my class who was making trouble for the rest of the students, and me. When Joe answered a question or issued a directive, it was usually in a tone of voice that would have sounded condescending or saccharine coming from any other man or woman, but not from him. It was because of that singular and sorrowful world within which he lived. He was the kind of man who saw beyond judgment, right through to forgiveness; he was Christ-like in the best sense. But on that day, not far from the end of the summer, he wanted to get at what lay at the heart of why I never seemed to trust, when all there was left was trust. I caught a rare flash of anger in his eyes. "If she gets here, she stays. They know the rules. No fighting. No weapons. You never know where Grace is," he said, as though student and gift were both some feral cat that made every inch of city its home. "You might want to think about that yourself. Give her a break," he said, and his face lit up again. "She'll be all right. Now why don't you make sure you've got those permission slips straightened out for the game tonight."

That was about as eventful as my summer in the Bronx got. But I wasn't complaining. Come the second week of August it was daily life with the Jesuits I would miss the most. The work, the prayer, the purpose. Nothing unexpected, except what I later believed was in fact the slinking, undeserved gift of grace.

When I returned to life on the Upper West Side that autumn, I slipped back into friendships, classes, writing.

"Where've you been?" Beverly asked.

"Oh, I had a little teaching gig in the Bronx," I said. I couldn't begin to explain now the path of prayer and discernment I had been on the past year. I wasn't being cagey so much as feeling that my search for an answer to the question of whether I was called to religious life had taken on a depth and complexity not easily rendered. Besides, Joe had paid me enough to keep up with rent, so my empty room didn't matter as long as there was a check in the mailbox on the first of the month. I decided that Beverly's question was more polite than probing and left it at that.

"Well, it's nice to have you back," she said. "You're looking good." Then she introduced me to her new boyfriend, who joked about wondering whether he'd pass the test with Bev's roommate, "a Columbia man."

But in the following weeks and months, I felt a sustained and growing eagerness, like when you just can't get someone off your mind. Or, as Bruce Chatwin wrote, like I had some journey mapped out in my central nervous system, and that seemed the only way to account for this "insane restlessness." Until I decided that what I wanted to do was to be a Jesuit.

And what about the monastery? a voice in my head countered when I believed that I wouldn't be hearing that voice again. So I tested it. When I thought of leaving school and going back to Abiquiu, New Mexico (as I had once considered), or Spencer, Massachusetts, I felt expectant at first to imagine the radical departure from the world, the silence, the labor, the prayer. But then . . . nothing. Not anything worrisome or nagging. Not any thing. No challenge. No difference.

And when I thought of living like Joe Towle and the other Jesuits in Hunts Point, at work and at prayer—like the monks yet in the world—then a flood of peace, like springwater down a desert arroyo. Like Christ our light, "our light . . . our light." Yes, that would be something, I thought. This is what I've been looking for, this kind of priesthood.

I knew the application process would be time-consuming and arduous. Vin had explained it to me once: physicals, blood test, HIV test, IQ test, psychological profile, four personal interviews, letters of recommendation, transcripts, an extended spiritual autobiography, and then the overall assessment of a committee.

But I had a graduate thesis to write.

So write it.

What if I applied and didn't make it?

What if?

And when would I tell my parents, friends, brothers and sisters about all of this?

In due time.

It had been six months since I had last spoken with Vin. He wasn't the kind of guy who'd check in on you. I called him in early October, almost a year since our first conversation. I told him about my summer in the Bronx and that I was back safely for my last year at Columbia. Then timidly I stammered, "I was wondering, Vin, if, uh, you could send me an application. For the society?"

He laughed through the phone, approvingly it sounded to me, and said, "Of course, Andrew. I can do that. Anything else you need?"

What else is there? I thought, and then said, "Yeah. Pray for me," which is the only way I can explain, in the end, how I came to the Jesuits at St. Andrew's in Syracuse that August.

T wo weeks might just as well have been two months within our novitiate life and routine. It was all Ordinary Time. Ordinary not in the sense of being boring but from the Church's word for the time between seasons, *ordinal*, a counting down, movement toward expectation of an event.

By Monday the tenth of September, we had already settled into "a proper order," as the *Constitutions* of the Society call it, the skeletal backbone of the novice's day, "as far as may be possible, for the time of eating, sleeping, and rising, and *ordinarily* all should observe it."

I got up at 6:00 a.m. and went over to the pool at Le Moyne for a swim, where I counted out laps in series of ten, like my own version of the rosary, until I got lost in my underwater meditation and had to begin all over again. Usually I walked the half mile from novitiate to gym. But that day I was the liturgist, which meant I was in charge of the secular as well as the sacred reading material. So I drove a house car, one of three Toyota station wagons. On my way back to St. Andrew's, I swung by the convenience store on East Genesee Street to pick up *The New York Times* and *The Post-Standard*. In line at the register I saw Tobias Wolff, one of my favorite living writers. You couldn't miss him with that mustache of his. *This Boy's Life* had been published the year before, and I knew he was teaching at Syracuse University. "Hey," I wanted to say, "I liked your book of short stories, *In the Garden of the North American Martyrs*. I'm one of them. A Jesuit." But I kept my mouth shut. It was the driftless boy in his memoir (not the short stories) who rattled and stuck with me. I haven't told you much about the Pennsylvania in which I grew up, but I knew guys like Jack Wolff. I studied them, envying them almost, and then did what I could to stay as far away from them as possible. For all I knew the man himself would say, "Shove off, choirboy," and leave me standing there holding the paper. (Later, when I saw that our library had copies of *all* his books and that they were signed by him with the inscription "To the Novices at St. Andrew's," I wished I had at least said, "Good morning, Mr. Wolff".)

By 8:00 I was showered and sitting alone in the darkened house chapel. I began what we called an Examination of Conscience, my first for the day and something I had begun to do every day at this hour. "What have I done that is Christ-like? Where have I failed yesterday and perhaps already today? How might I change?" It's a short prayer, fifteen minutes at the most, meant to be a corrective, a reminder that whatever I do this day will come down to a choice for or against the love of the Lord.

But, the endorphins from my swim wearing off, I drifted into a kind of torpor. I should want to pray without ceasing, even when my prayer is sleep, I thought and sank down further, wondering, What saint was it who said that? Then, not invitation but a rebuke. The words of Jesus from the Passion on Palm Sunday (a long way off yet): *Are you asleep? Had you not the strength to keep awake one hour?* I felt a breeze about me and believed that I was out-of-doors on this balmy morning. The door, I thought, then realized that the breeze was the door to the chapel opening and closing. I need to climb out of this. Climb, climb. There's so much to be done today . . . And then the 8:25 bell went off like a gong next to my head, summoning the house to 8:30 Morning Prayer. I should have rung it, but a *secundi* named Joey, who had also come into the chapel early, did me the favor, though more to remind me what time it was than to respect my contemplative sleep.

In a matter of minutes, the space went from somnolent to bustling, eighteen of us in a variety of nonreligious garb—feet shod and unshod, shirts tucked and untucked—dividing ourselves in half to create an antiphonal theater of prayer. I lit a candle on the altar.

"O God, come to my assistance," I intoned heavily as I read the invitatory from my breviary.

"Lord, make haste to help us," the rest of the chapel responded.

"In the name of the Father, and of the Son, and of the Holy Spirit . . ."

". . . As it was in the beginning, is now, and ever shall be. Amen."

I ate a breakfast of cornflakes and banana in milk, with a cup of tea and a glass of orange juice. Frank, Billy, and David sat down at the table with their own versions of the same morning menu.

"Do your Spanish homework?" David asked.

"He won't call on us anyway," Frank said, not resigned but by way of assurance.

"Maybe not," David said. "But I don't want to get behind."

"I'll learn it when I have to," Billy said, maybe knowing then that he would never speak a word of the language.

Mondays, Wednesdays, and Fridays, the five of us trekked over to Le Moyne for Professor Tony Vetrano's undergraduate course in Spanish, where we were drilled on forms of *ser* and *estar* in a room full of eighteen- and nineteen-year-olds. We knew the story of Ignatius studying at the University of Paris, a man nearly forty sitting with students not yet out of their teens, all for the greater glory of God. But we weren't so far removed from our classmates. Wearing shorts, T-shirts, and flip-flops during what was unseasonably hot weather that September and looking like fourth-year students who needed a language elective, we put on our new identity.

I liked going across the field for these lessons because it got us out of the house. But Spanish was also a required language in the Provinces of New York and California. More than half of the population we would most likely encounter in our lives as priests would speak Spanish as a first language. So we did the work, participated in class, and learned so much Spanish (some of us, at least) that Professor Vetrano stopped calling on us for the answers he knew we had.

"*Gracias, señores,*" he'd say to our novices' corner of the room, "*pero, yo sé que ustedes tienen la respuesta a mi pregunta. Alguien más?*"

The other students suspected we were up to something more than stacking credits for graduation.

As though all things within our "proper order" were drawn centripetally back to the work of the house and the house alone, the novice master stopped me as I got up from the table to rinse my bowl and asked if he could see me in his office for a few minutes. I would be late if the meeting took any longer than that, but I couldn't say no. There was no telling why I was being summoned. I gathered up my books and followed him down the hall.

Don Gannon was a balding, fair-haired athletic man in his early fifties with the build of a quick point guard. His accent came from somewhere between Brooklyn and Jersey City, though I was never sure exactly where he was from. He had been a priest for over twenty years. His quiet and unassuming demeanor belied his skill at assessing people and situations with stunning acuity. He said little and missed nothing.

He didn't keep a separate office in the house. He worked out of his room, which was spare with large, southern-facing windows, taking advantage of the natural light. Crime novels, contemporary theology, and Jesuit histories lined his bookshelves. It was said that he once did graduate work in mathematics, but there was no evidence of that in view. On the wall there hung the ubiquitous vow cross above his narrow single bed. In the center of the room, two chairs faced each other, as though constantly in the attitude of spiritual conversation, waiting for novice and master to provide the material.

"Come in. Shut the door and sit down," he said. He settled into one chair, and I took the other. "You're doing well?"

"I am, Don." We addressed every Jesuit, regardless of position, by his first name. St. Ignatius Loyola was "Ignatius" now. "I'm trying to get used to the quirks of the house."

"It does feel a bit forced," he said, his attention unwavering. He had an eye that turned out slightly. "But you'll appreciate the routine when you've got other things on your mind."

I said it was a lot like sailing, doing the same thing the same way each time you went out on the water so that the essentials didn't break down when you needed them most. He liked the analogy. Then he got to why he had called me.

"As you know, a large part of the running of the house requires my appointing someone to act as the beadle. That's been Joey's job during your two weeks of probation." (Ah yes, the bell corrects as well as summons.) Probation was the brief period during which we *primi* lived in the novitiate but were not yet accepted as novices. Probation was pro forma, yet it was not unheard of for a man to be dismissed for demonstrating right away that he wasn't fit for this life, which usually meant that he had no idea there'd be so much dish washing and toilet cleaning involved. Today was our last day of probation. "I'm going to announce at the next community meeting that I've appointed you the new beadle."

"Why me?" I asked with point-blank surprise. I thought that the beadle had to be someone who was outgoing, ambitious, and a good manager of time. Frank or David, either one of whom seemed destined to become a college president or the provincial, had to be a better choice than I. Don said that he thought I was even-keeled enough to do the job, and I thought his own response to my sailing analogy was pretty wily for a Jesuit. But I could sense what Ignatius called *agere contra*, doing what's contrary to your inclination, or that to which you're attached. Freedom *from* is freedom *for*. It was clear I didn't want to engage yet with my fellow novices on this level of responsibility, probation or no probation. My inclination—and temperament—was toward the fringe, while being careful not to cut myself off. Now I'd be dead center. Unbelievable how little time it took Don to see that.

The term *beadle* comes from the Old English word *béodan*, which means "to command," though more properly "to bid." When the number of Jesuits in a house of novices was in the hundreds, the beadle was a necessary link between the superior and the entire class, a conduit who made sure that the men knew and did whatever the superior wanted them to know and do. If something or someone was amiss, it was the beadle's responsibility to inform the novice master. With fifteen novices on hand, though, the beadle was in charge of typing the daily schedule, delegating roles for house functions, making sure everyone was pulling his weight on chores, and keeping an official journal of our own quotidian in the beadle's log (which still exists somewhere in that house).

Don said, "We'll check in regularly," then stood up to make it clear the meeting was over. "Feel free to come to me anytime with questions or concerns. All right?"

"All right." What could I say? I was, at least, grateful for his trust.

"So what is it that you and your friends do?" a shy but sultry-looking sophomore girl asked me as we both—somewhat awkwardly—walked out of Spanish class together and into the hall that day. I knew the encounter was inevitable. I wanted it to be. She had been taking the seat right in front of me for the past few weeks, hoping, I guessed, that if she sat on our end of the room Vetrano wouldn't call on her. She wasn't having such an easy time with her language studies, although by looking at her (which I did a lot of) you would have expected a native Catalan to pour out of her softly upturned mouth.

"My friends." I laughed. "Where are my friends, by the way?" My heart started beating as though it was trying to break down the walls of my chest.

"They've gone on without you," she said, with a slight hint of sarcasm. "Off to more classes to run?"

"No, Spanish is our only one, at Le Moyne, anyway," I said, aware now that her tentative classroom persona had given way to a more flirtatious and suggestive air. I knew that I had chosen a life in which I would live exclusively around other men, and avoid anyone or anything that might suggest the possibility of intimate physical contact with either sex. And then a young woman I might have gone to the beach or shared dinner with not two months before suddenly wants to talk to me. I didn't wonder if I could live as a chaste man at this point. I wondered what or who it would hurt if I played along while we walked together for a few hundred yards. That was all.

"So you *are* students."

"Of sorts, just not regular undergrads."

We came to the lower end of campus and stepped onto the main path toward St. Mary's dormitory, where she lived. From across the field, St. Andrew's came into view, lorn and separate, but somehow majestic.

"You see that house?" I said, pointing across the road. "That's where the five of us live. That's where we're students, I guess you could say. We're studying to be priests. Jesuits." Like distant Bedouins approaching a shimmering dune, the other four disappeared around the side of the house and gave my claim the credibility it needed.

She looked at both house and men, as one remained and four faded, then turned to me, wide-eyed. "You're kidding!"

"Swear to God. Really."

"Wow!" she said, then stared back as though she were trying to register the information. "But, I mean, that's not easy, is it? No sex, right? No crazy parties? Not that I'm doing much of either these days, but if I wanted to I, you know, *could*." She was fumbling now through a conversation that had taken such an unexpected turn. Suddenly I *was* a Jesuit, like her English or history professor. "But, if it's what you want to do . . . ," she said, and let her voice trail off. "I don't know. Are you gay?"

I felt the pull of trying to save a conversation, trying to let it go on as long as we both had time, because I liked her mousy Syracuse accent, the unkempt clothes that meant she had just rolled out of bed, and her own unaffected naïveté. My pulse lowered and my palms dried. "No," I said. "And it is what I want to do."

She blushed, and then said almost in a whisper, "It's not going to happen, like, tomorrow, though, is it? Becoming a priest?"

"Two years here, three years of philosophy studies somewhere else, a few years teaching, three more of theology studies after that. Then, if you're good, and still alive, you get ordained."

"Jesus! I mean, sorry, but . . . You're just starting out?"

"Few weeks into it."

"Ah, baby Jesuits." She had found her comfort level again. "That's so sweet." She leaned forward and touched my arm. "You guys'll have to come to a party sometime. I know so many people who would *love* to hang out with you. Would you be allowed?"

"Send the invitation. We'll run it by the Vatican," I replied, but the joke was lost on her.

As I turned away to cross that field for myself, I tried to decide if I was proud to be a Jesuit or feeling turned on by the fact that this sweet siren of a thing couldn't have me if she wanted me. Then I decided that it didn't matter. In time, it would. But on that day, while this might have been a first, I had a feeling it wasn't going to be the last. Another challenge, of sorts, I threw down in front of myself.

When I got to the house, I went right to the dining room. The other four were sitting at one table, waiting.

"AaaaJaaay," Chris yelled out when he saw me come in. "You dawg!"

"Tell me not one of you guys would have talked to her if she had said something to you." They all demurred.

I threw together a ham and cheese sandwich, then sat down and told them about our conversation and how I'd marked us all for good as "the priests." I left out any hint of how much I'd enjoyed our fifteen minutes of banter, hanging on to that feeling of having been handed something I was certain I'd lost forever, a loss of my own making.

"I'll bet she's got a broken heart," Frank said.

"Yeah, right."

"Sure. She's been looking at you since the first day of class, swinging all of that pretty black hair, *O-LA* the only word of Spanish in her head." Frank started laughing his deep, barrel-chested laugh.

"She sits by us to avoid Vetrano."

"So do I," Billy said. "For all Vetrano knows, I'm fluent in five languages."

"Five?" Frank said.

"If you count Long Island."

Our coed never did invite us to that party. We wouldn't have gone even if she had. The novice master would never have given us permission. (Don wouldn't have said no. He would have suppressed a smirk, looked somewhere between wry and derisive, and then said, "You can't be serious.") And while we would have been flattered by the invitation, not one of us would have been serious about wanting to go. I never said more than "Hello" or "How's it going?" to her again. Frank was probably right about her intentions, and once she crossed me off her list, what was the use of spending time and emotional capital on an investment that would never yield any return?

That afternoon we had an in-house conference in our library on the early history of the Society. I loved the library at St. Andrew's. The chapel was a negative to that room's warm and detailed photograph. It had a single large window that looked out onto the south- and west-facing backyard, so the full light of day poured in on those afternoons when there was little if any light in Syracuse. The bookshelves were made from hard yellow maple and held everything from rare eighteenth-century Jesuit texts to contemporary theology, philosophy, and fiction. And because it was a small room (slightly bigger than a bedroom), those shelves were packed tight with books from floor to ceiling. A bust of Ignatius sat on the windowsill facing the door, an old felt biretta resting on his head. With the hint of a smile carved into that likeness, it was as though he welcomed anyone who would set foot into such a cramped yet fulgent space.

But it wasn't just the architecture that drew me toward this room more than any other in the house, it was the feel of seemingly infinite intellectual and spiritual travel that this and any library always suggested to me. When I was an undergraduate at St. John's, I used to wonder what it would be like to touch a book's spine and know instantly what life, ideas, and loves lay between front and back covers. Of course that would sacrifice the pleasure of reading, and so I dispelled the fantasy as quickly as it came on. Better, I thought, to have a house one day wherein I could build my own library, walk in with this hope, and walk out again knowing something, if not all, of at least one book's promise. And it occurred to me on my first day in the novitiate, when I climbed the stairs to the second floor and saw this library, that I had in a way built the house I wanted and gotten my wish. Books, time, and prayer spread out before me day after day, as though they were the only sustenance I would ever need.

On that afternoon, Gerry was leading us through a close reading of a document called the General Examen. It was directed to men like us, "all who request admission into the Society of Jesus." We had gone for the lesser part of two hours and were finishing up a discussion on what the Jesuits call the subject's "manifestation of conscience" to his superior:

> It is a matter of great and even extraordinary importance that the superiors should have a complete understanding of the subjects . . . The more completely the superiors know these subjects' interior and exterior affairs, just so much the better will they be able, with greater diligence, love, and care, to help the subjects and to guard their souls from various inconveniences and dangers which might occur later on.

We all found this to be not only sensible but edifying, to know that the Jesuit's sense of *cura personalis*, the care of the whole person, began with the relationship to his superior. Billy (usually quiet) piped in with a comment about how, in his experience, no job is ever done thoroughly and well if even one person isn't clear about what's expected of him.

Then Frank and David began to spar about a point farther along in the text, in which Ignatius mentions how "it helps and profits one in the spiritual life to abhor in its totality and not in part whatever the world loves and embraces."

"Is this an ideal we're supposed to strive for?" David asked, rhetorically it seemed to me. "Or are we meant to take this as black and white?"

"What do you think?" Gerry asked.

Without waiting for David to reply, Frank said, "I think it wouldn't be here if Ignatius didn't mean for us to take it as real, and not an ideal."

"You're throwing around real and ideal as though they're exchangeable parts," David countered. "The issue is separation. We remove ourselves from 'whatever the world loves and embraces.' Whatever the world embraces *inordinately*, I take it to mean."

"Then what do you take 'abhor in its totality and not in part' to mean?" Frank asked.

"I take it to mean we let go entirely. What are you suggesting I'm missing?"

"I'm suggesting we do what the *Constitutions* ask of us."

"Then get rid of your clothes, your books, your music."

"If I got rid of my clothes, I'd be in jail, or a Franciscan. And I didn't bring any books or music with me." I thought about it and realized that Frank had moved in with a small suitcase. "I take that back," he said. "I brought my mother's collection of Irish poetry with me."

"Okay," David said, "so you're a man of simple needs. That world you're able to abhor, though, won't stop here. We put down, we pick up. We'll need to put down again."

I could see Chris gearing up to take a side (though I wasn't sure whose side he'd be on) when Gerry cut in. "You're both right." He sat at the head of the table, dog-eared copy of the text laid out in front of him, notes in Latin penciled into the margins. "Remember, this is a document meant to examine those who want to enter the Society. The infant order wanted to know not how a man was inclined but if he was *determined*. 'Determined and ready to accept and suffer with patience,' Ignatius says one paragraph later. So, Frank, yes, you need to have a real grasp of what you're giving up in its totality to embark on the spiritual life. And, David, you're right to say that the proper attitude, after this first sacrifice, is one of continually removing attachments." This would be the entire focus of the *Spiritual Exercises* and the Long Retreat, Gerry reminded us, his face set and his tone of voice unwavering, in order to suggest how serious this all was. Then we moved on to the body of the *Constitutions* to look at how its layout reflected the trajectory of the Jesuit's life.

Determined. What Frank and David were both right about was this. Regardless of what questions and convictions we had come to this house of novices with, what we all had in common, after our own personal periods of discernment, was the determination to *live* the life of the Jesuit. Not inclined to try it, not waiting for when it got so hard we would cut and run. Most of us were college-educated. All of us had known work. Not one of us was younger than twenty-one. At the outset or in the midst of what should have been our "professional" lives (consultants, lawyers, professors, writers), we embraced becoming novices again, and not by picking up another trade. We had to reorder our lives so that to be poor, chaste, and obedient meant fulfillment rather than frustration. And that doesn't happen overnight, regardless of how long you've been a practicing Catholic.

Gone—but not too long ago—was the harsh old theology of priests and nuns "dying to the world" when they entered the seminary or convent, taking new names, sleeping in cells on straw, wearing identical habits, and disappearing to family and friends. We didn't change our names or attach to one another's names the formal prefix "Brother." Our rooms in the house were simple but warm and spacious (though we moved from one to another every six months to avoid attachment). We wore the same clothes we were used to (Levi's and a Patagonia button-down were my habit). We received mail, were allotted a stipend for long-distance phone calls, and would be allowed to visit our families for two days after Christmas.

What we gave up *in its totality* was what the world said we needed: credit cards, bank accounts, investments, awards, connections, independence, and "the genital expression of intimacy," also known as sex. It wasn't that these things were perceived of as evil. We believed that a less attached life was not only possible but desirable, a life in which a man could live on a different kind of capital, a different kind of freedom, a different kind of affect. In everyone's story there was the example of someone who showed that it could be done. And not through a tortured existence of self-hatred, hair shirts, and leg chains, but through the ongoing journey to "Know Thyself."

That's what you might call the *real* ideal. It didn't take long, though, for the struggles to appear, struggles we all brought with us no matter how light we traveled. In that conference, listening to Frank and David duke it out over the finer points of Jesuit formation, I remained silent, indifferent, not caring one way or the other about whether I would be called out on what it was I abhorred according to the ideal of the General Examen or the *Constitutions*. I was content to study those finer points as a kind of historical exercise, but what was the point (I thought) of arguing over Jesuit legalese this early in the game (I, the boy in the Pennsylvania school yard who would rather find a quiet place to read, while the likes of Frank and David mapped out their territory by standing toe to toe and swinging for the face)? The Society of Jesus was meant to be an order of diverse individuals, yet harnessed according to gifts, talents, and the needs they addressed. The president of Le Moyne College lived in an environment entirely different from Joe Towle's in Hunts Point. Yet, in the ideal of community, they were the same. A public life of poverty, a private life of chastity, and a communal life in which each was asked to do one thing above all others: obey. This was the kind of radical simplicity that attracted me to the Jesuits in the end (or should I say the beginning), this notion—this powerful Christian tenet—that all is gained through sacrifice and self-emptying.

When I went for a walk to make my second Examination of Conscience around 4:30 (I went outside to get some air after the conference, and as a way of remaining in the world, even if I was no longer *of* it), the dialogue continued into and then took over my prayer. To obey seemed easy, as long as there was a library around. And what was poverty if you never had much to begin with? The reality that silenced me in those earliest days, for all of my determination and practiced monkishness, was chastity, already insisting that it wasn't going to be an easy traveling companion. Not four hours earlier I had convinced myself I was over the girl. Funny how profound the cliché is that we want only what we haven't got, especially when we're given so much time to think about it.

My first summer as a lifeguard, I woke up to find that I was an articulate, heterosexual male with my father's tall frame and square jaw. There was no lack of attention from the young women who graced the beach, and I took advantage of it. But I did believe in love. Now, a "few weeks into" my marriage to an ideal, I wondered if I wasn't the sailor who'd gouge the wax from his ears and head straight for the rocks. I was quiet in conference with my Jesuit brothers that afternoon because three things I could never abhor in their totality were a woman's voice, the smell of her skin, and the shape of her mouth. I thought of the girl from Spanish class, and while it wasn't she herself who captured my as yet disobedient and unchaste heart, the ideal of the woman did. And yet, at twenty-seven, there I was, praying for the strength to let go of one and embrace the other, trusting that I knew what I could and couldn't sacrifice. My morning sighting of Tobias Wolff suddenly came to mind, because I thought of a passage that had stood out for me in *This Boy's Life*, Jack Wolff thinking about his mother's life in hindsight: "Like anyone else, she must have wanted different things at the same time. The human heart is a dark forest." I had to convince myself that, having made my choice, I was determined to live it.

I made my way back to the house for 5:15 Mass, where Gerry presided and preached on the Gospel passage for the day, Luke chapter 6, verses 6–11: "Is it lawful to do good on the Sabbath rather than to do evil, to save life rather than to destroy it?" And in response to his own question, Jesus of Nazareth—in front of those who would seek both to uphold the law and to kill him—heals the man with the withered hand so that the man believed by all to be a sinner can get on with his life, free now to do with it what he will.

Sometimes we had to wait after Mass until Frank, our seventy-eight-year-old Polish cook, got dinner off the stove and into chafing dishes for us. Another bell rang when it was ready. We plucked napkins from pigeonholes on the wall outside the refectory, queued up, filled our plates with fish, rice pilaf, and a medley of steamed vegetables, then sat down at whatever round table of five had an empty seat. There was no rule to this; it was an understood courtesy, though often its own nod to unexpected grace when you realized you had gone an entire day in the house and not said one word to Tim or Martin or anyone else in the second year. No one was uninteresting or a bore. (Well, almost no one.) Besides, by the time dinner rolled around, we were all usually so exhausted that the best conversation we could summon was on an interesting headline in the newspaper, or the contents of the previous night's episode of *Northern Exposure*.

After dinner, small but efficient groups of four cleaned according to an originless ritual known in the New York novitiate as McQuaid. McQuaid was the name of a nineteenth-century bishop of Rochester, and of a Jesuit high school. Homesick or cynical novices from upstate found some reason to attach the name to the refuse, steam, cleaning fluids, and heat. But McQuaid also became a place of what we called lateral "formation." There was no hierarchy here, only a job to be done. Labor and proximity let us test our own sense of belonging against the others'.

I was assigned to McQuaid that night with Chris, Frank, and Peter, an older, slightly stooped *secundi* whose favorite form of fraternal correction in a situation like McQuaid, when someone might seem too caught up in his own spiritual angst to get the job of sweeping or mopping done, was "Snap out of it!"

Frank had slammed the dishwasher door shut, the machine's jets of water blasting away at the plates and utensils inside, when Chris left the food he was wrapping up to ask, "So what was going on with you and McCallum this afternoon?"

"Why should something have been going on?" Frank said and racked up another tray of filthy dishes.

"Come on. You don't care that much about the General Examen."

"I do. How do you know I wasn't testing myself by taking the position of devil's advocate?"

"Right. I didn't take you for such a conservative."

"What do you mean by conservative?" Frank asked. I was walking in and out of the refectory and the kitchen, sweeping. Frank didn't sound as though he was joking.

"You have to admit, the position you took was a little on the either-or side."

"The position I took is the one I always take. I don't know about you, Chris, but I'm doing this because what I'm giving up is so clear to me." I walked through one more time. "Ask AJ. That boy knows some things."

"I'm not talking," I said.

"Not talking, unless it's with Le Moyne coeds," Chris said and went back to his cellophane and Tupperware containers.

Frank put his hand on my shoulder. "Chris is a little shocked to find out that he wasn't the one she was trying to get close to." Then he pushed one last tray full of forks, knives, and spoons into the ceaseless spin, pulled down the door, and threw the switch. "Hey, Bellito," he shouted over the din as he leaned on the edge of the long sink awash in a mixture of coffee, milk, and soapsuds. "How'd you get in here anyway, if you're so indifferent about studying the *Constitutions*?"

Chris walked back into the dish room. "How?" he asked. "Or why?"

"How? I mean, forget the documents. Isn't there a height requirement?" Frank said and started chuckling.

"Fuck you, Evans," Chris said and hunched over a bowl of leftover carrots. Then, as an afterthought, he shouted back, "They replaced that with an IQ test. What's your excuse?"

"Me?" Frank checked the temperature gauge and walked over to where Chris was working. "I told the truth in the sex, drugs, and rock 'n' roll interview."

Chris pushed the refrigerator door shut and avoided a pile of dirt I had swept up. "What, that you're a classical-music-loving virgin from New Jersey who never once took a sip of altar wine?"

"Nope," Frank said. "When they asked me how often I masturbate, I looked at my watch and said: *What time is it?*" He walked back into the dish room, threw open the washer door, and stepped away as the windows fogged and the steam made it feel as though we were all in a Turkish bath.

"And that worked?" Chris said, trying to sound unimpressed.

"That worked."

"I'll tell you what would work," Peter said from inside the pantry he was mopping, "is you guys shut up and finish those dishes. That would work."

"What are you saying, Pete?" Frank asked. "That I don't work?"

"I'm saying, when I'm done with this mop, I'm done with this kitchen."

"And you'll get no argument from me, son."

I prayed my hour of prayer after the work of the day was done, but before I was too tired to do anything but sleep. Between 7:30 and 8:30 in the evening. Mornings were the preferred hours for prayer among Jesuits (because they inevitably became workaholics at whatever it was they did), but as a novice I liked waiting for the prayer of evening the way I waited for a good friend. Most days I focused on the Scripture readings from Mass. Sometimes a line from a psalm in the breviary, or the life of a saint whose feast it might be. Rare moments I just enjoyed being quiet: in the fold of the chapel (if no one else had the same idea); outside for a walk around our suburban neighborhood (best, if you can believe it, when the Syracuse winter howled); or sitting in my room, surrounded by things familiar—books, guitar, icon of Christ All-Merciful. But of all the places, I preferred the small side office on the second floor of the novitiate where we reserved the Blessed Sacrament in a tabernacle. *Tabernacle*, from the word for *tent*, reaching back to the days of the wandering Israelites. It was the place where they stopped, sat, and spoke to their God. Sitting cross-legged on a pillow on the floor, while a vigil candle burned to indicate the holy presence, I spent the hour in a kind of conversation of quiet, one I neither summoned nor created, but longed for.

We don't pray to change God, C. S. Lewis once said, we pray to change ourselves. Every day and every time you stop and enter into prayer, you set about changing yourself. What have I done? What ought I to do? Each time you ask these questions there comes with them the determination to continue, to return, to keep asking them again and again.

"You didn't call me to be a monk, did you?" I said into the quiet once I had settled (my back sore that day) by leaning against the wall.

The candle flame danced inside the red glass. No wind, yet somehow animated.

"I've said goodbye to others. One called me selfish, and she was right. It's failure I fear."

The flame whipped quickly and released a tiny puff of smoke into the air.

"Failing here. Not by doing something stupid but by not knowing what to do."

Now the flame stood still, looking like a light, not fire. I remembered that tomorrow was Tuesday. I'd be going to the hospital where I was starting work as a volunteer chaplain.

"It's feeling already like a long week," and this came with an exhale from me. The flame reacted briefly and then straightened. It shimmered like a sunset on a warm horizon, golden, liquid, and yet fragile. I could stand up and snuff it out with one move, extinguished as quickly as it was lighted. This seemed somehow to be a warning. Return to the room. This is a holy place, a holy time. I picked up my missal and turned back to the readings for the day. Slowing. Settling. Beginning.

Is it lawful to do good on the Sabbath rather than to do evil, to save life rather than to destroy it?

"Good question. Work if it means to save life." Something moved in me. Something down there, buried in a place where I'd have to dig hard to get at it. "To save it," I said to myself again, thinking of all that had happened this day. *Ordinary Time*, I saw on the schedule, which Joey had put up and which I would be putting up in weeks to come. Ordinary. "Counting down to Advent." The coming. To save life. *To save life rather than to destroy it.* To live like this, every day, that would be something.

The time expanded, contracted, and expanded again, until after forty-five minutes I began to drift, not disciplined yet to the full hour suggested for the practice of prayer. *"Are you asleep?"* A few things left to do as liturgist this evening, I thought to myself. Lock the doors to the outside. Father Minister checked these sometimes, and I didn't want to disappoint him right from the start. And turn off the downstairs lights. Around midnight. I could read in my room until then, or play some guitar. Unless some of the guys were hanging out in the kitchen. I was beginning to like the spontaneous gathering of Frank, Billy, and me in the kitchen for a beer after Night Prayer. Chris sometimes, rarely David, probably because of what had happened today. No matter. There was no real malice between those two. Anyone could see that. It was all trials and testing. At least Spud was in there fighting. Where was I, dreaming . . . *"You can sleep on now and take your rest."* I bet they'll all be in the kitchen after Night Prayer. Compline, as the monks call it. The close of the day. *Protect us, Lord, as we stay awake. Watch over us as we sleep. That awake we may keep watch with Christ, and asleep rest in his peace.*

S t. Jane de Chantal called prayer "a familiar conversation with the Divine Majesty in one's soul." By the time I entered the Jesuits, I had had an eclectic but scattered experience of prayer, not yet like the conversation promised by de Chantal. Still, the thinnest experience of prayer can open a pathway into a place that seems almost certain to be an inexhaustible font, and so something worth staking your life on.

I knew the Mass was prayer, perhaps my earliest form of the act, from the opening and closing blessings of the priest to the gradual understanding that the liturgy is the unifying prayer of the Church, as though it, too, were a person kneeling down to pray for the space of an hour. I got that much. At home we said the rosary, novenas to the Sacred Heart, and a whole host of devotional recitations many Catholics seem to absorb through osmosis. The meditative experience that comes with the recitation of a thing like the rosary regularly when one is young can create a powerful metronome in the heart and mind. So, while I had given up this piety by the time I entered religious life, the *prosody*—the song—of this prayer has never left me. And I was also taught to pray for people—the sick, the needy, the dead—but I never knew why, except that prayer might somehow change things. Prayers of petition, they called these, and as a boy I whispered, "O Lord, please . . ." countless times at night before I rolled over and went to sleep, not believing after a while that those prayers did anything other than somehow soothe a soul in need of any conversation, human or divine.

And yet, regardless of what Reason tried to teach the man I eventually became, the heart has its reasons, too. I couldn't forget that I had heard some prayers of my own petition answered, as though God wanted me not to question whether prayer could change "His mind" or "existence" but to wonder about the nature of *God* and *change*.

In my senior year of college, a friend of mine told me she had been diagnosed with a form of blood cancer. It would be slow, doctors said, but only a matter of time.

"What can I do?" I asked, helpless in the wake of her news, and not expecting an answer.

Twenty-year-olds don't often reach for the vocabulary of prayer. But she came from a southern family with deep Episcopalian roots. She knew, too, about my own Catholic, Eastern European upbringing. I suppose that's why she said, "Well, pray, I guess."

It was Lent, and because I was long-distance running at the time, I decided I would balance the physical with the discipline of what was then a lingering habit of saying the rosary. There was also nothing else I knew how to do that would impose order and give some focus to my prayer.

Then, I thought, as a dare to God rather than to myself, if I am going to pray I want an answer. I finished every decade of the rosary with a "Let her live." This for six weeks. And in May, a few days before my own graduation, long after I had stopped wondering if people are ever given what they ask for, she came to tell me that the doctors had misdiagnosed her. No sickness. No cancer. Her blood was hopping with cells as red as fresh cranberries. Once I thought through the actual time line of events, I told myself it all had to be a coincidence. Medicine is certain of these things. But then, shouldn't medicine also have gotten it right the first time? I decided then that this was the closest I would ever come to witnessing a miracle, tucked the thought away, and got on with where it was my own life was headed.

It was in college, too, during my year in Santa Fe, that I began *zazen*, the practice of meditation known as *sitting*. A man I worked for in the school library was a Buddhist, and after I told him one day that I had tried to meditate like this in high school but stopped after a week of frustration, he offered to teach me. Or I should say he invited me to *sit* with him. John was an intense old hippie raised in Santa Fe, after his parents moved out there from New York in the 1950s. He was reported to have been the first person to play the Beatles' *Sergeant Pepper's Lonely Hearts Club Band* album in the United States, at a party right there on the campus of St. John's College (he had a friend in London who sent him the album before it was released in New York). He knew I was a Catholic ("Like fish in a barrel in this town"), and I had been telling him about my admiration for the prayer of the Carmelite women at St. Michael's. But he knew the works of Thomas Merton, too, so there was never any question of conflict between the discipline of Zen and the faith of Catholic prayer. I would bike down to his house near Cerrillos Road after I ate dinner in the college dining hall. Sometimes there would be three or four other people gathered to sit for thirty minutes, then a cooldown of stretching and some tea. Other times it was just the two of us. Among the culture of tutors at St. John's, I began to think of this man as a kind of teacher. Not a master (he wouldn't have aspired to that) but a guide, a companion who knows the way a little better because he's been on the road a little longer.

When you practice Zen for the first time, you are staggered by how noisy, cluttered, distracted, and unfocused—like some bratty child—the mind can be. But I felt the determination that comes with greater discipline. When I wasn't meditating with the group, I kept to a daily schedule of my own, sitting for thirty minutes in my dorm room, half lotus, spine centered, watching my breath, thinking no thing, just breathing. And gradually, day after day, with no goal or need to accomplish anything, my mind quieted and the focus became more and more that one thing, which is no thing. It's as humbling as it is empowering. All of that distraction—ever present, mind you— dissipates with each breath, like no more than a handful of dust.

John was fond of saying, "When you meet the Buddha, kill him." But in my classes that year we were reading Hume, Kant, Milton, and Newton, and I found that sitting helped me to *see* these difficult texts better. I think I always maintained a certain low-grade anxiety during my four years at St. John's, never believing I was as smart as the rest of my classmates. They understood—the books, the ideas, the philosophizing—and I didn't, at least not right away. And so I couldn't help but feel as though there was something I was missing, some conclusion I was expected to reach and present in our seminars and tutorials. During my year of *sitting*, however, that anxiety—like a distraction—also dissipated. I read the books in what contexts previous discussions had given me, asked questions that concerned me, and remained open to the insight of anyone seated around the table. It was as though I was learning to be patient with my mind as well as my body. My whole self.

Should I have killed the Buddha? Other desires were at play, making my practice slack off. That was the year I went up to the Monastery of Christ in the Desert for Easter. And when I came back, I realized that emptiness as a practice is different from emptiness as a belief.

A Catholic's core stance of faith—the belief that Christ has died, risen (the fullness of the empty tomb), and will come again—gets lived out in the inherently day-to-day nature of community, the road to Emmaus, the recognition in the breaking of the bread. People come together in churches to pray the liturgy (whether the ritual is a reflex of rote memorization or not), to meditate on the Word, and to receive the real presence of Christ in the Eucharist, which means literally a "thanksgiving." Catholics return daily or weekly to this community because we are drawn not to emptiness but to a fullness we believe in, which compels us toward, and keeps us returning to, that conversation with the divine. Which is to say that, whether we turn to prayer in private, with two other people, or with an entire congregation, we look as the many toward the one. Breath, yes. No life without it. But no Buddha to kill either. Rather, a God to speak to, like Moses, the Psalmist, the prophets, and anyone else who's ever said, "O Lord, please . . ." in the night. Prayer radiates like breath and desire as intensely outward as it does in. It seeks the communal, the only way it can prevail, while it also seeks the quiet of retreat. The monk's cloister is a smaller version of the world. No man is an island, and no prayer is uttered out of vanity or in vain. There is no change without changing others. That can be the miracle of cancer cells turning from white to red, or it can mean the realization that we need to be doing this for more than just ourselves.

This change in my prayer came when I made the decision to apply to the Jesuits. While the stimulation of an entirely other kind of community—urban: aural and physical—surrounded me as a graduate student in New York, I used the discipline of Zen "to turn my mind," as Augustine says, "on the things of God." I sat like a Buddhist with a passage from Scripture (recommended by my spiritual director) in front of me. Inevitably, exhausted or distracted, I would lose my focus and my nerve, shake off the drowsy state that I had fooled myself into believing was meditation, and almost bellow into the silence of my room: "What am I going to do?" There, I realized, was that moment of address when God is present in the emptiness. I wasn't expecting some voice to say "Do this!" and then lead me on my own way. I was examining in myself what it meant to ask. With that I began to see how the spiritual discipline I was cultivating supported and shaped the events of my life that led me to this kind of work as a profession.

Each month in the novitiate we sat down for another round of faith sharing. The marathon life stories had all been told by this time. Now, in October, we each got five minutes to talk about what place we had come to in our prayer.

This is a particularly Jesuit notion, the "place" of prayer, putting yourself into the boat in the storm on the Sea of Galilee, walking along the road to Emmaus with those disciples who do not yet recognize the risen Christ, or crying out to God in an emotionally dry and weary landscape. The idea is to compose a scene in your mind, enter it, and track how you are *feeling* as you act and react. Affect is a strong indicator of health and growth in Jesuit spirituality. Ignatius called it *sentir* in Spanish: "For it is not so much knowledge that fills and satisfies the soul, but rather the intimate feeling and relishing of things." And so our long narratives of journey were replaced with snapshot descriptions of what we felt as we retreated into and returned from our one hour of silence each day.

A string of *secundi* spoke that afternoon before it was my turn. The *secundi* as a group would be leaving the novitiate for their "long experiments" in working Jesuit communities in a few months. The move was crucial toward their discernment of whether they wanted to take vows and live in those same kinds of communities for what might be the rest of their lives. Feelings seemed to be rising, if not already running high.

Men like Charles and Martin were champing to get on with it and were frustrated by the constant routine of the novitiate. Nick, Peter, and Rocco had made strong friendships in the work they did in Syracuse. They were feeling a tinge of sadness in the anticipation of moving. And Tim, a journalist who used to write for the *Catholic Worker*, was focused on what was yet to be done here. He spoke of wanting to cover the sloping front lawn at Le Moyne with several hundred white crosses to symbolize *los desaparecidos*, "the disappeared," in El Salvador, and to remember the first anniversary of the six Jesuits who were murdered outside their residence at the University of Central America in November 1989. Their deaths—shot in the head and their brains splattered as a message to those who sought to educate the poor—reverberated among Jesuits, moving every man in the Order, and those about to join, to consider the fact that this life might require a wholly other kind of sacrifice.

"The students will wake up and see this *field* of crosses, like a graveyard, and not know what it means," Tim said with a kind of infectious glee (although I noticed that not everyone in the room was infected by it). "Then they'll be forced to ask: *What's going on?*" Tim liked to confront complacency, and I suddenly had an image of the girl in our Spanish class rising from her bed, going to the window, and wondering what was going on.

The night before, in the reservation chapel, I took for my prayer the reading for Mass that day, Luke 11:5–13. "And I tell you, ask and you will receive; seek and you will find; knock and the door will be opened to you." I wandered for the entire hour back and forth over the last three verses. "What father among you would hand his son a snake when he asks for a fish? Or hand him a scorpion when he asks for an egg? If you then, who are wicked, know how to give good gifts to your children, how much more will the Father in heaven give the holy Spirit to those who ask him?"

These "familiar conversations" are hard story lines to distill, especially in the company of seventeen. I felt, I told the others when it was my turn, as though I really have been among men—fellow Jesuits—who would hand their sons and others bread and fish, the good gifts, even though we sometimes showed what less-than-good gifts we were capable of giving. Some laughed at that in their attentiveness.

"I just got here," I went on, "so while I can appreciate, Charles, your desire to get going and, Rocco, your desire to see this time through to January, I want to do what I'm doing. Study, pray, and complain about McQuaid."

To my *primi* brothers, I admitted that for a while after I had been "given" the chance to flirt with an attractive young woman, the video loop of what might have happened in another time, another place, had played itself out. I had entertained some fantasies, but I held no sullen regrets. "Not indifference," I said, "but this surprising *desire* for something else I've also been given. Does that sound crazy?" David shook his head, and I saw a smile of recognition on Gerry's face. "I've never understood what that Spirit in Luke's Gospel might be, but it seems as though the answer is not to know but to trust. So that's what I'm working on, because I can say I feel as though it's brought me to a good place."

Summer ends now; now, barbarous in beauty, the stooks arise
  Around; up above, what wind-walks! what lovely behaviour
  Of silk-sack clouds! has wilder, wilful-wavier
Meal-drift moulded ever and melted across skies?

I
t's a poem rarely cited by Hopkins lovers, one that was "the out-
come of half an hour of extreme enthusiasm" as the poet-priest
walked home alone after a day of fishing on the Elwy in Wales. It
was autumn now in Syracuse, and I was reading Hopkins not for
prayer but for my pleasure, in the afternoon, outside, bundled in
a fleece and sitting in an Adirondack chair on the shore of Lake
Cazenovia, leaves turning, dropping . . . "And the azurous hung hills
are his world-wielding shoulder."

We came out to Lake Cazenovia on Wednesday afternoons to a
stately villa owned by the Le Moyne College Jesuits. It was a rest
from the daily *ordo* of the novitiate. We ate pizza, watched movies, sat
on the back lawn in warmer weather and drank a beer while the sun
set. Some men didn't like the nineteenth-century grandness and old
money the house suggested, contrary to a vow and life of poverty, and
so stayed away. Others drove out here for the day (though we were
back at St. Andrew's for Night Prayer). I came because I loved to be
by the water. After the years I had spent on the ocean or never more
than a few miles from it, landlocked Upstate often felt empty to me.
"These things, these things were here," Hopkins wrote, "and but the
beholder / Wanting . . ." So, that house in Cazenovia gave me some of

those things I missed from my "old" life. Not only water but a place where I might do some physical labor—paint, chop wood, sit by a fire, for the sake of providing order and shelter, or perhaps just to take care—as well as rest.

But in spite of that, there was little I could say I missed from my former life. Late October and I was feeling, day after day, a continually growing desire—determination—to live *this* religious life in the motions that felt more mundane than ordinary now as we moved closer and closer to Advent, which meant for us imminent change in our stage of formation rather than the coming of a savior. The mundane is not to be discounted, though, when a life is performing the act of beginning again. Because, inside or out, the candle flame flickers and you realize that the prayer, the poetry, the conversation isn't over. In fact, it's barely had a chance to begin. What's more, for as difficult as you think your own struggles are, they're as difficult, if not harder, in others who are trying in their own way to make sense of these beginnings and to come to their own peace.

Once a month two novices spent the night at the Oxford Street Inn homeless shelter on Syracuse's down-and-out West Side, helping the men who ran the place, although there was nothing for us to do but be a presence, and then I was never sure to what end.

The OSI, as we called it, was a warehouse-size hall of eighty-five beds, open from 7:30 p.m. to 8:30 a.m. They never seemed to turn anyone away, regardless of condition, unless someone intended physical violence. Winters it was crowded, summers (I was told) were sparse, which made sense in the logic of street survival.

As beadle, I made all the schedules now and doled out positions and chores according to my own calculus of numbers and chance. Frank and I were on to volunteer for our first time at Oxford Street on a Friday night during the last week of October. Friday meant nothing to us. It was just another night.

Tom dropped us off at 10:30. It had begun snowing, wet, heavy flakes in the early storm. There were some tenacious leaves on the trees. They'd be gone by morning. In front of the shelter, men were coming and going, some determined, some hesitant, trying to assess their own needs against the ferocity of the weather.

"The Jesuits are here," one of the other volunteers yelled to someone inside when Frank and I walked through the door.

"Safe for Democracy," Frank whispered to me under his breath.

"New guys!" a young, twitchy man in a filthy Orangemen sweatshirt said. He was missing front and back teeth on the top and bottom, and his eyes looked glazed and bloodshot under the artificial light. He moved off in a spasm to another corner of the floor.

Whoever was in charge that night came out of his office, introduced himself, and told us to make ourselves at home. I couldn't tell if he was sincere or if that was his attempt at a joke. There were two aluminum urns: one for coffee, the other for hot water. Frank and I took off our coats and stirred packets of cocoa into foam cups.

Everything about the place seemed edgy and harsh. Bare lightbulbs, steel-framed cots, blasts of hot from poorly placed heaters, shards of cold everywhere else, outbursts from "guests" annoyed by or protecting themselves from another visitor, the smell of smoke and alcohol both subtle and hard in the clothing and on the breath of someone walking in late, deciding that, yes, tonight winter was on its way.

I'm not a smoker, but I've always loved the smell of fresh tobacco, maybe because my father in middle age smoked a pipe. Two cots down from the drafty front door, a wan and distant-looking man sat on his bed rolling cigarettes out of finely cut leaf. His fingers trembled slightly, but he sat in an otherworldly silence as he produced those fags, their faint, leathery smell the one welcome scent in the air. He was, I thought, laying up a store for tomorrow, when they would open the doors in the morning and send the inn's inhabitants back out onto the streets, for another day at least. *Where your treasure is, there will your heart be also.*

At midnight, everyone was in who was coming in.

Once I realized that this wasn't some courtesy call, that I wasn't going to stay until two o'clock and then haul ass back to St. Andrew's, I suddenly felt an uneasy claustrophobia about the place. Frank and I had been talking to a volunteer who was a medical student at SUNY Upstate. He had gone to Georgetown and liked the Jesuits, hinted

ANDREW KRIVAK

that he had once (maybe still) thought about joining but was now too busy with school.

"What's your day like?" Ken asked. Frank looked at me as if to say without trying to be snide, "Never thought about that before." Our days appeared to be no different from the days a man like Ken might spend in Syracuse, and yet they were, too, like no day he would ever live without living inside our community. Rather, I thought with a calm resignation, we were antipodean to the men who lived here. We chose poverty and their circumstances had forced it upon them, yet we were homeless all; we looked to some higher, spiritual love in lieu of a particular physical relationship and they knew the destructive violence and lonely addictions that let them love no one, yet we believed in the love of the stranger regardless; and while we were all men who valued our independence with a certain pride, we needed— and wanted—someone to tell us where to go at the end of the day. Such a close equatorial line.

"That's hard to say," Frank said. "We study like students. We clean like housewives. And we still have to find the time to pray like monks. Aside from that, we kind of get on each other's nerves."

Ken laughed, but I could hear the unease. "What's your prayer about?"

"It's about an hour long, and generally in silence," Frank said. "Except when I shout in ecstatic rapture."

I said, "I heard you last night. I wish you'd saved those mystical outbursts for the afternoon."

"Then when would I get any sleep? Huh?"

"Well, not tonight."

"You must get that all the time," Ken said in a self-deprecating tone.

"We're giving you a hard time because we're jealous," Frank said.

"Jealous?"

"That you'll do more good in your life than we will," I said. Frank nodded.

I saw the cigarette-twisting sage turn out a flashlight he had been using to read with. He put his back to us and climbed under the blanket on his bed.

"I guess you pray out of the belief that you'll both remain constant and somehow change, you know?" Frank said, as though he owed Ken a decent answer to his question. "Or that you'll figure out whether God's called you to this before it's too late."

"What do you mean by too late?"

"Too late to do anything else with your life."

"What if God wants you to do what you will no matter what the life?" Ken asked. A man who had clearly thought about this.

"Bull-SHIT!" The shout came from the far corner of the shelter. We all looked up. "It's mine, MUTH-er FUCK-er!" A figure was rising in the shadows toward the back of the warehouse.

"Someone better come out here!" Ken yelled into the office.

But the director was already on his way out the door and down the rows of beds. "Danny! Dan-ee." He held the man by one arm. Danny was walking in a tight circle, looking down as though he had lost something on the floor. Every now and then he would swat at himself with his free arm and hiss, "BITE me . . . don't BITE me!"

"Hey! Shut up over there!" someone else yelled from another part of the cavern.

"We're tryin' 'a sleep." It was the twitchy guy in the dirty sweat-shirt.

"Danny, it's okay. It's right here. Whatever it is, it's right here." The director called to us, "Ken, bring me some water!" I looked over at the sage. He turned his back to the commotion and faced us. Eyes closed, he seemed to be shivering under the covers. His nicotine-stained beard in the half-light of that space made the sheets look whiter than I believed they were.

"Happens," the director said as he walked over to where we'd been talking and sat down. "He'll be up again later, but that should be it for the outbursts. I know old Danny. He's been coming here for years. Slid through the cracks a long time ago."

And that was it for the outbursts. Nothing more to contend with that night than a few cacophonous blasts of loud farts and long snores. These men's lives are also as anticlimactic as ours, I thought, though not feeling any closer to them than the opposite poles I had felt before. With two extra volunteers that night, we could swap off a few hours and get some sleep on a cot near the door, two away from where the sage now slept soundly. Frank offered it to me first, but I said I wanted to stay up. So he flopped down on the top blanket and drifted off to the intermittent roar of industrial heaters, while I sat and wondered what, in their own ordinary time, these souls were counting down toward.

When I got home that morning, I went right to bed. Saturday was a cleaning day, but men who spent the night at the OSI were exempt. The rest had their schedules. The house ran itself.

I slept for a few hours and then went down to the kitchen for a cup of tea. I found a note in my mailbox from the minister, the priest in charge of house administration: "Guests this afternoon for Mass and dinner. Second-floor bathrooms missed! Bill."

Father William Sullivan, SJ, was a big man, six foot four, deliberate in his speech from his earlier days of teaching English in the Philippines, and deliberate in his moves. He went to the famed Jesuit high school Brooklyn Prep and spoke with nostalgia about the days "when Brooklyn was the world." Although younger than Father Sammons back home, Bill had entered religious life in the still-palpable shadow of the Second World War, another young Catholic man who wanted to give his life to the Church, which I realize now was what I wanted to do as well.

With Bill, though, in those early days, I clashed, always running afoul of his meticulous administrative ways.

Out in the world, as we called it, I had bought and owned three secondhand cars, managed my own credit-card accounts, and made rent on time in every place I had ever lived. I had punched a time clock, taken out loans, paid them off, and I knew what it was like to spend my last five dollars on a plate of pasta and a beer. Others in our community had done far more: owned houses, managed stock portfolios, inherited six figures. Now we were all given a twenty, two tens, a five, and five ones on the first of every month. This was the stipend on which we were to live. It wasn't a hardship. It was spending money. Anything we needed was paid for as a formation expense. It was a tangible exercise, though, in that intangible religious ideal of communal poverty. You consumed what you needed and examined if you could get by on less.

Bill seemed to think this was the first time we had ever held fifty bucks in our hands. The range of denominations suggested a false sense of greater quantity within the fixed sum. The formality of dispersal was meant to ensure that we knew who held the coin of the realm. There was something quaint and "old Society" about this when we first arrived, but as the novelty wore off and it became clear that there was quite a gap of years between what Jesuit formation was and what it had become, it all began to feel downright infantile.

While this was easy enough to live with (and overlook), as the beadle I had to deal with Bill for assignments, repairs, credit-card purchases for the house, and the reporting of those purchases, all of which I did, but never with any indication that I enjoyed doing it. That's where, I realized, in Bill's eyes, I fell wide of the mark. Joey always knew that some acting was needed, and he played the part of the beadle well. My indifference toward the job, however, was an indifference toward Bill. My lack of response to the gestures of his system meant a lack of response to his role as a *formator*, a Jesuit in charge of another Jesuit's formation. There was never open conflict. He didn't sit me down and straighten me out. I never thought to consider my role in the matter in prayer. Instead, we talked obliquely, if at all, when I had to report to his office. Other requests, transactions, or critiques were done by way of notes in my mailbox. A measured coldness grew between us as the months wore on.

On a day trip to the Auriesville Shrine of the North American Martyrs (those eighteenth-century French Jesuits who were tortured and killed by the Hurons, and whose faces lived in stained glass in our chapel) one of us novices, in a mix-up over who would pay for the gas (I knew at the time but don't remember now), left the house credit card at an Exxon station on the thruway. David, driving the last section toward home, noticed around the Hamilton exit that the card was gone. I wanted to go back and get it, a backtrack of a few hours, but the others said it was better just to cancel. Or maybe the station owner would drop it in the mail. "Call him when we get home," Chris said.

"Why weren't you on top of this?" Bill asked coldly when we returned and I told him where we had left the card.

"I wasn't driving."

"You're the beadle. You're in charge of these things. You should have made sure everything was in order before you left the station."

"We've all paid for gas before. I'm not going to stand over someone and make sure it's done right. If you want me to say it's my fault, okay. My fault."

"I don't want you to say anything you don't mean," he said. "I want you to know that I now have to cancel a credit card." He sat down at his desk, turned briefly to a stack of papers, and then looked back at me where I stood by the door. "You may go."

Sometime after that he started asking Joey to take him on bank runs (Bill never learned to drive) and to make sure Billy inspected the furnace or dropped off one of the Toyotas at the dealer for repairs, leaving the schedule to me, and my regular check-ins with Don. He wasn't relieving me of my duties because I had failed him in some way. He was taking a path of least resistance. Ministers saw them come and saw them go as well. Maybe he hoped I'd be gone come January. Let it be, I decided. I'd rather have less of this kind of work to do. So I didn't bother to see who had been assigned to the second floor that Saturday morning. I finished my tea, grabbed a squirt bottle of 409 and a toilet brush, then cleaned the bathrooms and vacuumed the floors myself.

This day, of all days, lives in my memory from that time because of the seamless way with which I moved from one world to another in the space of twenty-four hours, no more than five miles apart. The ordered imperium of Jesuit formation, elite, like-minded, secure within its boundaries, and unflinching in its direction; and a shadowy assembly of broken men, pugnacious, addicted, and transient. One believed the other was in need of salvation because it had gotten lost somehow along the way. But who was in need of whom? I wondered. Was the getting lost as obvious as the having gotten? *What if God wants you to do what you will no matter what the life?* No matter what way you've chosen, or believed you were given. There was no ideal morning or ideal night, no certain task or way to pray that captured this life. I've always hated the expression "There but for the grace of God, go I." God doesn't pick and choose who'll be a drunk and who'll be a Jesuit, who'll suffer from the DTs and who'll read a Hopkins poem before going to sleep. I required and received as much grace as the broken Danny and the nicotine-addicted sage. We all did, and that's what I accepted on that day—somewhere between wiping shit off the rim of a toilet bowl and vacuuming the floor of the chapel (after which I sat in that silence and prayed, hoping, as St. Paul says, that the Holy Spirit would intercede "with sighs too deep for words")—the realization that the work of my novitiate had just begun. I no longer felt homeless myself or wondered where I belonged, because, in spite of everything, this house was where I longed to be.

The work I did look forward to in my first year as a novice was at SUNY Hospital in downtown Syracuse. I was a chaplain under the supervision of a cherubic Slovak American priest named Father Al. Every Tuesday and Thursday morning I got the bus on Salt Springs Road with Tom, Joey, Rocco, Charles, and Tim and spent the day wandering the wards, hoping to find every one of my spiritual "patients" well.

I didn't like it at first. I felt uncomfortable in the airless, antiseptic halls, calling on people whose wracked and failed bodies made them vulnerable, angry, or unnaturally passive. I wore a shirt and tie (never a Roman collar, which wasn't given to us to wear until we had taken our first vows) like some wrong preacher in a Flannery O'Connor story. Timidly, and going on their admissions chart that they were Catholics, I would ask patients if they'd like to talk, pray, or receive viaticum, the Church's distribution of Holy Communion to the sick, literally "for the way." Sometimes there would be no response. Sometimes they would start yelling. Most times they said, "Thank you, yes," or "Thank you, no." Sometimes they would ask me to stay.

Helen was in her late sixties. Her husband, John, was the same age, and he sat with her in the hospital all day, every day. She had been diagnosed with cancer the form of which I don't remember anymore, but she was clearly on the short road of a fast decline. When I met her and John in October, they always wanted to receive Communion together. Then they would ask not why but *when* I had begun my studies for the priesthood.

"Oh, the Jesuits!" Helen would say. "They're the good ones."

When Anne or Beverly, the two regular nurses on Helen's floor, came in to check on her, Helen would sing, "Andrew is going to be a priest. Don't you think he'll make such a fine one?"

Anne would give me a wink on her way out the door and say, "Ah, Helen. I think it's a shame. Now try to take a little nap."

When Helen did sleep, John and I talked in the waiting room, mostly small talk. He always seemed preoccupied with when he might lose his wife.

Come November, a bowel obstruction had developed in Helen. She was attached to an IV and couldn't have any solid food, which meant that she couldn't receive the Communion host either. Still, she listened to the readings for the day, then prayed the Our Father sotto voce and watched wistfully while John—as though alone already—closed his eyes and consumed the consecrated wafer I took from the guarded interior of my chaplain's pyx.

One day I walked into Helen's room and she started weeping. I noticed that John wasn't there, and I thought something had happened to him.

"What's wrong?" I asked in a panic.

She said, "I can receive today!"

Her doctors had discovered the previous afternoon that the obstruction had somehow gone. So we sat in silence for a moment to collect ourselves, said the Our Father and Agnus Dei with palpable anticipation, and as I placed what we both believed was the body of Christ into Helen's outstretched hand, she looked flushed with the color of some new life she had long been waiting for. It was a vision I had seen before, when my mother used to take Communion to my grandmother, sick in bed at home in the long, drawn-out last years of her life. I remember standing off to the side (I was a teenager and about to leave home for college), watching daughter and mother share this act of faith passed on. And my father is now something of a legend at St. Therese's for having taken viaticum to so many of the parish sick during the years of his own retirement; he and a few other men of the parish acted as self-appointed, unordained deacons to whatever priest walked through their doors. This Holy Communion and its effect on a person was a healing I understood to be a kind of tenacious spider's web of strength that led us not into Jonathan Edwards's fiery Hell but along that final, sacramental stretch of road toward Heaven.

The week before Thanksgiving, all us novices made a five-day retreat in the house.

For the *secundi*, the retreat marked the last consecutive month of novitiate life, before they left for New York City and the Jesuit communities of Fordham University or Xavier High School, with new apostolates that gave them a glimpse of their future in the Order.

For us *primi*, these five days were a precursor to the Long Retreat, the first shift into extended silence and a new level of prayer.

On the first day, the contrast of our former schedule and the new silence seemed to cover the novitiate like a pall. Where once we spoke freely or lingered in groups over tea, coffee, or a beer—in the refectory, at the kitchen table, or in front of the TV—there was an empty wake. We couldn't build or travel (yet) to a new novitiate, so we constructed around ourselves rooms of silence as we were summoned to Mass in the chapel, or left alone to wait on God elsewhere.

Snow fell for the next two days. Don reminded me to put up a schedule for shoveling. "Make a morning and a noon shift. But make it voluntary, in case anyone's working on personal things."

I have the notebook that contains my reflections from those days. They're in a journal I kept the summer before, when a captain from MacDougalls' asked if I could help him and his wife deliver the boat they were skippering from Nassau to Falmouth. I arrived in the islands on a one-way ticket with a letter from Howard saying that I would be leaving by sea. Now every day I looked at the cartoonish "Commonwealth of the Bahamas Inspected Baggage" sticker I had placed on the cover of the notebook as a keepsake.

Inside, after my personal ship's log (which ends on August 11, 1990, and thoughts on Thomas Merton's essay "Rain and the Rhinoceros" in the midst of a Maine fog), I began: "11/17/90: 7:15 a.m. to 8:15. Luke 11:1–4, 9–13: At first I was glad to listen to the sounds of the voiceless morning. Then, I turned to the first verse: 'He was praying in a certain place . . .' "

The same passage I had been focused on in my prayer when it came up in the liturgical cycle in October now centered those five days of my first novitiate retreat. I had come to this *certain place,* I realized then, because it was, after I had knocked and asked, what had been given: the instruction to pray, the persistence and community, the good things that were as much as and more than *bread, fish, eggs.* All had become a kind of *Holy Spirit.* And while my prayer periods ventured out into other reflections aimed at shoring up the novice for the experience of the *Spiritual Exercises* (Psalm 139, "Lord, you have probed me, you know me"; John 15, "Remain in me, as I remain in you"; Romans 8, "We wait with endurance. In the same way the Spirit too comes to the aid of our weakness"), I always came back to the peace that I had found in this *certain place.*

When we came off silence on Thanksgiving Day, Chris, our self-assured Italian boy from the Bronx, told us that he would be leaving the Jesuits. As a class, David, Frank, Billy, and I were surprised to hear about Chris's decision. We thought he had been happy in the novitiate. He was certainly engaged with it. I don't remember if he gave any particular reason for leaving. Weeks after he was gone, word was he missed the girlfriend he had left back home more than he believed he was called to be a priest. And that, in the end, I think, turned out to be the truth.

One month later, on the day of Christmas Eve, I went down to the hospital for Father Al's small staff party to say my goodbyes. I wouldn't be back in Syracuse until mid-February.

Before the party, though, I went up to the sixth floor. I wanted to see Helen and say a prayer with her and John. I bolted out of the elevator and down the hall. Her room was empty. I walked over to the nurses' station. Anne and Beverly saw me coming and feigned a preoccupation with charts. I knew what had happened, we had all been waiting for it, but it's never real until the absence is there, yawning and clifflike, something close to a favorite piece of music cut short, but with the added pain of knowing that you'll never hear those notes again. I was trying not to cry.

"She died early this morning," Beverly said before I could ask. "He was here, so she wasn't alone. Left an hour ago." There was a fresh bouquet of flowers on the counter. The card inside, placed slightly askance and facing out, read: "To the Nurses, Thank you. Love, John." I wanted to do something, something human, I wanted to hold them both, hug these two women who must have felt what I was feeling, if not every day, then enough days to make it an emptiness you never get used to. But they went back to their charts. Any move from me toward them now would have seemed awkward and foolish. "Well, Merry Christmas anyway," I said and walked back toward the elevators.

At the novitiate, we had fresh-cut, decorated fir trees in the living room, refectory, and chapel. We were each allotted fifteen dollars to spend on a gift for the novice whose name we had pulled out of a hat. I picked Charles and bought him a CD of Debussy nocturnes. Before dinner on Christmas Eve we drank spiked eggnog and exchanged our gifts. It was forced and felt somewhat childish, not at all how I had imagined spending the holidays in religious life. But no one said a word in protest. What words would they be from us who professed to live a life of poverty? We were all too tired. I got a navy and paisley tie that I liked. I put it on and kept drinking eggnog until I discovered the end of that tie soaking in my drink. Time for something other than this clownish attempt at cheer, I thought, got up, walked back to my room, and lay down to sleep, hoping the liturgist would wake me for Midnight Mass. But I couldn't sleep. Instead, I stared at the ceiling and wondered what would come of all this in the new year, while the wind beat in blasts against the window.

Christmas Day we woke up to an unusual sight in Syracuse. The sun. The newspaper had already said that from mid-November to December 20, Syracuse had seen something like nine hours of unobstructed sunlight. Finally, this dawn sky was cloudless. I dressed for outside and walked downstairs. The snow-shoveling schedule had cut off in the evening. There would be another eight inches on the ground.

"Morning!" Tom said as I opened the door. One of the dutiful, he had been out shoveling since 7:00 a.m.

"Almost done?"

"Not even a dent."

We considered dividing the driveway in half but decided against it. So we started together at the top, by the garage, and began to work our way down toward the road.

David and Frank came out to join us an hour later. Standing in jeans and an Irish wool sweater, Frank said, "Damn. Never see white stuff like this in Jersey."

"In Buffalo," Tom said, "this is a dusting." He pretended to adjust his cap and then dug deep into a drift.

It was almost ten o'clock when we finished and went back inside. Gerry and Joey were in the kitchen, at the work of baking and cooking for the holiday feast that would come later. At that hour, a Polish mother's poppy-seed roll was in the oven, an Italian grandmother's red sauce on the stove. Don had brewed a fresh pot of coffee and was walking back to his room, breviary in hand. I left the other three in the refectory. Classical music was coming from Bill's office, and I felt a rush of contrition for my part in the cold war between us. "I'll go to him for confession later on today," I said to myself, peered out of habit into my empty mailbox, and went upstairs to get ready for the Christmas Mass in daytime.

The Jesuit Retreat House of St. Isaac Jogues in Wernersville, Pennsylvania, sits on a high promontory above horse farms and potato fields, and overlooks the town of Sinking Spring. The South Mountains of Berks County lift and drop in the distance. On nights when there is no wind, you can hear the old Reading Line trains moving along the tracks of the Great Valley.

The entrance to the grounds is a black wrought-iron archway flanked by white stone pillars, shrubs to the right, and a large overhanging tree to the left. Drive too quickly and you'll miss it. From this gate a single-lane paved road winds for a quarter mile, ascending past stands of birch, shaded lawns, and a few benches placed at strategic points for the peripatetic. At the top, the house occupies its incongruous summit like an Italian villa. Stairs lead from the circular drive to a long southern-style porch and the entrance of two massive double wooden doors. The roof of the main chapel pushes its peaked center higher in the front. A bell tower rises above that. Three stories of dormitory-like rooms sprawl symmetrically from the north and south wings of the house. Hints of terraces, gardens, and cloister walks emerge from behind a modest protection of large boxwood and privet hedge.

The four of us stepped out of the car we had driven down from Syracuse and surveyed the building and these grounds. This was how I had imagined the retreat into religious life should look. Paths approaching a summit. The end point a quiet yet majestic place. I

thought: If only I had joined the Maryland and not the New York Jesuits, then maybe the past few months of novitiate wouldn't have felt
so mundane.

That was when the Maryland novices came out of the front doors
and greeted us with the same mixture of confidence and goodwill our
secundi brothers had shown us at St. Andrew's in August. No visible
difference in the way we looked or the clothes we wore. They were
an older class, though. There was a Ph.D. in philosophy, a Ph.D. in
physics, and an ex-lawyer with several years of practice behind him.
Three of them hurried down the stairs toward us. Two of them broke
off halfway. The last three, with the philosopher among them, remained on the porch.

On the novices' wing of Jogues, where there were easily enough
empty rooms to accommodate us, we each disappeared into two connected six-by-ten studies. Cubbyholes really. There was a desk and a
chair in one, a single bed and a radiator in the other. Outside, I could
hear the staggered sound of bags hitting the floor. The magnitude
of what we were about to undertake suddenly struck me, and I
felt lonely and afraid, in spite of the others there with me. What I
wouldn't have given then to go back to Syracuse and not face the spiritual unknown that awaited us all in this place. Then we emerged at
the same time a few minutes later, four dazed watchers spread evenly
along a football-field length of hall.

"Ahh," Frank said, his voice moving down the walls like a bowling
ball. "Always prefer to stay in the luxury hotels."

"There you go, AJ," Billy offered uncharacteristically. We had argued in the car on the way down about the need to study a language
systematically. Billy said he could learn Spanish just by listening, immersed. I agreed with the immersion but said that you had to know
how the pieces fit before they'd make any sense. I hadn't wanted to
pick a fight but wouldn't let go once I did. I didn't stop to think that
maybe Billy was feeling self-conscious about the new kind of work he
was, for the first time in his life, struggling with instead of having it
come naturally and easily. "Thirty days to be as much of a monk as
you'd like," he said.

I pretended to survey the hall. "And you, Billy?" I asked.
He shrugged. "What's not to like?"

It was the second of January, 1991. Twelve novices from the New
York and Maryland Provinces, along with three priests acting as spiritual directors (Gerry was ours), would live for a month of silence on
one floor of this house, which in 1930 would have swelled to capacity
with seminarians, and make the *Spiritual Exercises of St. Ignatius Loyola*. Removed from work, play, any distraction, we shifted to this next
phase of our training: the Long Retreat. We were to have no contact
with others, including fellow retreatants, except forty-five minutes of
conversation a day with our director and whoever might greet us with
"Peace" at Mass. We would pass people in the halls, see them stroll-
ing the grounds, or hear them crunching away across from us at meal-
time, but their thoughts, their voices, their actions should be no
concern of ours. Studying, dish washing, visiting the sick—they were
all set aside now, and our lives would be marked off in stages the *Exercises* called the Four Weeks.

That year, though, peace—or the lack of it—was on everyone's
mind, even those of us who were about to disappear for a month from
the world. Far away from the snows of Syracuse and the fields of
southeastern Pennsylvania, American troops in Saudi Arabia drilled
and then waited for what would be the first Persian Gulf War. Diplo-
mats were attempting to dislodge Saddam Hussein's sudden occupation of Kuwait five months earlier, a few weeks before we began
religious life. Now there was an appetite for battle. Military planners
were employing the phrase "full, decisive and overwhelming force."
Saddam, a man whose face and actions the world would come to see
a great deal of, referred boastfully to the impending fight as "the
mother of all battles," as though the desert would be host to some
epic struggle between the forces of good and evil. It was, but not in
ways anyone ever expected.

We went into silence on the third of January wondering if we
would emerge to find that we were living in a time of war. Yet I don't

remember the conflict looming over us in a manner that would suggest a poignant theme for men preparing to follow the life of one of the Church's great soldier-saints. Our own battlegrounds were being prepared. The evening that began our retreat, after a subdued and reverent Vespers, Gerry, sounding like the author of Ecclesiastes himself, instructed us that there was a time for concern about the things of the world and a time for meditation on the ways of the heart. "You've come here to search your hearts, not books or the newspaper. You've certainly not come here to have a good time." Word had gotten out that some of the Maryland guys wanted to have a little pre-Retreat party, but the directors put the skids to that fast. Gerry said he would brook no deviation from the rules, notes, and prayer of the *Spiritual Exercises*, nothing that wasn't taken up and discussed with him first. These thirty days were crucial, he insisted, for knowing not only *if* but *how* we should continue as Jesuits. Master and commander now of our little New York army of four, he held his index finger up as though to indicate one rule alone was written in stone, and said: "Don't fuck with the Long Retreat." Then we finished with a prayer for the Holy Spirit and were dismissed to our rooms.

Invective aside (persuasive as it is at times), this was what I needed to hear. A directive. A purpose. A reminder that I was about to undertake an endeavor greater than myself, one in which I could place my trust with the sole intent of knowing at the end of this time that a vocation to religious life—a life within the Society of Jesus—wasn't someone else's idea or desire but mine.

The First Week

The *Spiritual Exercises* are at a glance little more than notes for how a person might engage in a method of prayer. Ignatius Loyola's "Introductory Observations" themselves are written in ordered blocks that contain pragmatic terms such as *examination, facts, summary explanation,* and *inordinate attachments.* Unlike the monk's *lectio divina,* reflective reading that inclines "the ear of your heart" to a word or words in a sacred text, the *Exercises* require mental and spiritual participation in that "place" we were taught to compose in our prayer, and then an after-reflection, which we did in the form of a written journal.

This was how the founder of the Jesuits discovered God dealt with him. Recovering from a near-fatal wound to his leg, Ignatius the soldier began reading a life of Christ, the only book around in the Loyola family castle. In time (and with nowhere else to go but "inside"), he discovered that imagining he was a poor follower of the Lord brought him more joy than imagining he was a dashing knight. The healing body brought with it a changed and restless heart. And as the man moved further and further away from his old life and into his new, he tracked, literally, how it felt at each step of the way, the notes of which laid the foundation for the *Exercises*.

My method of prayer on retreat was no different from the hour-long periods of prayer I had been working toward as a novice that fall. I began at first in my room, as I had at St. Andrew's, sitting upright in a chair with a new candle in its holder on my desk, an old crucifix stark and solitary on the wall above it. Gerry had directed me toward Psalm 23, and so I settled into a "mental representation of place," proceeded by imagining a time and space to accompany the prayer, seeing, listening, feeling everything in and around me. But I found no verdant pastures outside my window, no restful waters, and in the small plot of that unfamiliar room, no repose. For the next period I moved to the novices' chapel and prayed there in the dark, expanding physically in the space but not in the valley of my soul. Afterward, when I sat down to record the direction and feeling of my prayer, I wrote of *continual distractions, mental wanderings, near sleep*. My thoughts were elsewhere—the Caribbean, Cape Cod, New Mexico— my feelings the feelings of a man second-guessing a life he had chosen as it unfolded right before him, and I discovered what was at stake for these next thirty days: How determined was I to pass through the second-guessing and doubt, and change?

This kind of beginning is to be expected. I had gotten a hint of it during the five-day retreat in November. The most distracted and wandering meditation period holds something of what Ignatius calls the "fruit" of prayer: Now that you've imagined and *felt*, what will you *do*? How *will* you change? What stands in your way? For my part, it was precisely in my stubborn unwillingness to believe that what I had been given and, from that, what I had been able to make were both things worth accepting and carrying to their fullness and end. Which is precisely the aim of the First Week, to know and to feel where and how I—my individual soul—have strayed from what Ignatius calls the "First Principle and Foundation": "Man is created to praise, reverence, and serve God our Lord, and by this means to save his soul." If anything should get in the way of this, we risk the greatest loss of all. So "our one desire and choice should be what is more conducive to the end for which we are created." The choice is simple after all. But simplicity doesn't translate into ease.

Thomas Merton tried to work through the *Spiritual Exercises* on his own in the cloister of his Perry Street apartment in the West Village. With a mixture of the bohemian he had been and the Trappist he would become, every afternoon for a month, Merton wrote in *The Seven Storey Mountain*, he sat in dark and silence, in the back of the house where there was no street noise, cross-legged on the floor, the blinds drawn "so that there was just enough light left on the wall to see the pages, and to look at the Crucifix on the wall over my bed." Merton thought, "The Jesuits would have had a nasty shock if they had walked in and seen me doing their Spiritual Exercises sitting there like Mahatma Gandhi." But Ignatius would have said Merton was adapting the *Exercises* "to the condition of the one who is to engage in them." And although, in the end, Merton found them "too big and simple and radical" for him, this one key insight from Ignatius Loyola impressed itself upon the young man: detachment from those things "which tended to get me in trouble."

January 5, 1990 (11:00 a.m.): It's wonderful to see so much light day after day. G has been having me meditate on what he calls "the gifts of the Spirit" in my life. What have I been given? What am I grateful for? I'm trying to get used to the schedule, the most difficult change of which is waking up for the midnight meditation. Afterwards, it's impossible to go back to sleep. On the other end of the day, after dinner, vespers, and another full hour of prayer, I'll emerge from the corner of the choir loft I've been using for my meditations (where I half expect bats to engulf me) and find that it's only 7:30, pitch black out, and so quiet not even incidental noises puncture the silence. Would that sleep came then. I feel like a freakish cross between a narcoleptic and insomniac.

I prayed for an hour immediately upon rising, reflected on the experience in my journal for five to fifteen minutes, then showered and went down to breakfast as though it were a day like any other. When I returned to the novices' wing, I fell back into prayer. Lunch the same, then an afternoon meditation. Mass, dinner, another period at 8:00, waking again at 12:00 a.m., returning to sleep, if I could, until morning. That was the routine: a burgeoning interior life of contemplation. What I hadn't expected, though, as hour moved into hour and I sometimes sat and counted minutes until the end of a period, was the danger of a withering exterior boredom.

I brought this up to Gerry, and that was when he had me turn to a contemplation on what he called "the gifts of the Spirit," the ways in which I had been shaped, moved, and called by God from the earliest days of my life. "And I want your prayer to be an hour of writing," he said. "No sitting in the dark. Be as creative and as animated as you'd like, as long as you're writing. That should cure your boredom."

Maybe it was because Pennsylvania now surrounded me. Maybe it was the more direct fact that the "gifts of the Spirit" had taken me back to the town north of here where I had grown up. I began to think more seriously about this journey, the road out of Dodge, which was the town of Dallas, Pennsylvania, and that place composed itself with grace on the page: the small one-story house we lived in that always seemed larger than it really was; the closeness of family, at least when we were young; the fall Saturdays when I split logs for our cast-iron, ceramic-fronted Pittston stove with my father; the heat that stove pumped out, along with the hints of burning apple, cherry, and oak, all winter; the springs and summers Matthew and I stole down to Toby's Creek, "a place of retreat for Toby the Indian, whose haunts were once along the creek to which his name has been given" (or so Peck's history said); our grandmother, my mother's mother, who lived up the street from us, dried fruit on a radiator, brewed sassafras tea, and came to Mass with us; St. Therese's Church, a place in which I felt at home, the liturgy a sort of ritual storytelling that served to make sense (I was taught) of the week that had passed and the week ahead; and, as I realize the uniqueness of their presence now, the books that surrounded us as we all got older (though not all of us took to them), suggesting that there were other places, people, ideas yet to be found, and a faith that never wavered.

> January 6, (8:00 p.m.): There's both a certain creative release in my prayer and yet a nagging, unsettling sense of guilt. G is suggesting stories and poetry to focus me. I find myself returning to where I grew up in Pennsylvania, the Back Mountain. The summers I spent outdoors. The winters when a coal-stove burned perpetually in our basement (and the ashes I was given the job to shovel). The love, both tough and tender, that defined my family. I was too bookish to have many friends—Christine, who fed me the Beats and the Brits; Jim, with whom I played guitar—but that pushed me to look beyond the small-town horizon. Then, I shifted from the good presence of Nature around me at home to the intense boredom—there it is again—I've often felt when I returned as an adult, as though the way to happiness was a way out. Once I accepted that there was grace as well in the leaving (believing that the Spirit was sending me) I dwelled upon the odd ways in which I had discovered roads that led somewhere, and got on roads that wound up a dead end. "You grew up on a dead-end street, remember?" I said to myself. Is this the essence of my vocation, knowing the heart's origin, while the body journeys on? Perhaps what we think are dead ends can become through streets in ways we'd never considered.

The true mark of the tyro is mistaking the sky reflected in the surface of water for the genuine depth of the sea. As my meditations continued, I began confusing gifts received with the smug and dangerous pride of having gotten out of that place and gotten a better deal than those who always said they wanted to stay, "Because it's home," but who had no choice. I could see, out of the corner of my mind's eye as it were, that I was beginning, as I wrote in my journal a few days later, "to control my own story of the Spirit near the end" (but I hadn't begun to examine it yet), and so turned that directive for my prayer into a license to create my own distractions, without realizing that the whole point was to turn me toward what God had given, not what I might make.

So, because the food served in the retreat house dining room was defiantly bad (I stuck to cold cereal at breakfast, salad and a thrown-together sandwich for lunch, then took my chances on the main course of the day at dinner: dry chicken, baked pasta, limp vegetables), I began studying the kitchen staff as examples of the kind of life I had managed to avoid as a Pennsylvanian. Listening in silence to the chatter coming from where they worked as I stirred honey into weak tea, I started making up stories about what brief lives and character sketches these men and women—cooks, washers, food preparers— offered in their faces, which were like a gallery of portraits I had grown up staring into.

I called the stout dyed blonde in charge of getting the food out to us, Rita Grobowsky, and imagined that she began working at Jogues Retreat pushing carts and washing dishes when her husband up and left her in '82. As with everyone else on staff, she got hired through the friend of a friend of Father Somebody, SJ. It was either the kitchen or welfare. She had two children. An older son named Ricky and a daughter named Rose. Ricky was always on the verge of trouble during the years just after the divorce, but he settled down, thought briefly about enlisting in the Air Force, and then got a job doing cable TV repair. He had a good area, a swath of suburbs south of Reading, away from the blacks and Hispanics who had strangled that small city's once-grand downtown with their guns, drugs, and "loud ways." His wife gave birth to a baby girl, Megan, last August.

Rose, though, was Rita's darling. Smart, attractive (the real Polish blonde), and ambitious. She had the grades to go to Georgetown, and that same Father Somebody said he knew the president there. In the end, though, Rose visited Penn State's main campus and fell in love

with it. She got her degree in marketing and is the new public rela-
tions liaison for the Yeungling brewery in Pottsville, Pennsylvania. She
puts on a crisp navy suit and very little makeup (she's that pretty), and
takes visitors for a tour of America's oldest brewery, entertaining them
behind the bar at the end of the visit with one glass per person and
the closing chapter of how the oldest and the *best* beer is made right
here in Pennsylvania. "No, she doesn't have a boyfriend," Rita says to
anyone who asks, "because she works too hard." Besides, she's thinking of going to law school in a few years. "She won't do this forever.
Not my Rosie," Rita says and pushes the dessert cart back into the
walk-in refrigerator.

But when I brought these up to Gerry, hoping that I could deceive
him with a gesture toward benevolent humor, he saw right through
me, as though to the bottom of that sea. "Uh-huh," he said, trying to
look patient but unable to hide the stone fixture of his otherwise animated face, a signal to us all that the man wasn't in the mood to be
messed with. Then, "Look, AJ, I didn't give you this latitude for you to
have fun with. If you can't distinguish the difference between the gift
of an imagination and the grace of the Holy Spirit, then you've some
work to do." I was sent back for a repetition on the First Principle and
Foundation, and then, in the sleepless haze of the midnight meditation, I was to ask again for what I genuinely wanted to receive.

The purpose of the First Week, as it moves along in these fits and
starts, is to face the reality of sin. From his own experience, Ignatius
knew that this initial stage of recognition was the darkest and most
painful room to enter. So it had to be for us as well.

The gifts—my own as well as the Spirit's—I had been mining
were a catalyst. Gerry must have known where they would lead. He
was from Pennsylvania himself. Or maybe he knew from experience
where God would take me. Days later, I couldn't shake the edgy pride
that pricked at me, and this as the meditations moved into an extended Examination of Conscience, with its categorizing of insidious
faults: Pride, yes. The deadliest of all the deadly sins. But there was
also Envy (the fear that Rita and Rosie both were happier than I),

Avarice (what gifts my brothers had that I wished were mine), Wrath (in the guise of uncharitable words and deeds that were meant to give offense), Greed, Lust, and Sloth (deeds left undone because I was too damn weak to take a stand). What sort of box was being pried open here? It was the one question I could ask with no conclusions yet to draw, and going on faith that God must somehow be guiding me.

The idea in these "exercises" is not to count the quantity so much as to recognize the patterns of sin, to remember, and to find a sorrow in that memory that eluded me in my blindness the first time. Yet, as the hours and days of prayer and examination wore on, my conscience entered into a free fall of awareness, sensitivity, and focus, until the memory of the past and the contemplation of the present seemed to conflate into one and move side by side to the ticking of a clock.

The first meditation is on the sin of the angels, the Fall, "seeking to remember and understand all the more to be filled with shame and confusion when I compare the one sin . . . with the many sins I have committed." Every angel created the same, all of them serving God, and yet some longing to be greater than the others, imagining a rival power. Lucifer—attractive, ambitious—wanted it all. "To reign is worth ambition though in hell," Milton wrote of his protagonist. Not even my own prayer could escape this same damning mix of pride and envy (such deep roots) I had dragged for twenty-seven years around with me, until so comfortable was I in its skin that I believed it was a harmless exercise. "To set himself in glory above his peers." I knew the sin of Pride is the sin of the self, I who believed that I was always smarter and better than the people of Dallas, one step ahead, able to get out, and yet to where?

More and more I remained in my room for these prayer periods, especially at night, as though wanting not to stray from the place where some meeting had been prearranged. Chair. Candle. Desk. Crucifix. Then the second meditation, as Ignatius himself seemed to lead me like a Virgil leading Dante, "that of our First Parents, who sinned by violating the command not to eat of the tree of knowledge." They lost "original justice," Ignatius reminds us, "and for the rest of their lives lived without it in many labors and great penance." How I confused the work my parents put into raising their family with the feeling that I ought to be entitled, somehow, to more. Why can't I go to that school? or Why don't we buy that car? I pressed my parents when I was a boy and a young man. I knew. We were caught in the middle of getting what we needed, never what we wanted. Never what I thought I deserved. If there is such thing as an "original" sin, the sin of Adam, it may be mapped according to this parentage: want, the opposite of sacrifice (and how my own parents sacrificed). We're takers by nature. We survive according to it. Eat or be eaten. And to choose another path, to go against what we've been "taught," can prove deadly. Ask Socrates. Ask Jesus. Ask the Jesuits in El Salvador.

Finally, "the record and gravity of my sins . . . What am I compared with all men? What are all men compared with the angels and saints?" Ignatius asks: "Consider what all creation is in comparison with God. Then I alone, what can I be?"

What can I be to those I had hurt willfully, choices made that I knew averted justice, right paths I had not taken because they were the more difficult choice, and confusion I brought upon myself? *In what I have done, and in what I have failed to do.* And the risk of a lifetime of living in this wake.

I hadn't known any great evil at that point in my life, or so I thought. I'd had my share of fights, aggression on all sorts of levels, active and passive. I reveled in and was confused by the unconsummated fumbling of adolescence, with all of its petting, self-pleasuring, and empty longing. I've told my share of lies and spread deceit, sadly aimed at times at that same sacrifice of my parents, who in their own awkwardness wanted what was best for me. I felt the strong temptation once in the presence of cold, hard cash to steal, but then heard my father's voice, the social worker as Robin Hood: *"If you're going to steal money, make sure it's millions so that you can fill the pockets of someone who needs it."* Perhaps the most insidious evil that plagues me is the constant comparison with and covetousness of anyone and anything that isn't, and will never be, my own.

It's no surprise that my journal entries tracking these periods are tellingly vague and nonspecific. ("I began to fade and must have fallen asleep . . . Poor sleep has taken its toll on me . . ."). I convinced myself I was no better and no worse than your average sinner. Make the list and get on with the retreat. I avoided genuine sorrow well because I failed to see at first what Ignatius was trying to get at: it's the weak yet constant turning away from sacrifice and love that sin accomplishes, if you can call that an accomplishment. Slowly yet surely it happens, until you realize you've gone too far, and that it might be too late to turn back.

Midway into that First Week, with the suddenness of a river approaching steep falls, I entered the descent into the meditation on "the length, breadth, and depth of Hell."

FIRST POINT: To see in the imagination the vast fires, and the souls enclosed, as it were, in bodies of fire.

SECOND POINT: To hear the wailing, the howling, cries, and blasphemies against Christ our Lord and against His saints.

THIRD POINT: With the sense of smell to perceive the smoke, the sulphur, the filth and corruption.

FOURTH POINT: To taste the bitterness of tears, sadness, and remorse of conscience.

FIFTH POINT: With the sense of touch to feel the flames which envelop and burn the souls.

In our rooms we were instructed to close the windows, pull the blinds, and be careful at all times for a period of two days to avoid distractions and not to make any unnecessary noise. The effect was truly some kind of paradise lost, "The seat of desolation, void of light, / Save what the glimmering of these vivid flames / Cast pale and dreadful . . ."

I conjured a Hell that roared through my senses with synesthetic overload. Rancid, aching shouts that approached in terrifying increments, like the New York City subway in August, deafening and piss-smelling, a humid waft crawling beneath clothes and onto every inch of body, to settle there like a second skin. The *No Exit* terror of a homeless shelter, with its fetid stillness, disembodied shrieks, and tense boredom. Then, bodies around me became the body of a drowned man I had seen once, skin emptied of pigment, the stomach bloated and pushing out vomit, eyes rolled back and staring at none of us who stood over him. Go on, Ignatius seems to say, think of what you know of as misery, and know that this is *unimaginably* worse.

Worse, were I like the Fallen, unredeemed and unapproachable. Though not yet. Where I might go depended on the acceptance of what could and *could not* be changed in the predictable morass of sin I had stumbled into over and over again, attachments that I clung to and that never failed to get me in trouble.

Sleep came, and I dreamed eternal punishment stretched out before me as though I were a man alone in a boat on a vast mountain lake. No sound, no voice, no feel. Everything frozen. I became colder and colder, and I remember whispering, "But I don't deserve this." *No? Don't you remember? Your aloneness? Your desire for it? Not what you have done, but what you have failed to do.*

I awoke startled, disoriented, and in pain. I had fallen asleep in the worn-out chair each of our rooms was furnished with, my lower back bent tortuously and nearly collapsed. But I knew where I had been in the dream, and where the pain had come from. On the desk in front of me was the candle I had lit an hour before, burning and stalk-still in the airless room. I got up slowly and blew it out. How right that this should all come back to me now in the complete absence of light.

The summer I graduated from college I went back to South Carolina to lifeguard because the money was good, and I liked the lifestyle of sand and sun.

Pen—short for Penelope—and I had met the first summer I came to the beach. She was a southern deb of Irish descent, tall, dark, eyes an azure blue. We danced together at the Afterdeck and fell in lust, bumping and grinding on hot nights in the shack she shared with classmates from the University of Virginia. Somehow we resisted sex. Guilt, most likely, the Catholic's prophylactic. After a few months, though, instead of becoming closer, more comfortable with each other, we drifted apart. We were both mercurial, introverted, and fiercely independent, getting angry at each other over nothing, and then trying to make up because we wanted there to be something.

When summer was over we went our separate ways, wrote to each other for a few months, and then stopped. I knew only that she was applying for an internship in the summer and thinking about graduate school.

In early July of the following year, she showed up unexpectedly one afternoon at my guard stand. I thought she had left the beach for good. She was down for the week, she said, and wondered where I might be. She invited me to dinner with her mother, a great conversationalist on the subject of southern literature, and I never turned down a chance to talk about poetry.

Back at the rented condo, we sat on the balcony and watched a waning moon rise late on the water.

"Such a pretty night," Pen's mom said wistfully. "Why don't you two go for a walk? I sure don't need you here with me."

In the near-darkness, we talked about where we'd been and what we'd been doing since we'd last seen each other, and why we hadn't kept in touch. Time, distance. But then the conversation turned to why I hadn't felt as much for Pen as she was now saying she felt for me, which surprised me. I told her about Santa Fe, about my studies, my experiences of prayer "in the desert," and tried to tell her with as much clarity as I was able that I had discovered a sort of peace, if not happiness, in my quiet and unattached life. The beach was a chance to make some money before I could move on. I was hoping to do some traveling by boat. I wasn't sure when this restlessness would wear off.

We had walked about a quarter mile down a deserted stretch of undeveloped strand. No lights, no people. Just the moon. Pen stopped me and pulled me toward her. She seemed to want to say something but couldn't. We kissed, not tenderly. Then she peeled off her top, undid her bra, and slid her shorts down until she stood naked, white, and beautiful on the sand. "Come on," she said and ran and dived into the surf.

About a month later, a Friday morning at 7:00, as I was heading out the door for work, Pen called and told me she was pregnant. Could I get some time off to come to Charlottesville to talk?

When we did, Pen said—without emotion—that she was going to

terminate the pregnancy. She had played the scenario out in her head and decided that there was too much she had envisioned doing before becoming a mother, and if she didn't do it now she never would. I felt emptied, emptied of possibility, wondering what I, too, might have done before becoming a father.

And I felt far from her. I wasn't sure what I was expecting to hear her say when it came time to lay out the options: Marriage and live happily ever after? Say goodbye and have the baby on her own? But I didn't expect a stark announcement of abortion. She doesn't want me to be a part of this, I thought, knowing that, while we had been attracted to each other, we were not in love, and there was nothing that could sustain us for any long period together. She seemed to be suggesting the same. But where did that leave us?

"At the time," I said to Gerry, sitting before him in spiritual direction with this as my all-consuming reconciliation, which came at the end of that First Week, "I wanted to say, 'Don't do it. We'll think of something.' But I didn't. It was as though I couldn't move. All I remember is thinking, We need time. I need time! A little more time to figure it all out. And then, before I knew it, it was September. So much for the endless summer. But I wasn't looking for more time. I was hoping it would all go away. So I did nothing, said nothing, and wanted nothing but to be left alone."

Gerry kept his eyes fixed on me, his head nodding with no indication of what he might be thinking. This was where I thought it would end. Not the guilt but my life as a Jesuit. Before he could respond, if he even intended to respond, I added, "On my way through Annapolis that fall I stopped at the Redemptorists' and went to confession. It was all I could think to do, though it felt like a formula to fall back on. Once I got in there and told the priest this same story, I nearly started bawling my eyes out, I was so sorry. He absolved me, but I swear I never heard a man sound so sad in his entire life."

After the silence of what seemed like seconds protracted into hours, Gerry said, "Maybe what you heard was all he could do to let you know you're still loved."

He's being kind and pastoral, I thought. But I didn't want to prolong things. "I have to leave now, don't I?" I said. "I know that it's an impediment to ordination, the abortion."

He suddenly seemed more quizzical than surprised and said, "No. You don't have to go. Not for this. It's a horrible thing, AJ. You wouldn't have brought it here if you, too, didn't think so. Might you both have acted differently given the grace? Yes. You didn't force her to do this, did you?"

"No," I said.

"I wouldn't have thought so. Sure, there's sin layered upon sin in this one. When isn't there? But the grace, it seems to me, is in your coming here, to this life. Don't you see? We *need* men who know as much about failure as they do about love."

I left the room torn as well as forgiven—again. I would continue this Long Retreat, fully aware of my failings, but the love I was supposed to know something about felt as though it was a long way off.

The Second Week

A few days of silence sound as though they would be a welcome change from all of the concerns any person has to balance day to day. But go a week, ten days, or more with a strict routine of prayer, food, walking, sleep, and prayer again with never more than five hours between the last period and the first of the next day. There is nothing relaxing—in the common notion of "retreat"—about it. It's a headlong confrontation with all those thoughts, hopes, fears, and desires we push aside by listening happily to some other, more benign noise. I knew now why this disciplined spiritual workout was called the *Exercises*.

Around mid-month, winter closed in with a snowstorm moving up the coast. And far from the fields of Berks County, a different kind of exercises were getting under way, the precise and measured work of F16s, Jaguars, Harriers, Patriots, smart bombs, M1 Abrams, and satellite feeds. On January 17 our spiritual directors told us that Operation Desert Storm had begun at 2:30 that morning. I sneaked a look at *The*

New York Times on the periodicals table of the novices' reading room, browsed the front-page headlines and grainy photos, then left off to go for a walk along the frozen potato fields. I'd have time enough to learn all I could about this war that seems now like a short prequel to the events of the early twenty-first century. My best, last chance to outwit another kind of enemy—a tenacious voice that kept whispering every now and then, *Who're you kidding? You're not cut out for this*—needed attention for the next few weeks.

Part knight-errant, part soldier-saint, Ignatius Loyola was a man squarely in and radically ahead of his own time. His conversion story follows the classic hagiography of riches to rags, honor to humility, like those of St. Francis of Assisi and Bernard of Clairvaux. But Ignatius embraced a life of poverty and pilgrimage at a time when the dome of Christendom was cracking and the authority of Catholicism was being challenged by the Renaissance, Reformation, and the rise of the New Science. It's a mistake to think of the man's life as merely a response or reaction. Rather, he unfolded along with it. For, if the end toward which all strive is "God as understood by Holy Church," the means toward that end should be the created world within which that Church constantly finds herself.

Sections of the *Spiritual Exercises* taken out of context have been fodder for some of the myths and legends that surround the Jesuits: military language and imagery that suggest Inquisitorial torture (Ignatius himself was held by the Inquisition while they examined his writings); a macabre belief that every Jesuit is given a human skull with which to contemplate his own mortality (documented in a few cases, not a bad idea in general); and the rule "What seems to me white, I will believe black if the hierarchical Church so defines," evidence of not Christian but casuistic motives driving this most ambitious Order of priests to conquer the world for the Pope ("What seems," Ignatius writes, not "What I know").

Beneath the vivid imagination and unwavering loyalty of St. Ignatius, though, is the modern realization that we are in possession of a cluttered sense of ourselves and ourselves in relationship to others.

Almost four hundred years later, Freud would suggest that there is a narrative of the unconscious that runs parallel to our conscious lives. Learning how to read the former will help us reorder and live with the latter, all toward a certain kind of human salvation. The *Exercises* are meant to do the same: reorder our narratives so that we'll find, in the end, *eternal* salvation. For Ignatius, there is only one sickness that needs to be overcome: sin. And there is only one story about it worth telling: the one that ends with God. All of the clutter, hindrances, and attachments are like an antagonist's attempts to thwart that story's end for his own gain.

After the upheaval of the First Week, our meditations turned to the life of Christ: Nativity, Presentation in the Temple, Hidden years, Baptism in the waters of the Jordan, that "Ordinary Time," counting down now to an entirely different kind of passion.

We were offered another "election" not far into this Second Week. The Meditation on the Two Standards. The Standard of Satan, "the chief of all the enemy in a vast plain about Babylon seated on a great throne of fire and smoke, his appearance inspiring horror and terror." And the Standard of Christ, "standing in a lowly place in a great plain about the region of Jerusalem, His appearance beautiful and attractive." In the midst of prayer we are asked to watch how Satan proceeds, "how he goads his demons on to lay snares for men and bind them with chains," effected through the desire for riches, honor, and pride, that for which all of us willingly strive.

Then we turn to Christ, "sovereign and true Commander," yet surprisingly unglamorous, and we're asked to consider the reality of what choosing to follow under *his* Standard gets us: "the first, poverty as opposed to riches; the second, insults or contempt as opposed to the honor of this world; the third, humility as opposed to pride." What could it mean to pray for loyalty to and companionship with this Christ, hoping that I might get what I prayed for?

January 18 (9:35 p.m.): The Standard asks a great deal and it is not so easy to respond. Satan tempts with riches, honor, and pride, but consider all the ways, shapes, and forms these temptations can take. Christ asks for poverty, insults, and humiliation, but in all of our pursuits in life, will we constantly seek such difficult and unacceptable tasks? Will I? Then, difficulty in the temptation masked as a virtue. I may be so wrapped up in poverty that I'm never humbled. This is a losing battle! The extremes of these Standards seem to me to be the key points: humility and pride. Accept the former, avoid the latter. Yet, I must record this: my feeling of shame, sadness and helplessness at the realization of what a humanly impossible Standard Christ's is. In all reality, lived outside of these *Exercises*, there can be no greater or more demanding task. Yet, I'm not certain I understand it fully. Am I ready to accept? How is it possible to say yes? Will I, when my own brothers seem to have forgotten this Standard? Will they when it is I who have dropped it?

I'm no monarchist, so I had my problems not with the notion of "election" or "making a choice of a way of life" that Ignatius sets out as the purpose for these meditations but with the idea of kingdoms and rulers and men in their service. Gerry and I sparred over the language of "Standards," appearances, the fact that poverty was rarely a visible trait of any Catholic religious order. "Why such resistance to the means, AJ, if you understand the ends intended?" he'd say. "You know literary history. Put it into context." Then he'd send me back to repeat the meditation over and over again.

But there was more than language, history, and a means to an end at work in this prayer. A few days later, while walking through the graveyard of an old Protestant church nearby, I realized that at stake was my entire understanding of what it meant to be a follower of Jesus. Catholics who were born on the cusp of Vatican II (and older) tend to be uncomfortable with saying the words *Jesus* and *friend* in the same sentence. It's too southern, too much like the anti-Papists. God—in the churches of a Northeast rife with Eastern Europeans and Irish—was more father figure than friend, and fathers rarely confused discipline with friendship. In the gulf between heaven and earth, one knew where God sat, powerful and mysterious, perhaps a bit vengeful at times. The Blessed Mother interceded when we needed a hand, and the saints were ever-available for their own community service, but a personal relationship with Jesus was, well, at best the watering down of a powerful mystical theology. Worse, the stuff of hubris.

But how would any man or woman wanting to leave the attachments of the world behind and follow Christ be able to do so without recognizing that the apostles themselves—those who were "sent"— were "friends of the Lord"? Ignatius called his fledging order of pilgrims, in Spanish, *la Compañía de Jesús*. In spite of its militaristic setting, the choice to proceed as a companion of Jesus was at the heart of this meditation on where I would place my loyalty. *No one has greater love than this, to lay down one's life for one's friends.* Like a man and woman who renew their commitment in their own daily love for each other, the religious turns to Jesus in prayer in order to say, "Yes, I will live under that standard of friendship. I will lay down my life in this way." I knew, too, that as a Jesuit novice I had already been engaged in this companionship and its renewal for the past five months, slowly coming to the kind of trust any relationship requires. Now, here I stood in the intense quiet and contemplation of this retreat in yet another meditation face-to-face with a life in which I had one choice to make: Did I have the strength and love necessary to live knowing that my single intimate companion would be this Jesus who is both God and man?

That day, I said yes. But that didn't mean I was released and sent on my way to live as a Jesuit. The *Exercises* require four weeks and thirty days of settling into the decisions about life we make. Two weeks and fifteen days had merely set the stage.

There was a man in the boatyard on Cape Cod where I once worked who adjusted compasses. You would think that a compass wouldn't need adjusting. Floating in oil, encased in glass surrounded by wood, free from outside magnetic interference, it points north with the near-exactitude of science. The problem is that magnetic interference is a fact of life not only on any boat but in the earth's rotation as well. Compass error, or deviation, can't be eliminated so much as minimized. The adjuster corrects these errors and reorients the compass toward magnetic north, the closest one can point to true, so that the sailor can proceed with the knowledge and confidence that he's on course.

I was praying in the large and lofty chapel that is the heart of Jogues Retreat one morning, warding off sleep by trying to turn any distraction that entered my imagination into a scene from the life of Christ. I was about to doze off when I suddenly thought of Ignatius Loyola doing the same—the Spaniard himself in need of a strong coffee—as he jotted down his "points" in "The Mysteries of the Life of the Lord," somewhere in sixteenth-century Spain. I said "Hah!" out loud in that flinty space and heard an annoyed "Shush!" come in a woman's voice behind me. I resisted the urge to turn around and continued with my prayer, in which I now connected an Ignatius at work on his notes for the *Exercises* with the image of the compass adjuster. Had he been a mariner, and born later, the saint undoubtedly would have suggested the connection, too. Yet, what I laughed at was the grace that reminded me to make the *Exercises* my own. I remember my brother John once pointing out that compass adjuster as he walked through the boatyard at the end of a day: "There's the kind of work you want. No one but the Pole Star telling you what to do." John meant self-employed and living on the water, with an entire industry dependent upon your expertise, something I most certainly would have turned to had I stayed in Massachusetts and not moved to New York with hopes of becoming a poet, and then a priest. But now here I was, contemplating life in a religious order the very founder of which was instructing me through words five hundred years old to get myself right with Jesus and sail by that northern star. Because, when all of the distractions and attachments are taken away, it's not what you do or don't do, but why you do it.

> FIRST PRELUDE. This is the history of the Three Classes of Men. Each of them has acquired ten thousand ducats, but not entirely as they should have, for the love of God. They all wish to save their souls and find peace in God our Lord by ridding themselves of the burden arising from the attachment to

the sum acquired, which impedes the attainment of this end.
THE FIRST CLASS. They would like to rid themselves of the attachment they have to the sum acquired in order to find peace in God our Lord and assure their salvation, but the hour of death comes, and they have not made use of any means.
THE SECOND CLASS. They want to rid themselves of the attachment, but they wish to do so in such a way that they retain what they have acquired, so that God is to come to what they desire [. . .]
THE THIRD CLASS. These want to rid themselves of the attachment, but they wish to do so in such a way that they desire neither to retain nor to relinquish the sum acquired. They seek only to will and not will as God our Lord inspires them [. . .] As a result, the desire to be better able to serve God our Lord will be the cause of their accepting anything or relinquishing it.

For all of the language of "desire" and vivid *mental representation* that has accompanied the *Exercises* and its meditations up to this point, the detachment of the Three Classes of Men comes as something of a surprise. Along with the medieval vocabulary of these contemplations, I struggled with the introduction of the word *indifference*. This was something as unwelcome in my assent to Jesuit life as the desire for humiliation. I had been indifferent about plenty up to this point: a respectable profession, acquiring of a lot of money, political causes, commitment in general. What I wanted to do now was make a goddamn difference. That was why I had joined the Jesuits, out of the hope that I might make a difference by setting my sights "not on the things of this world." But suddenly, amidst all of this visualizing and Ignatian *sentir*, we were told, essentially, to float ourselves in oil.

All three classes of men are faced with what to do with "the attachment to the sum acquired," knowing that the money is a magnet before a compass. The First Class is straightforward. They have the desire but not the will to do anything; they go to their deaths unchanged. The Second Class actually does something, but in their detachment they create another attachment, never realizing that, regardless of their apparent shifting, obstacles remain. They are like *takers* who want to be perceived as *givers*, and so manipulate a situation accordingly. In the Third Class, the compass points unswervingly, to such an extent that metals and magnets may come and go from the pilothouse of the soul but the person remains pointed toward God and God alone, in thought, word, and deed.

This isn't some lazy attitude of indifference, though, where we accept as God's will whatever direction in which we're pushed. It's the hard work of constant watching and trusting. Which I came to realize through another act of remembered grace.

One morning in Wernersville, around the time of these prayers of election, I experienced in a kind of waking dream the realization that I had, by twists and turns I couldn't yet explain entirely, been led to this life. It came with a vivid memory of a few long days that belong back in my account of the time after I parted ways with Pen. A fragmented and chaotic tale, it seemed like a back eddy in which I had gotten caught, until someone somehow pushed me out. On retreat, though, the hours of that story rose to me, as jarring then as their sudden presence is jarring now.

It happened like this.

Sleeping fitfully in my room at Jogues one particularly cold morning, I saw at around 7:00 a ball of red sun rising over the snow-covered eastern valley. It was so large I felt as though I could touch it, or at least warm up if I got closer. I put my coat on mechanically and went out. I followed the drive that led down to the fields, then set out across them.

I had been in the midst of a prayer on the fifth chapter of Luke's Gospel, verses 1–11. So, as I walked, I composed the place for myself: the sea, fishing boats, nets, a man named Peter, and the itinerant preacher who wanted a boat for a stage from which to speak. But the words addressed to me were those addressed to the would-be disciples: "Put out into deep water." And I remembered a beat-up forty-foot sailboat on which I had been a crew member when I lived in Florida briefly in the fall of 1986. I wanted to sail to the Islands and found an old man who needed hands for a run to St. Thomas. There were four of us: the captain, me, and two others, Harvey and Kathy. We were paid with passage.

We left Port Everglades and set out onto the Atlantic with the wind blowing at a near-gale force of thirty-five knots out of the east. We beat into it all that day and night, making little headway, determining that we were somewhere south of Bimini. I say "somewhere" because the captain, a gray and taciturn man, had begun to suffer a bout of what? Depression, we figured. It might have been heroin. He locked himself in his cabin, leaving us with instructions to follow the chart to St. Thomas.

Harvey, an ex-chef who had replaced the kitchen with a ketch a few years ago, set up a navigation station. He plotted the course. The slightly mannish Kathy (who may or may not have been Harvey's girl-friend) and I secured the deck and reefed the sails. We punched along on four-hour watches, settling into the necessary routine.

On the third day out, I had the 4:00 to 8:00 a.m. shift. The night was particularly rough. Just when we thought the weather was going to break, it picked up. I tried to sleep for the few hours that remained before my watch, but as I climbed forward and into my hammock, the boat dropped off the top of a wave and lurched forward, sending a bag of festering apples on top of me. The smell was putrid and sickening. The boat rose and dropped off another wave, and I ran up on deck in time to get a whiff of clean sea air, the taste of bile, though, at the back of my throat. Harvey was at the wheel but didn't say anything. I went below quickly to grab a sleeping bag and came back out to rest curled up in the cockpit. I got up at 4:00 for my watch, which meant making sure the autopilot remained on course and staying alert to what changed and didn't change on boat and ocean. In a few hours it was morning.

In that place of wakefulness and sleep—the rising sun and the brightening waves whipped up and tossed by stiffening winds, flying fish shooting from the surface and landing on deck at my feet—I felt as though I were in a strangely normal state, as though this were how I would live out my days, muscles deprived of all but the most essential motion, the body's frame used now to the pitch of the sea under-neath, the mind heavy with the desire for more sleep but working with a lighter intensity out of a duty to rise to the challenge. I had no choice, but that, too, seemed natural, as though someone had said, "Put out into deep water," and I had listened. But I wasn't thinking in terms of the life of Christ that day. I was clinging to the vaguest no-tion that if I kept moving, I might discover where I was being led.

When our captain emerged from the hell only he himself can speak of, and we found (after he decided to motor into the now slack-ening wind instead of sailing just off of it) that the cooling pump im-peller on the engine was shot, we turned around 180 degrees and returned to Fort Lauderdale, discovering that in twenty-four hours at sea we had sailed a few miles east of the Florida coast (which now seems like some improbable adventure to me).

Back onshore I went to visit some friends who lived on the New River. One, a good sailor and seasoned traveler of the Caribbean, told me he was surprised to see me again, and he didn't mean surprised by an early return.

"I know that guy, AJ," Bob said. "He hasn't got all his marbles. I wanted to tell you that before you took off, but I couldn't catch you."

"I'm not sure I would have listened," I said. "I wanted to go too badly."

"Go where?"

"The Islands."

He scoffed. "People die out there, and smart people die as fast as the stupid ones. You've got to figure out who you can trust, man. That's the way you survive."

"How do you know, if you haven't been sailing with him?"

"You don't need to go sailing. Look around. Watch someone, talk to him, work with him. Hell, ask him to do a meaningless favor. Who's he looking out for? Himself? If he is, then don't walk away. Run." Bob cracked open two beers and placed one in front of me. "Here. Good to see you back." He took a pull on his own. "When you're done, go get your shit off that boat. You can stay here for a few days while you sort out what you're gonna do next."

I must have walked a long time away from Jogues on the morning this all rose to me, because, as I looked over my shoulder, I could see one straight path of footprints in the snow. My own. I glanced up at the retreat house and reoriented myself by the bell tower, an unmistakable and distant lookout on the hill. The sun, directly in front of me, was smaller. The morning was brighter, the air felt warmer. I turned around and retraced my steps.

I had—I've marked it in my journal—made my decision to stay in this Order and become a Jesuit on that morning, after I returned, settled with some tea, and sat down to record that waking confluence of past and present events. I say a decision, but it was more like that moment of discovery I had been hoping for, believing that I was being led into and through this life, and all I needed to do was trust. *When they brought their boats to the shore, they left everything and followed him.* "And so will I," I said to myself out loud in my prayer, as though practice for my vows to come. "So will I."

Mass that afternoon was celebrated by the Maryland novice master, Father Conroy, who we all knew had been in Vietnam before joining the Society. He preached on the battle with trust and aloneness, as though it was something we were all struggling with together. We sought to be alone in our contemplation for the space of a month, he told us, because the *Exercises* require it. And, should we choose this life, there would be times when we'd find ourselves grappling with the physical and spiritual reality of being alone—an aloneness we hadn't necessarily chosen. "Yet, always, we move as companions whose companionship rests ultimately in the Lord," he said. "Even if circumstances mean that we are companions only in spirit, we must live as though we are a community, and one in which we can all place our trust.

"Look at the brothers to the right and to the left of you," he went on. "Alone in our prayer, in our rooms, the chapel, outside, wherever, we are told to make a material representation of the place, so that prayer becomes a tactile encounter. Don't forget the end to which it's all directed. We are a community of fifteen for this month, but we belong to the Society, to the Church, and to the Body of Christ as one.

Regardless of where our prayer goes, or where we might go when we leave here, we cannot be separated from this. Remember, the question we ask in our aloneness—*Where* is God in all of this?—is not a question at all, but rather the truth that *There is God* in all of this, and all we can do is trust."

I looked at the brothers to the right and left of me. The silence seemed to suit Billy. He was drawn immediately to the brother who ran the entire physical plant of the retreat house. He walked outside as much as I did, so I saw him in passing a great deal. But he gave away nothing. No glint of consolation, no burden of desolation. He took to retreat as he did to any task: quietly and steadily, until it was done.

David's face was a barometer of where we were in the *Exercises* from week to week. Sin and the depths of Hell? Serious, gloomy, ashen. The life of Christ? Settled and yet somehow searching. Meditation on the Two Standards? Decided and at peace. A good artist, David used to draw and paint small prayer cards, which he would give to Gerry to give to us so as not to disturb our retreat space. Tucked into my old copy of the *Exercises*, I still have a small pen-and-ink of the face of Christ, with "Strengthen us!" written across the top. And in my journal there's a photograph mounted on a frame of construction paper. It's of a snow-covered tree from the grounds in Syracuse, with a line from Hopkins printed at the bottom: "God shall o'er-brim / the measures you have spent . . ." That was David. A giver in the world of takers.

Frank never seemed far from breaking into a smile, as though a critique of too much self-pity, his own brand of irreverent reverence. In the late mornings sometimes I could hear him and Gerry both chortling in the room Gerry kept for spiritual direction, across the hall from my own. It never bothered me. I waited for that sound, and felt as though I had missed it if it never came.

What would the others have seen if they looked sideways at me on the day we all pondered the depth of Father Conroy's homily? A tentative man whose nature it is to mark the outer edge of things without stepping beyond the pale of those boundaries. Aloof, some might say. Others, introspective. But I hoped—I hoped—that they might, too, see something in my silent gait that led them to decide, If this one will remain, so will I.

After all of this contemplation about what kind of man one sought to be, what kind of banner one should live his life under, there was one more prayer we had to turn to in our aloneness for the sake of discerning what course we should take in life: the Jesuit's memento mori, the meditation on his own death.

I began in my room—dark but for the light of that single candle—after Vespers.

THIRD RULE: This is to consider what procedure and norm of action I would wish to have followed in making the present choice if I were at the moment of death. I will guide myself by this and make my decision entirely in conformity with it.

And, after considering this "rule," I succumbed to the exhaustion of the day, the week, the entire month, and slept. I woke at midnight (if you can call it "waking"), summoned the strength to pray, and drifted back to sleep just the same.

In the morning I tried to recollect my desire to embrace this particular meditation with the intensity and alertness it required, and so, after remaining another hour in my room, I took a walk to the graveyard of the priests and brothers who had gone before, a few of them reinterred bodies of novices who had died in the flu pandemic of 1918. Then, into the night and after Mass the next day, I continued to contemplate the same point, until I found myself kneeling in a side room off the main chapel where the late Mrs. Brady, who had paid to build Jogues Retreat, was said to have attended Mass out of sight of the novices, like some Carmelite behind a screen. There I turned over and over in my hands the apocryphal Jesuit's skull, wondering what kind of story would be told when all that was left of me was bone. After an hour, I imagined a scene in which a nurse taking care of me in an antiseptic and barren infirmary asked: "Did you ever regret, Father, not having children?" The voice seemed familiar. The question shook me, and I felt a wave of sadness. Is this what it will be like at the end? I wondered. But I sat still for a long time before I heard my own voice say that I regretted the times when fear and inaction had replaced love and faith. Aside from that, what else from the past had I any control over to retain? No, from now on, I told myself, this will be my way, this decision I'd already made, this life already begun and offered, as Ignatius says, "to God our Lord."

The Third Week

I prepared for the final meditations on the life of Christ with longer walks outside. In Ignatius's text, the Passion, the climax of the *Exercises* and the retreat, was approaching, and I was expecting the same mixture of resignation and dread that any man facing his execution might. The identification with the life—and death—of Jesus was now that strong.

I had decided on a new direction in my outdoor wanderings, down an access road on each side of which grew a continuous row of maples. Some of them already near a century old, they were beginning to lose branches, if not die altogether.

During what coincided in the *Exercises* with Holy Thursday, I noticed on my return to Jogues that an older priest who lived in the house (separate from the novices) was splitting logs from one of the maples he had felled with a chain saw the day before. I don't know how much he had planned to chop. It was one o'clock, and he hadn't much wood in front of him. He reminded me of my father, though, dressed in a red-and-black plaid coat, a wool cap cocked on his head but not covering the ears, each stroke of the ax landing home and rending the solid log in two. I slowed to admire his work and then moved on.

"I've got another ax," he said behind me. I turned, and he pointed to a handle propped against a healthy tree.

He knew that I was on retreat and that I shouldn't be talking. But the rules are made for the man, not the man for the rules. He wouldn't have asked for help if he didn't want it. I walked over and hefted the ax, and he directed me to a separate pile of two-foot logs next to a chopping block.

I had seen him in the dining room and passing in halls throughout the past month, indifferent to every group activity that was going on, but with a surety that gave him an unmistakable presence. He wasn't from the infirmary. That was obvious. Who was he? I wondered.

"Gil," he said, holding out his hand. "Gil Sweeney."

I shook it. "Andrew Krivak." He approved, and the two of us set about splitting logs in silence until 4:30. I remember him looking at his watch and then the low sun in the west, as though to confirm visually that the day was in fact over.

"It'll be time for Mass in a half hour or so," he said. The regular Jesuit community celebrated Mass at 5:15. We novices had it at 11:15 every morning in our own wing, but I didn't say anything. "Leave the wood here and grab the tools," he said. We walked back up to the house with the axes and rakes, tucked them in a shed he reserved for groundskeeping, and went off to our same and separate lives.

January 26 (12:00 a.m.): The life of Christ as the carpenter's son seems so far away now. Not weeks but years, and how distant, too, it must have felt as he was marched from Gethsemane back into Jerusalem and in front of the Sanhedrin. Tonight, Peter's denial. A man he prayed with, talked with, traveled with, and in the hour of death, not even silence. Rather, "I do not know him." It isn't malice but fear that does this. It is denial that leads to death. The *Exercises* note: "Take care not to bring up pleasing thoughts, even though they are good and holy. Rather I will rouse myself to sorrow, suffering and anguish by frequently calling to mind the labors, fatigue and suffering which Christ our Lord endured from the time of His birth down to the mystery of the passion upon which I am engaged at present." My shoulders ache from chopping wood, and I'm exhausted. Labor. But how good! No, tonight it must be: "My friend, I do not know what you are talking about."

In the morning, the weather was as springlike as it had been the day before. But it was my Good Friday. I walked back along the line of old maples, hoping to find Gil at work again. He wasn't there. Had he ever been there? But I saw the logs that we had left, and that Gil would no doubt return for, and knew the work and prayer were real.

Death hadn't yet taken unexpectedly anyone I loved. Both my grandmothers had died the year before, one after a long illness, the other after a long life. The closest I had ever come to the kind of grief that rips a hole in you was when my brother Matthew was nearly killed in a bicycle accident when we were boys. Literally shattered by a car, and right before my eyes.

Boyhood. That's a story all its own, one that can't be told in its entirety here. So much we had gotten into when we were young, my brother and I and the kids we hung out with, it astounds me that we escaped death. But I remember the dry terror I felt staring at him on the road that day, early October, on our way home from soccer practice. After the earsplitting sounds of braking tires, crumpling metal, and shattering glass, Matthew lay so quietly in the street in a pool of his own blood that I could think only to ask a man who said he was with the fire department: "Is he dead?" Then I listened to my brother's otherworldly screams in the ambulance as the paramedics cut away his clothes to examine his body and he writhed in pain. I sat in the emergency room waiting area alone and cried until my parents arrived. Though no one ever spoke it, they and my brothers and sisters back home all wondered, if, come morning, we would still be a family of nine.

How much worse the beatings from the Roman soldiers to within an inch of Jesus the Nazarene's life, I realized when I turned to the meditation of the Death upon the Cross, the coarse and splintered wood of that torture rack pushing into the bloodied pulp that was his back. And the actual work of a body being nailed—unfinished strips of rusted iron bludgeoned through flesh and bone, the blood, what's left of it, covering everything—to that cross. Raised up, then, in an act of suffocation. *"It is finished." And bowing his head, he handed over the spirit.* The pain, the thirst, the hunger (no food until tomorrow's breakfast). At the time of my brother's accident, I can't say I would have thought that even the death of God could bring me to more grief than I felt then. But with one shedding light on the other ("SECOND POINT: The sun was darkened, the rocks rent . . .") I *could* find that grief for the one with whom I sought to be friend and companion. I could imagine and feel the emptiness. In the weakness and exhaustion of my midnight meditation, I thought, This is death. And yet how much worse.

I wondered if Ignatius expected us to defy his directives during these long meditations on the Crucifixion. Was part of his psychology the fact that we could not *not* turn to the promise of the Resurrection? But I wouldn't, if it was out of the need for comfort. Rather, I wanted to behold the miraculousness (*"Woman, behold your son . . . Behold your mother"*) of the fact that I was surrounded by so much of the living while I had been contemplating so much death.

It was then that I turned to the names. Early on in the retreat I had begun a back page in my notebook that contained the names of family and close friends I wanted to pray for. I had a few pages from those first days of January when the only other things I was writing were reminiscences of Pennsylvania and character sketches. Now, though, the idea of the names came back to me as a way in which I might connect every living person I could think of with this still point in salvation history. It wasn't an act of mental proselytizing. It was an attempt to remember, so conscious was I of the turning this prayer represented in my own life. Remember that I am never alone. So I began writing in my journal every name of every person that I had ever known. I rewrote the names of my immediate family, then my extended family, which took some time. After that I wrote down the names of everyone on retreat, all Jesuits, priests, and religious—men and women. Teachers I'd had at school the year before, and teachers I remembered back to kindergarten. Friends I'd kept, and friends I'd said goodbye to. From there, the long distance of memory. People I grew up with and hadn't seen since. People I might have been introduced to once and whose names, as though caught like pieces of clothing on a branch, I remembered. The list went on and on, hundreds of names, a notebook full of them, my mind opening up and out as though I had trained a telescope—a thing that *sees* to ends and beginnings—on my memory. I filled page after page. "I will," I promised myself, "leave no one out," as though this exercise was in itself proof of at least the possibility of a resurrection.

The Fourth Week

The meditation that precedes the Resurrection is a retelling of the events of the Passion. That's how, in a sense, the Gospels, the "good news," began, the startling details of Jesus of Nazareth's death told with his life attached retrospectively to it. I went back through all of the Ignatian points from the Last Supper to the "Burial of Our Lord." I imagined the washing of the feet and the first Eucharist as though I, too, were in the upper room, drifting from a mixture of fatigue and claustrophobia (I was, literally, in an upper room of the choir loft), and thought briefly that I should finish the meditation and pick it up at another hour. "No!" I said to myself. "There is a story to tell, and I will stay here for as long as it takes for me to pray through the telling of it."

From that point on my whole attitude, and with it my attentiveness, shifted, and the vividness of the Passion that I had evoked earlier returned with the same feeling and emotion: the love this Christ showed his disciples when they broke bread for the last time; his grief and sorrow as he prayed outside in the garden; the unrelenting brutality of the Cohort and their treatment of their prisoner before the high priest throughout the night; the man's presence before Pilate and Herod, and the insignificance of those rulers before him; the physical pain of the Crucifixion; the emptiness of death; the grief of those who loved him, and their own suffering as they took him down from the cross, cleaned his wounds, wrapped him in a shroud, and placed him in the stone sepulcher.

I felt a strength, then. It would be wrong to say that I was aware of it all of a sudden, because it came on increasingly with every stage, every momentary decision to stay put throughout this retelling. That seemed as much the point of the prayer as any remembering. But with it came another remembering, another story in the constant back-and-forth of histories that this retreat had been calling me to reveal for much of the past thirty days. Now, on the cusp of an imagined Easter, as this silent desert landscape of retreat in the middle of winter came nearly to its end, and at a moment when I felt, as I once had as a boy, that some new life was possible again, I went back to Dallas, Pennsylvania, and the hamlet where I grew up, called Fernbrook. Something about a Holy Saturday there emerged as a grace—like a light—when I ran to a place because of what others said but found what I was looking for elsewhere. You could say that was the first time I felt called to a life like this, as though someone had looked me right in the face and asked, "Why are you looking for him here?"

Toby's Creek was swift and high. Big late-season snows were melting under weeks of steady rain, and torrents of water made the stream that snakes along Lower Demund's Road and through the center of Fernbrook a river. The weather that day, though, was beautiful, Easter weather in a part of the Northeast where spring never comes too soon.

Matthew and I ran down to the old railroad track beds on the woods side of Toby's, across from the Fernbrook Inn. We had gotten word from our friend Jeff that a group of four other boys had converged on this section of the creek with an inflatable raft they'd found discarded in a Dumpster at the cement factory. They wanted to float it at the swimming hole by the inn and see who could take it as far as the bridge across the street from the Back Mountain hardware store, a stretch of about three-quarters of a mile along the straightest section of this local tributary of the Susquehanna.

We each wanted to have a run, but Matthew and I couldn't go first. We weren't on the inside of this group, most of whom came from Shavertown. And we'd gotten there too late, after the idea to pump up the raft and test it in the creek had been hatched.

But we didn't want to get stuck going last either. We had to be home for supper and get ready for church. All week my mother had been baking and preparing the Slovak bread, ham, sausages, and cheese that we always had on Easter, which she arranged in a basket and took to church to be blessed on Saturday afternoon. Later, we'd pile into the car and drive back for the Vigil.

Matthew pushed himself into the scrum of older players. "What are you arguing for? I'll go."

"Yeah, right, little man," Charlie, the bully, said. I was proud of my brother's tenacity, but he didn't understand what was going on, the jockeying not for first, where there was the potential to fail, to be made a fool, but for second. I put a hand to his shoulder and mumbled that he ought to "cool it."

Then, a brash but likable kid named Ray said, "All right," and swaggered down to the bank.

At the water's edge, the current seemed to have gotten faster, or at least faster than we thought. Four of us had to hold on to the front and back of the raft. The whole endeavor suddenly seemed crazy to me, but Ray settled in, grabbed the board we found for a paddle, and yelled, "Let 'er go!"

He shot like a rocket out into the middle of the stream.

We climbed back up the bank and sprinted along the track beds to keep up, catching glimpses of the raft through the trees as it plummeted downstream farther and faster into a funnel of water shaped by the large rocks that lined both sides of the creek. Ray's pealing howls rose intermittently above the roar as he bounced along.

We ran like that for about fifty yards to make some headway and get to a place where we could watch the raft approaching. It was moving at a good clip when it came back into view, rising and falling in the peaks and troughs of current. But Ray looked oddly as though he was shrinking in the middle. His hands were over the side, and he was paddling, but his balance was off and the raft was moving erratically. As he rushed by, he yelled, "It's losing air!"

We took off again, Jeff hollering, "Bring it ashore at the pines!"

The creek swept around in an arc at this point, so we had the shorter distance to run. As the others put on a burst of speed to outstrip him, I watched Ray try to navigate the faster water in what would be, on any other day, a gentle bend. Heading in an unnaturally straight line, he careened off one rock, pushed back out with the board, dropped over another rock, and came up sideways into a standing wave that hit him broadside. The raft flipped up and over.

Ray managed to hold on to a thin rope woven through eyelets along the raft's edge. His head bobbed above the water's surface as he tried to gulp air and not let go. He wasn't a strong swimmer (a football player pushing fat), and he was being dragged downstream and under. It dawned on me that he might be in trouble. The others were yelling "Hang on!" as they left the tracks and bushwhacked their way back down to the bank.

The Pines was a small peninsula on the creek created by a stand of fir trees. The roots were covered by a dirt mat and fallen needles, but eddies had cut away at the bank, creating a ledge. Jeff grabbed Ray as he rushed toward us, then we each got a hand on him. He was soaked and heavy, and he wouldn't let go of the raft, which seemed to want to take off on its own now that it had lost its rider.

"Leave it!" Jeff yelled.

Ray coughed. "No!" His wet, exhausted weight began slipping from us.

"Fucking leave it!"

"No!" he choked.

Then his hand let go of the rope. The raft popped up like a beach ball, settled on the surface of the water, and floated away.

We pulled Ray onto the bank and leaned him against a tree. He was heaving, as though laughing at some private joke, but he looked ragged, and he was shaking from the cold.

"What the fuck were you thinking, hanging on to that piece of shit?" Jeff was almost screaming at him, out of breath and panting. "You could have drowned!"

Ray stared through wet hair across his eyes and smiled. "I didn't want to let go."

"Yeah, of that?" Jeff pointed downstream to where a limp mass of blue and white plastic impaled on a sharp branch strained against the force of water rushing beneath it.

Ray pushed himself up and stood in the pool of water forming at his feet. "Next time, you go first." He was looking at me and throwing down the challenge so that he might save some face.

I had some saving of my own to do. "I'll fucking do better than you," I said, and turned away as though disgusted that I wouldn't get my chance to prove myself in the company of these others.

Tired, wet, and flecked with dirt, we emerged from the woods by Merl's Garage at the bottom of Franklin Street and went our separate ways.

In church that night, wearing white cassocks, those of us altar boys who'd been on the banks of Toby's that afternoon said nothing about the raft. We were leading a slow, streamlike procession with candles and a censer.

Under the watchful eye of Father Sammons, I set fire to the paper and wood in a deep brass pot, the Easter fire from which the priest lit the Paschal candle that burned until Pentecost. Ray was next to me with a piece of charcoal for the incense. As the dry fuel caught, he leaned over the growing blaze and brought his hands up to the flames. He had that same smile on his face as when we'd pulled him out of the water. I wanted to tell him to stop screwing around, that he should light the charcoal, but I couldn't bring myself to disturb him, he looked so intent on getting warm.

Then, from over our shoulders, Father Sammons said: "Raymond! Let's go, young man."

Ray's smile disappeared. He scowled and made an odd motion of leaning back and away while reaching into the fire with a pair of tongs, as though he'd been cautious of the heat all along. When the charcoal began to sputter, he dropped it into the censer, lowered the lid, and fell back into line.

"Brothers and sisters in Christ, on this most holy night," Father Sammons began to intone from the back of the church. The pews were bursting. People were standing everywhere—nave, aisles, doorways. And I knew them all. There wasn't a sound except for the crackling of burning sticks and the priest's voice as he finished the Vigil prayer and proceeded down the aisle, singing, "Christ our light . . . our light . . . our light."

I don't know about any of the other guys (as I write, those I've contacted to ask if they remember the raft have said that they recall nothing of that day), but that night I felt the kind of gratitude a kid feels when he gets something good that he doesn't deserve, as our army of servers fanned out and into the crowd to bring that light on thin tapers to everyone gathered in the dark.

FOURTH POINT. This is to consider all blessings and gifts as descending from above. Thus, my limited power comes from the supreme and infinite power above, and so, too, justice, goodness, mercy, etc., descend from above as the rays of light descend from the sun, and as the waters flow from their fountains.

On the third of February we remained under silence for the entire morning, but there was levity in the air. We ate breakfast quietly and dispersed to a final period of prayer.

The day before I had been poring over what Ignatius calls the "Contemplation to Attain Love of God" and its "Fourth Point." I was mystified by it, as though standing beneath those very waters and fountains in the closing hours of retreat. Then, on that last morning, I returned to a meditation on the Resurrection I had done a few days earlier. This line is from the sixteenth chapter of Mark: "He is going before you to Galilee; there you will see him, as he told you." The Ignatian visualizing had become second nature, and the words, directed at me, came through as both anticipation and promise. There were places I had to move on to from here, beginning with the drive back to Syracuse. It would be a long journey to whatever Galilee awaited, but I felt as though I had caught a glimpse of it already, and I wanted to go there. I was ready. What can I write now that would capture the peace, desire, and conviction that surged through my heart and body as I sat on a bench on a promontory they called Sacred Heart Hill, the weather springlike, Easter before its time? "I am changed," I said out loud to no one and to God.

We gathered for Mass at 11:15 in the main chapel, where we were welcomed back into the world, resurrected and hungry.

At lunch in the dining room, the conversations were animated, casual, humorous, rarely broaching the spiritual. There had been plenty of that. Others at the retreat house who were not under silence— priests, members of the spirituality center, waitstaff, visitors—said that they had been thinking about us and praying for us. Had we known about the war?

"Take it slow."

"Don't watch too much TV."

Gil came over to my table to tell me he had finished clearing the maple, and then disappeared.

The five of us split up into two cars and drove from southern Pennsylvania into New York State, the false spring gradually giving way again to winter. Ten miles outside of Syracuse, from the last rise before the road drops in, gray snow clouds hung over the skyline, outlined and distinct, as though they had been painted onto an immovable curtain.

Frank the cook was in the kitchen making us a welcome-home dinner. The *secundi* were gone until May. The house had been sealed up tight for the past month. Now, a new echo of the old routine was in the air: pots banged, feet hit marble stairs, warm radiators ticked away. Here there were no long corridors or lofty ceilings against which the slightest noise echoed without position. Each unavoidable sound that rose was local. You could identify who or what was at work, and where. Any vague disdain I'd had for this place, or envy for another, remained where it belonged. In the past.

When we sat down to dinner at 6:30, there was already a foot of snow on the ground.

"What would you say, Father Master," Bill asked Don with a wry bow to hierarchy as we all sat at one crowded table, four novices and three priests, "if Father Minister purchased a snowblower for the house?"

"I'd say the men were getting lazy," Don said with a nod in my direction.

"It wasn't my idea," I said, protecting my status as beadle and a kid raised in a part of the world that knew snow.

"Well, I wish it was mine," David said with a chuckle. "I'm not sure I've got much of a back left after sleeping for a month on a mattress that was new in 1950."

"Don't worry, David," Don said. "We'll get you back into shape. Never thought you'd be glad to come home to this place, did you?" David said no, he didn't, and we all laughed, although I noticed that Gerry, Frank, and Billy weren't as animated as the rest of us.

"Weather report said it'll be gone by the morning," Billy said, and then there was silence around the table.

It was an odd segue, but I suppose there was no other way to bring it up. Frank said, "It's not easy to tell you guys this." He was looking at David and me. "I've decided to leave the Society." The snowstorm suddenly seemed to be inside. David and I put down our forks, the question *Why?* too obvious on our faces, but we knew the answer was coming. "It was the work of the retreat," Frank said. "I realized I entered because I thought I should. You know, surrender all to God. But when I really examined it, I was able to see it's not the Jesuits I'm called to. I want a family. Once I was able to admit that, somewhere during that week we were supposed to *pretend* we were in Hell," he said, trying to make a joke but then regaining his seriousness, "it became pretty clear that this life isn't for me."

There's no real response you can give at a time like this. It's a moment of decisiveness and permanence that cannot be withstood. I noticed then that Billy, too, was unresponsive to Frank's news in a way that suggested more a summoning of his own decisiveness than resignation.

David saw it. "Billy," he said, not a question but a statement.

"Yeah. I'm not called to this," he said. "I can do the work, but you guys"—he singled out David and me now—"take all of this intellectual stuff seriously."

"I'm sorry, Billy," I said. "I had no idea."

"No, no," he said. "It's not your fault. It's what Frank said about the retreat. It helped me see that I want to go back to a regular job, regular life." Then, as though to remind himself of why he had turned down this road and away from that job and that life, he said, "I'm still gonna pray . . . for you guys most of all," and his eyes swept the table to include Don, Bill, and Gerry as well as David and me. "You gave me a deeper faith."

When Chris left the novitiate, I felt something closer to shock than to loss, realizing that some of us hadn't come here to stay. But because he had departed so soon, his presence at the beginning seemed more like the anomaly than his absence. When Frank and Billy announced that they were leaving, I felt that same initial shock. But once we finished dinner and McQuaid, and headed outside to shovel snow, I felt resolve. For them as well as for me. I've heard other Jesuits speak of departures as being "devastating," but you can't begrudge a man a choice like that. After all of the discernment of God's will to enter or to leave this life, in the end it's a choice one makes in what turns out to be an ongoing response to what others mistakenly view as some indelible and undeniable call. I learned never to take a leaving personally. Decisions like these are complex, layered with all manner of telling and retelling. My response then, and over the years that followed, became simple. We work out our own salvation, a stance I attributed to the *Exercises* as much as to St. Paul. "If I were at the point of death, it is *this life* I would have most wanted to live," Ignatius directs the retreatant. And *life*, remember, is meant to be all that would have come before us if this meditation were done on the cusp of the next.

A few days later, Don sat David and me down and talked about the reality of friends leaving, the difficulty of interpreting it as a time for self-doubt: If *he's* gone, what am I doing here? But I felt a tenacious and almost selfish desire to remain a Jesuit in the day to day, stronger than the sheer determination I'd felt in November and December. David felt the same way. In fact, I see it now as the moment at which we drew closer, friends as well as brothers. We made a pact over beers in the kitchen that night: if one of us felt as though he was no longer called to remain a Jesuit, he had to tell the other before anyone else.

.

The first thing I did after we returned to St. Andrew's was go to Bill Sullivan for the reconciliation I'd never made between us. I knocked on the door of his office Monday morning and asked him if he had a minute. He seemed to be waiting.

When I sat down, he asked me how my retreat was, knowing that, for anyone who has made the *Exercises*, this is an impossible question to answer. Yet everyone asks it.

"It was good," I said. "But, listen, I want to apologize for . . ." I had rehearsed this, but now felt conscious of sounding too wooden. He wasn't going to believe I was sincere. I broke off and started over. "What I want to say, Bill, is that I'm sorry for what tension there might have been between us in the fall. Honestly, I had no idea what the *fuck* I was doing." He grinned broadly, as I'd hoped he would. "So, I'd like to start over, right here, clean slate."

The thing about Bill is that I had gone from being frustrated with him to admiring him. What I'd once avoided as aloofness I came to discover was a profound irony. For all of his stilted mannerisms, there was an equally disarming sense of humor, frequently directed at himself. And for the benefit of the entire community, there were his homilies. He preached like I'd always imagined mid-century Lutheran and Congregationalist ministers who had read a lot of Karl Barth had preached to their Iowa and Missouri congregations. Smart, direct, layered with their own human and divine complexities from Scripture, and yet always somehow tender, as though there was no mistaking the fact that we were at heart believers who needed help with our unbelief.

After my confession of sorts, he pronounced in a deliberate voice he often affected, "Brother Beadle? Done." Then, and as a way of offering his own reconciliation, he said, "Now, Frank the cook needs the refrigerators stocked again. I'm having him come in to prepare dinner for the entire week." Bill opened his cash drawer and pulled out a wad of twenties. "Find the rest of your class, do an inventory in the kitchen, and go get what we need from Wegmans." He put the money in my hand. I didn't count it. When I got to the door, he said, "AJ." I turned. "Thank you." I bowed my head as if to say, "Father Minister? Done."

"By the way," he said, "you'll find there's more money there than you'll need for groceries. Make sure the two of you stop for lunch somewhere on the way home. My treat."

David and I never did stop anywhere to eat on Father Minister's dime. Instead, we finished what shopping we needed and raced back to the quiet of the house, where we were content to cook for ourselves. Long periods of silence create a kind of sensory awkwardness. It comes with having spent time in an unimaginable place that has pried open the imagination. Suddenly, the outside world is one vast intrusion. Every sight glares, every sound is noise. Highways, stores, and malls are one massive overdose of excess. So you do what you can to retreat again, protecting yourself, taking time to get used to the kind of movement you once took for granted. With the awkwardness, though, comes a clarity, a natural and heightened sense of awareness, that you wish could last forever, after having reached it by moving over such difficult ground. But you realize then that it's the choices you made in silence, not the place of retreat itself, that have become important to you, that have shaped you, and so eventually you find yourself tentatively stepping out into the world again.

After a week of settling back into the novitiate's routine—Mass, conferences on Ignatian spirituality, private Spanish tutorials with a new teacher from Le Moyne, and our own ongoing prayer—we resumed our Tuesday and Thursday apostolates. David returned to the grade school where he had been assisting. I showed up at the hospital. Father Al was glad to see me. The work seemed not easier but more comfortable. I no longer stumbled for words with my patients. If there was nothing to say, I said nothing, or left with a promise to return if they needed anything.

During my time as chaplain the previous fall, I had noticed

around the halls a woman my age who was working with the internal social work staff. She was fair-haired and angular with an accidental beauty about her, something like the delicate features of a china doll on an athlete's toned frame. More striking than pretty, her face lingered in the mind after you saw her, like an image before a bright light. When I watched her walk down the hall one day, Anne the nurse (unprompted) told me that her name was Ruth.

Back at the hospital in February, I saw this same woman turn a corner on the orthopedics ward and start in my direction. When she was near enough to touch, she said to me, "Hi. Where've you been since December?" I almost turned around to see if she was talking to someone behind me.

"Umm, I've been on retreat," I said, "with the Jesuits. It's part of my training."

"Training? With the Jesuits? That's far too much for a girl to hear standing outside of physical therapy," she said with some administrative authority. I always wore a regular shirt and tie to the hospital, although my ID badge read "Volunteer Chaplain" and had a photograph of me in black clerics and a Roman collar. So she must have known *something* about me. "What time do you go for lunch?" she asked.

"Twelve thirty, twelve forty-five. Depends on when Mass is over."

"Mass? Sounds like your story's going to take a while," she said, but I could hear, too, uneven tones of humor and nervousness. "How about twelve forty-five? Meet you outside the cafeteria."

"I can do that. See you there," I said as politely as I could without betraying the giddy delight I felt shooting beneath the surface of my skin.

We took a long lunch and talked until 2:00. It turned out she had asked Anne about me, so she knew I was a Jesuit but didn't know how, or if, she should say that she knew. She spoke of being a single professional woman working in Syracuse (where she had lived all her life), the man to whom she was almost married (called off), the doctors who fawned over her, and the brother she adored. I told her about working on the Cape and writing in New York. I was avoiding the specifics of religious life. We had, at least, our generation in common.

"Why social work?" I asked. She didn't seem to fit the bill in her cashmere sweater, wool slit skirt, and elegant pumps.

"I went to SU to stay close to home and to party. And when I graduated I had a nagging feeling that there should have been something more. I had been thinking about social work. So I went back for my master's, finished last May, and got this job at the hospital in August."

"My dad was a social worker," I said. "He's retired now."

"Then I know you didn't grow up rich."

"We always seemed to get what we needed."

"I do all right, too," she said. "I've got my freedom, my car, and some nice clothes. The real question, my friend, is why the *priesthood*?"

Of course it was. I drew a long breath. "If we had met two months ago," I said, "I might have told you that I wanted to do some greater, more heroic thing with my life."

"A celibate hero. That's a new one."

"No. Heroic in the way you described wanting to be a social worker. Some way to make a difference."

"Why has that changed from two months ago?"

"This retreat we had to go on. It's *rewritten* me somehow. Poverty, chastity, priesthood—these don't feel like a play in three acts anymore. Beginning, middle, end, and you know how it all turns out. I see it more like, well, I'm not sure. Like the past month has been how it all should, in some way, be lived. I don't mean total silence, I mean not avoiding the hard stuff or taking a path of least resistance. More like living as though an encounter with God is unavoidable. When I think about it, it's as though life itself has become a long retreat."

She looked puzzled as I spoke, and I realized that I was going off on religious things most people cared little about, or kept to themselves. "I'm sorry," I said. "I'm babbling."

"No," she said, a slight smile spreading now across her lips. "A long retreat. I like that."

From then on, every Tuesday and Thursday, Ruth seemed to make a point of finding me in the hospital and asking me how my day was going. We didn't always have lunch together. I had to join the pastoral care staff in the cafeteria on occasion to make it look as though that was where I belonged. But I preferred the time with Ruth when it seemed appropriate. And while I looked forward to going back to St. Andrew's on those days and doing things that were both a return to the old and an adjustment to something new—improving my Spanish, studying the original documents of the Society with Gerry, cooking with David for just five now, and getting out of the house with him for a movie or a beer in town at Clark's Ale House—feeling a pattern of community, in a sense, where once there wasn't one, I became more dedicated to my work at the hospital because I knew I would see Ruth there. Talking to her filled a gap I thought I had closed six months back, when I entered religious life. I didn't think to ask her then how she saw it, but I told myself it was a kind of friendship I was missing, friendship that was different from what I might know with a man. And why should I avoid that if it wasn't leading to anything more, anything particular? The "particular friendship" was forbidden in the old days of the seminary in order to keep a young man's focus on his vocation and God, and to discourage homosexual relationships. But David and I were both helplessly hetero. We weren't "particular" friends. We were a class of two. And as for women, we had both known them as lovers and friends. If a friendship was the reason why I looked forward to hopping on the bus into town on Tuesday and Thursday mornings during the cold and numbing Syracuse winter to sit and pray with hospital patients, there must have been some good in it.

PART II

In binding us, the vows set us free: [. . .] to use whatever resources we may have not for our own security and comfort but for service; [. . .] to be men for others, in friendship and communion with all; [. . .] and to follow the lead of our superiors.

—32nd General Congregation of the Society of Jesus

Novitiate became a trial, and I don't mean that pejoratively. With our election to continue on the path toward taking vows in the Order, David and I began moving from one task to another with what seemed at the time like a spiritually Herculean purpose of trying, testing, tempering the soul so that we knew what we were capable of. We still lived in the matter-of-fact ordinariness of work, school, chores, prayer—the life of any novitiate community—but having been shaped in the crucible of the *Exercises*, we began working toward an understanding of our capacity for weakness. We prayed for and wanted to learn failure. "Poverty, rather than riches; insults, rather than honor; accounted as worthless and a fool for Christ, rather than esteemed as wise and prudent in this world." Failure, that is, of control over more than ourselves. The Jesuit might affect a certain bearing of worldliness, success, and invincibility, but inside, if he isn't humbled—"mortified," Ignatius called it—he is of no use to anyone.

And so, in other provinces, men made a pilgrimage or a kind of mendicant journey during this first year of novitiate. It's laid out in the *Constitutions*: "The scholastics before becoming approved and pronouncing their vows should for the love of God our Lord beg from door to door for a period of three days at the times assigned them, thus imitating those earliest members." Taking longer periods in the summer, novices from Maryland, Missouri, Oregon, and the other provinces walked, bused, or hitchhiked well-laid routes with stopping points but no end point in mind. They relied on the kindness of strangers for food, shelter, money in some cases. Some discovered a purpose: a place of religious devotion, a birth home; one man who had been adopted shortly after he was born (we had heard) found his biological father. There was a certain lore that accompanied these pilgrimages, new chapters in a Jesuit's ongoing autobiography. And if nothing epic happened, it was enough that a man learned not to "take gold or silver or copper for your belts; no sack for the journey, or a second tunic, or sandals, or walking stick. The laborer deserves his keep."

In the New York Province, the idea of pilgrimage had been reconsidered and transplanted. Most of the New Yorkers knew urban lives, and in that landscape hitchhiking and relying on the kindness of strangers could prove, well, less than kind. If the larger purpose of the pilgrimage was to contemplate one's weakness and desire to turn his will over to the will of God, this could be done through a change of language and culture. In the New York novitiate, that meant traveling to the Dominican Republic to live with the poor in *el barrio* and picking up more of our required Spanish along the way. It wasn't a pilgrimage as such. It was more a time of immersion, wherein we stripped down our needs in order to examine our souls and learn to trust, facing an entire island of beauty and failure in the process.

In hindsight, "face" it is all we were able to do, looking on from a close distance, feeling its heat as it were, but at the time that closeness seemed as real as any mission to a foreign land for a lifetime of service and alienation, something I in my thoughts about a life of total sacrifice to the Lord (accompanied by Ennio Morricone's soundtrack to *The Mission*) believed I was capable of and in my heart desired. I looked forward to this trip with the anticipation of an explorer about to set foot on an unknown but long-sought-after land.

Don, Gerry, David and I arrived in Santiago de los Caballeros for Semana Santa, Holy Week, when the people of El Egido were immersed in their own rituals of Holy Thursday and Good Friday and invited the new "Americanos" who had moved in for another spring to do likewise. Aminta, a thin, powerful Dominican woman with coal-black eyes and a smile like the inside of an oyster shell, was in charge of our

Spanish program. She matched us with our families on Calle Ocho, a process that amounted to nothing more than a coin toss.

El Egido was one of the poorer barrios in the city of Santiago. The houses were made of piled cinder blocks, two bedrooms at most, living room, kitchen, tin roof, wood-slat windows. Some were nicer, if not larger; they might have had proper sitting rooms. The streets were dirt. Most of the people who had jobs worked in the U.S.-run factories in the "free zone," sold eggs and chickens door-to-door on motorbikes, or cleaned for families in a neighborhood where a cleaner was affordable.

David was sent to a large concrete house on the corner with the extended family of Doña Francisca. She was a tough but magnanimous old grandmother who had yet to show a streak of gray in her thick jet hair. He had a private room attached to the roof of the house with a terrace by the stairs. Doña Francisca took him in without any ceremony or alteration to her life. One afternoon David stopped at the foot of the stairs on the way to Spanish class, eyes transfixed on the *abuela* as she stuffed a crazed and helpless chicken into a cloth sack, cinched the top, snapped its neck with both hands, and left the sack to flop about on the bottom stair for the last few involuntary minutes of that chicken's life.

"*Ah, Daveed,*" she said, looking up at him without surprise. "*Shhh! Tranquilo. La gallina está durmiendo,*" she whispered and walked into the kitchen singing quietly to herself.

I lived on the opposite end of the street with Nana and Chéché in a four-room one-story tin-roofed house. They had two small children (whose names I have forgotten, and never thought to record), a boy of five and a girl who was a precocious three. I took the children's room (they piled in with their parents) and slept under a mosquito net.

Chéché was a wiry, cheerful young man, amiable and talkative. I learned a good deal of Spanish listening to him and his friends in the house at night, trading stories about life in the D.R. for stories about life in New York. Nana was Chéché's physical and emotional opposite. She was a large, imposing woman. There may have been, when she was younger, that same coal-black gleam to her eyes that all Dominican women seem to have, but it had faded. In the seven weeks I lived with them, she said four words to me. *"Andrés. Tu comida"* and *"Tu café."* I was no more than the American for whom she would cook three times a day and receive thirty-five dollars a week. At roughly ten and a half pesos to the dollar, that came to a little more than 367 pesos a week. Physicians, though, couldn't make that much in a month.

Their son was a dull, myopic boy with a round head and a vacant stare. Nana doted on him when he cried in front of his supper. The daughter was destined for either the freedom for which her parents longed or trouble. One afternoon, while I was sitting in the house talking about baseball with Chéché, she rode through on a broomstick for a horse.

"Cómo se llama tu caballo?" I asked, wanting to sound as though I could move from one conversation to another without effort in Spanish, especially with a three-year-old.

She stopped and looked at me. *"Se llama culo."* "His name is asshole." Then she rode off through the kitchen and out into the backyard. Chéché said, *"No sé,"* and shrugged.

On the streets, the island country and its people seemed to live according to this truth: *No hay nada seguro.* Nothing is certain. Rolling power outages, called *apagones*, which sometimes rolled for several days, meant electricity and water would come and go without warning. When there was electricity, the intrusion of MTV and American soaps blared from every living room that had a Sony Trinitron. Streetlamps lit up the corners where men the Dominicans called *heavitos* and *tigres* leaned against their cars, drank rum, and blasted merengue from opened doors.

When the power was off, houses were silent, streets dark. Families came out onto their porches. You could hear children laughing, someone playing a guitar, people singing, and the low hum of a generator at the *tienda* keeping the beer cold. To me these were two worlds I was constantly trying to reconcile. To the locals it was life in the D.R.

Now, away from home and on the road, we had to learn what becomes the survival of every Jesuit: to create an *ordo* out of your day so that you never cease, in spite of your work, study, or illness, to turn to prayer. So, our lives found an order not unlike what we had left behind in the novitiate. In the mornings I studied with a *café con leche* in front of me, then spent an hour before lunch in languid prayer, which usually meant a meditation on the readings for Mass that day, but often became a Zen-like awareness of the present-moment sights, sounds, and heat of the country that came in through the slats in the window of my room. In the afternoon, David, Gerry, Don, and I walked to our four hours of Spanish class at a convent school. Then we had Mass with the nuns and either walked home or went into Santiago for dinner. If we weren't too exhausted after that, David and I would meet on his roof for a beer and some mutual examen of the day. Hardly a lesson here yet in immersion or enculturation, but it took longer than we expected to settle into some semblance of that *ordo*, not necessarily on the outside but with an internal acceptance. There was the language barrier (we were used to expounding on philosophy and literature. And now? Baseball, bowel movements, and the weather). The unfamiliarity, the heat, the boredom. All of these things were a kind of constant thorn in the side of comfort. As it should have been, I suppose. The most difficult thing, though, what we missed most and could never seem to approximate, was privacy. That was the greatest luxury we took for granted in our lives as religious in America, the lack of which was jarring in the D.R. Privacy is a luxury the poor rarely realize they're missing.

So where was the opportunity to fail on our exotic island pilgrimage? Not in the vow of chastity with some cinnamon-skinned Dominicana, not while there were the real threats of syphilis and AIDS. Besides, there was nowhere we went unnoticed. Poverty? The economic gulf was too wide. We ate what the locals ate, and no more. I lost fifteen pounds. And the *guagua* (a small van, called that for the sound the horn makes) that drove us around the countryside was a utilitarian convenience. We knew, too, that we were leaving this place one day. Disobedience was always possible, especially in the brain-scrambling sun, where judgment failed and tempers flared. But Don and Gerry were good and fair men. We didn't want to resist them, we wanted to become them.

Failure came instead in the tiny frustrations of life in a culture not

our own. Death by a thousand paper cuts. Or nearly. Jesuits in missions all over the world had known this from the beginning, and part
of our eight weeks in the D.R. was meant to be an initial exposure to
this particular Jesuit sense of mission. "This battle," Jonathan Spence
writes at length of Matteo Ricci in China,

> could not but be more lonely and protracted than the major
> sieges launched during full-dress campaigns. One can only
> guess at the levels of endurance Ricci needed in this pro-
> tracted war of spiritual attrition, when so often the Chinese en
> masse must have seemed the enemy. He tells of how he
> watched as Chinese passengers and crew on a river boat joined
> together in throwing his baggage onto the shore because his
> travel papers were not in order; of the sound of an endless rain
> of stones on the roof of his house in Zhaoqing, thrown by
> schoolboys from the commanding elevation of a nearby tower;
> of the dejection felt after a Chinese crowd playing musical in-
> struments and shouting their victory cries smashed his doors,
> windows, and furniture and tore down his newly erected gar-
> den fence. Was it through such small harassments that the
> devil showed that "consummate malice" of which Ignatius
> spoke?

This was what we had been sent not to discover but to glimpse, the
"lonely and protracted," the "consummate malice" that we want to believe we are stronger than but that thrives on our hubris and pride. I
realized this one day, halfway through our mere two-month mission,
which was never meant to approximate a life sentence, regardless of
how long it felt.

On the way home from our daily Spanish lesson one afternoon in
early April, the clouds opened and dumped rain in what began as
drops but soon became waves. When I got to Calle Ocho and ran under the cover of Chéché's porch, I saw that my watch was filled with
so much water it looked as though the hands could be replaced
with goldfish. I had had the watch for ten years; it was a Pulsar div-
er's watch, a high school graduation gift from my parents (I loved it,

knowing what it had cost them). I had never known it to lose time, let alone take on water. Now the second hand weakly tried to push past "4-4-4-4" but got nowhere. It had been a long day. It had been a long month, and I cursed the rain, the house, the whole fucking country out of pointless anger and frustration. Later, someone told me that if I rubbed the crystal it would generate heat that could evaporate the water. "Bullshit," I said. The watch was ruined.

The next day David and I went into Santiago to find a repair shop, but the merchants all seemed to think I wanted to sell my worthless timepiece and spat before they shooed me away. Stepping out of one shop, I tripped over a mongrel in the gutter.

"*Mira!*" the man behind the counter yelled after me. "*No lo molestes!*" Then he called after his mutt. The dogs on the street understood more Spanish than we did.

That night I crawled out of my mosquito netting and into the backyard outhouse, where I sat, doubled over, on the edge of the rimless toilet bowl, growing delirious as I began retching and shitting, wondering if death wasn't a better option. I must have been there a long time because I pulled my head out of my hands when I heard the surreal, third-world sound of cocks crowing before first light. It's a haunting sound, dreamlike while it disperses dreams. The roosters are not close, not at the house next door. Rather, it's as though their calls are carried on the wind throughout the country. And no two roosters crow at exactly the same time or with the same pitch. They are always off by a second or a tone, so that, once they begin, a stream of cries flows up and down on the night air, making sleep impossible if you have opened your eyes and ears to their call.

Then I heard, rising from somewhere in the corner of my brain, "neither to retain nor to relinquish." The close green walls around me began to swim. A wave of warmth moved up from my diaphragm, and I could feel beads of sweat on my forehead. I lurched over hard and vomited toward the toilet through the space between my legs. I remained still for a few minutes, trying to regain my strength, listening to the cries of roosters.

When I opened my eyes and focused, I saw a river of black ants marching single file across the outhouse floor. They moved slowly, but with a steadiness that gave the appearance of speed. They carried at the head of the line a chicken bone, a drumstick. We had had chicken for dinner; the bone must have fallen out of the garbage in the yard. For what seemed like hours, I watched them carry the bone, moving up the entire length of the wall, over a ledge at the top, and then across the ceiling of the shack, never once faltering. As the line moved forward, the ants were rotating their formation, those at the front carrying the load for a while, then moving to the back of the line, while those in the back moved forward for their share of the burden.

"*Las hormigas,*" I whispered to myself, admiring them. The ants. They lived in this culture that had given them such a beautiful name. They defied gravity in this country that was slowly weighing me down. They accepted and digested the food that tonight was conspiring to kill me. And they did it all as one. I would have given anything to be able to step into line with them and do the same, moving forward to work, backward to rest, forward to work again.

What I came to realize, after I recovered and started eating solid food again, was that I had already stepped in line, joined the march of laboring ants, retaining what helped me to defy gravity along the path, relinquishing what tended to get me in trouble. And it began right there with our class of two, David and me. The D.R. had thrown us together even more intensely, and we were each beginning to rely on the other, almost without speaking, to pick up the slack when one of us was failing. In the barrio, older kids started calling us Starsky and Hutch. My Spanish was slightly better than David's because I had the benefit of listening to Chéché's Marxist buddies deride the "free zones" and American trade, asking what questions I could, offering corrections when they were needed. Then I'd take these conversations back to our own nightly beer and cigar on David's roof. For his part, David in a way took us back into the people. He was the outgoing and welcoming one. *Abuelas* loved him; children flocked to him.

One evening we got caught on the fringe of a house party, and David started moving to the music with everyone else. When the kids saw his wide shoulders and curly hair bobbing up and down at half the speed of the quick-tempo merengue, they called him "*oso bailando,*" the dancing bear, which got shortened to "*el oso.*" We couldn't walk down the street without some *niño* who had just been pissing in the gutter chasing after us, yelling, *"Mira! El oso! Ven aquí, oso!"* The novices who went on pilgrimage spoke of discovering grace when they freed themselves to trust a person, a direction, a challenge they might not have placed in front of themselves by choice. What was this Jesuit calling, this community of vagabond intellectuals who insist that "the road is our house," if not trusting that those I might not have chosen as friends could nevertheless become companions willing to change and be changed in the long retreat of life on this earth? My answer came again from the *Exercises*, although this time I felt not a specific and dramatic *I am changed* but a slower, dawning awareness of wanting to do what I was doing.

Before we left the D.R., David and I went to live for a week with the Jesuit community in Dajabón, an agricultural town near the Haitian border, where the Jesuits ran a college of agronomy. It was nothing more than a chance to see how another community in the Society of Jesus lived.

The passengers traveling from Santiago to Dajabón by bus were mostly Dominicans who were visiting family or spending time for some reason in the city. There were some Haitians, too, either making their way to the border or going home to the *bateyes*, which was where Haitians who worked on Dominican sugar plantations lived and, for the most part, died.

It's said that nearly a million Haitians live and work on Dominican sugar plantations. They are paid half of what the Dominicans are paid (itself not much), and they do the labor of cutting. In 1990 they were receiving the rough equivalent of one dollar per ton of cane cut in a day. The average man—working from 5:30 a.m. to 7:00 p.m.—can cut one to three tons of cane. They work spread out in the fields, so as not to hit one another with their machetes (though a few men with amputated arms or legs wander compounds idly) and load their cane stalks onto carts often drawn by oxen.

David and I were taken on a tour of the *bateyes* one weekend by two older French-speaking nuns who were trying to bring educational and economic reform to the Dominican Haitians. The tough but still somehow feminine sisters seemed to emerge on cue from a nicer hut among the shacks of the *batey* and gave their talk through a translator, although there was no need to translate the emotional fatigue in their voices.

In one *batey*, the nuns announced with their own indifference that prostitution and syphilis were rampant, as though one could do little else in stifling boredom behind four walls after a day of punishing labor but pay for sex and die slowly of madness. In another they introduced a Dominican teacher they had trained, and we got a promising lecture on the history and improving living conditions of the *bateyes*. This we heard in one of the blocks that doubled as a community hall. We had to break up a domino game between two old men, who moved to a bench off to the side and waited for us to leave. The room, dark and hot, smelled of stale sweat and tobacco. Outside, the constant chatter and laughter of children created a bizarre undertone of what sounded like the rattle of a cheap air conditioner. The discussion—if that was what it was supposed to be—swirled about in four languages: Spanish, French, Patois, and English. After a half hour of it, my head began to throb from the heat, the smell, and the linguistic puzzle. When we finally walked back out into the compound, I saw children playing in a river fifty yards downstream of where a man was squatting to shit.

On the way to Dajabón that day, David and I found seats at the back of the bus. It was a three-hour ride from Santiago, which passed quickly enough thanks to the Hollywood action film the driver slid into a VCR and projected onto a TV mounted at the front of the bus. The movie was in English with Spanish subtitles, and this turned out to be a great way to see and memorize idiomatic expressions, especially expletives.

We were an hour outside Dajabón when a patrol of Dominican soldiers stopped the bus. Because this was one of the few roads that led to the border, the patrols were common. They boarded and asked the driver something we couldn't hear. Then they walked slowly down the aisle, inspecting each passenger as they made their way. They stopped at David and me.

"*Son Americanos?*"

"*Sí.*"

"*Adónde van?*"

We told him that we were Jesuits going to the College of Agriculture. The soldiers flipped our passports back and turned around to question two Haitian men sitting in front of us.

"*A Dajabón?*" they asked, and the Haitian men said yes.

"*Porqué?*"

To cross at the border.

"*Tienen papeles?*"

As they produced their papers, one of the men overextended and touched the fingertips of the guard. The guard swung the butt of his rifle around and hit the man square in the head.

"*No me toque!*" the guard shouted.

David and I flinched from the close sound of wood on bone. I could see David starting to rise, so I grabbed his arm and pulled him back into the seat. This wasn't the time to stand up for the downtrodden.

The guards perused the Haitians' papers coldly, then asked the one sitting by the window how much money he had.

"*No mucho. Veinte, o veinticinco pesos.*"

"Twenty-five each?" the guard asked. His voice was incredibly even.

"*No. En total,*" the Haitian lied.

"*Mentiroso.*" The guard held his rifle butt up again. "Give it. All of it."

"But we'll need it at the border," they pleaded.

"You'll need more than that," the guard said. "*Vamos.* Off the bus."

The soldiers grabbed both men by their shirts and started to pull them out into the aisle. But the men, stubbornly, wouldn't go. They clung to the seat in front of them. Neither one made a sound. Then, as though he began to calculate what would be lost and what would be gained in this standoff, the Haitian closest to the guards said, "Okay, okay! *No más!*"

The guards released them. Each man pulled a wad of bills from his pocket, and the one sitting on the aisle handed over fifty pesos.

The guards counted it and walked off the bus. The driver looked back at us through his rearview mirror, then accelerated out onto the road.

When we pulled into Dajabón, David went to a pay phone to call Father Roman Espada at the college and tell him to pick us up at the *tienda* across the street from the station. Then we walked back inside, found the two Haitian men speaking in Patois (presumably about what they were going to do next), and handed them the forty pesos we had expected to spend for the week.

"This will help," I said in Spanish. They started to thank us profusely and wanted to talk. I told them we had to go and good luck. "Poverty, rather than riches; insults, rather than honor." These men seemed to live it every day, and not by choice. Why shouldn't we try to tip the scales, however slightly, if we could? But then they began to follow us, asked us where we were staying, and wanted to know if we could buy them lunch, too. When the false sense of magnanimity wore off as quickly as it had come on, I realized that we had entered a town in the D.R. where more drugs than people crossed over a flimsy border, and the last thing I wanted was to be seen by Dominican police giving money to a Haitian. A jail cell would have been the paper cut we needed to teach us about some real poverty. Forget about chastity. We legged it out of there fast.

Arriving at the agricultural college was like checking into a five-star hotel after our seven weeks in El Egido. The Jesuit Residence was as basic and unadorned as what our families offered in Santiago. But it was a home to us in ways that were immediately identifiable. We ate the same yucca and eggs, beans and rice, but we ate as a community at table, and the priests spoke in a deliberate Spanish that we could understand and respond to. Our rooms had the same slat windows through which mosquitoes poured like smoke, but there were good reading lights, new mattresses, and netting without any holes. The school had a library, and on the grounds there were shade trees, courtyards, and fields that spread out with whatever plants the students were learning to grow. There were no cars bleating merengue into the streets, no power outages (the institute had its own generator), no TV to bring American English into Dominican living rooms.

There wasn't much to do there except visit classes and use our now acceptable Spanish by giving brief presentations to the students on why we were Jesuits and why we had come to the D.R. ("*Solamente para vivir y ver,*" we told them. "Only to live and to see.") So, perhaps wanting to show us more of the countryside, two days before we were to say goodbye to the Jesuits in Dajabón, Father Espada asked if we wanted to drive into Haiti to visit a friend of his, an American priest who had been living there and running a school "for a long time."

The next day we crossed over the Massacre River with Espada and a Puerto Rican Jesuit. Espada had me drive—a beat-up old Toyota Land Cruiser he kept at the Jesuit Residence for teachers to take on errands—while he dealt with the Dominican guards. Then, on the bridge that separates the two countries, I opened up the throttle and shifted from second into third gear.

"*Coño, Andrés!*" Espada yelled. "*Despacio!* Slow down! They'll shoot us!" I ground down to a crawl. The Haitian guards scowled at me, but when they saw that Espada was a priest, they let us through.

The roads turned from paved surface to dirt ruts. On some stretches the holes were so deep it seemed as though they had been dug by hand. We were traveling ten miles into the interior, but it took us almost forty minutes.

The grammar school run by the Oblates of Mary was a few wooden pavilions surrounding a large white bungalow that looked as though it belonged in the movie version of a Graham Greene novel. We parked the Land Cruiser and walked around the classrooms first. The blue and white uniforms of the students and cleanliness of the school stood out against the starved and filthy conditions among the few homes we had passed on our way there. In a space with no lights and no walls, only a roof for shade and cover from rain, twenty ten-year-old boys sat bolt upright at their desks while a young priest showed us his students' handwriting lessons in their copybooks. Meticulous cursive French. Each paragraph written out three times before moving on to the next. When we were about to leave, the students stood and sang the French national anthem.

In the bungalow, we met Father Leblanc, the principal of the school and the superior of the house. The four of us—tanned, unshaven, wearing dirty khakis and boots—were unlikely visitors in the almost pristine conditions of this jungle retreat. Ceiling fans lopped away slowly in the afternoon heat; a houseboy came and went with iced tea and napkins. Leblanc, his left toe swollen from a fungus infection, kept his foot elevated on an ottoman. He greeted Espada and the other Jesuit in a flat, confident Spanish. When Espada introduced us and said that we were Americans from New York, Leblanc switched into English.

Father Henry Leblanc was an American member of the Oblates of Mary. He was from a mill town outside Boston, Massachusetts, and had been in Haiti as a priest for thirty-six years. When Espada mistakenly told us thirty-five, Leblanc corrected him slowly and severely.

"Thirty-six years, Roman. Thir-tee-six yeahs." His northeastern accent had not disappeared in spite of them, and in fact was made more distinctive by the presence of habits he must have picked up speaking Patois. In a monotone voice hoarse from smoking Marlboros since his first year in the seminary, he said, "Bevalee. Dat's da tone nawt of Boston."

The monotone became a monologue. Espada seemed to me a forceful man, impatient with the Caribbean culture he had adopted as home, but his attempts to interrupt never fazed Leblanc. He conversed with a thread that wove his story from the North Shore of Massachusetts to the Germans who had taken to the Dominican Republic as their personal engineering hobby.

"Dey'll fix anything," Leblanc said, "but dey want to do it demselves."

David remarked that this technique left little opportunity to empower the indigenous and teach them to manage their own affairs.

"Empowa?" Leblanc scoffed. "Empowa, my arse! Empowa cawruption. At least da Germans get da damn job done." He took a sip of iced tea, and no one moved or said a word. He put his glass down and went on as though we had granted the pause. "Aristide may be a good man, but he spent so much time on da left to win de election dat now he can't find any outside financial help. Let da Germans be." And we all sat in silence.

I wondered how Espada had come to know Leblanc, and why it

was important that we should come by for a visit. When I asked him later, Espada said something about the fact that Leblanc once saved him, and he felt an obligation to visit the man as he got older and lonelier in his Haitian exile.

"Te duele?" the Puerto Rican Jesuit finally asked Leblanc, pointing to his foot. Leblanc brushed the air with his hand, more as if to say, "Stupid question. Of course it hurts," than to indicate that little, if anything, pained him anymore.

That seemed, somehow, an appropriate note on which to end our stay in the D.R. A glimpse into the reality rather than the ideal of the mission. No priestly duties or exercises of good works (which you might be surprised to find we did little of there) could have opened up the place more to us than the living and the seeing that we did for eight weeks. If there was God in all of this, it was in those communities of the quotidian, however beaten down or beautiful they were. It wasn't only my own capacity for weakness that I examined in that country but the capacity of others to live with a poverty and failure thrust on them day after day, those who, unlike Matteo Ricci and all the Jesuits since, had no choice, no election, to make about where they sought to find "the Kingdom" of the Lord. It was here, or it was nowhere.

On our last day in Dajabón, David and I drove to the beach in Monte Cristi. We gave a lift to a woman and her daughter who were carrying full jugs of water, then bucked along in first gear for nearly a mile behind a herd of oxen too large to move to the side of the road so that traffic could pass.

On the flats where they evaporate salt from the sea, we speeded up to forty-five miles an hour and blew thousands of hungry mosquitoes out of the grille and wheel wells of Espada's rusting heap. At the end of the road, we powered over some rock and sand, and parked at the base of the actual promontory called Monte Cristi, where Columbus is said to have caught sight of the New World. The beach was sixty yards off, white, immaculate, and deserted, stretching away from the mountain and along the coast for several miles beyond what we could see. There was no one around in either direction, and we had no bathing suits, so we stripped and waded into the Atlantic, the air warm but the water numbing. I thought of William Carlos Williams's *Spring and All*: "They enter the new world naked, / cold, uncertain of all / save that they enter." Poor, chaste, and obedient, but free.

On the way back David pulled the Land Cruiser into a *tienda* on the shore road. We bought two beers and sat on the hood watching the sun set. A prostitute came out and asked us if there was anything we needed, anything at all, and we said no. She wanted to know where we were from. David swung his hand over the side of the truck and slapped the fender twice. *"La jeepeta,"* he said, one of those slang words we'd learned in the neighborhood and liked. She smiled and shook her head, thinking he hadn't understood her Spanish. Not *what* brought us, but from *where* had we begun? *"Sí,"* David said. She shook her head and disappeared into the store.

The sun was a larger, weaker inferno now, more color than heat as it hung like a stilled pendulum above the bay. The tiny, abandoned fishing boats, whose fishermen we never saw, bobbed gently in the harbor.

"Maybe we could petition to finish our novitiate at the agricultural school?" David said. "I'm starting to like this place."

"Hard to believe. Do you remember why we were even sent here?"

"Not offhand," he said.

The prostitute came back out, winked at us, and started down the road toward town as the last pomegranate blotch of sun disappeared.

B e careful what you pray for, they say, because you just might get it. For all of the weakness and failure sought dutifully in the D.R. and glimpsed from a safe distance, the real test waited for me when I returned to Syracuse looking like some version of a desert hermit, with sunburned face, scraggly beard, and shrunken belly.

David and I would soon be sent off on our first summer assignments, but until then we were given a few weeks to rest up at the novitiate, the last week of which consisted of vacation, or "villa," at the lake house in Cazenovia, by then my favorite place to retreat for a day or two. I shaved, got a haircut, eased back into three meals a day, and bought some clothes that fit me. The two of us said Morning Prayer and went to Mass every day with priests from Le Moyne who were staying at the house, and we read, studied, and prepared meals as though vacation, too, should mirror our lives in the novitiate.

Then, midway into the week, I called Ruth. I wanted to hear her voice. Early in my D.R. journal, weighed down with the loneliness of low-grade sickness and being surrounded by a foreign land and its language, I had created her presence on the page in my initial assault of that loneliness, wondering whether she might mean more to me if I were in a place where I could give that relationship a chance. But I knew enough, too, now to trust the process of spiritual direction. So I talked to Don, who said that he understood the feeling and told me not to discount it, though neither should I discount the work I had done to remain a Jesuit, if that was what I wanted. Hadn't I, after all, before the August I entered the novitiate, been able to explore freely other relationships? Novitiate wasn't a time to wait for a better offer. It was where a man came to begin living a life of the vows in the Society of Jesus.

I needed to hear that, because being a Jesuit was what I wanted.

But therein lay the weakness, the thing that tended to get me in trouble. I told myself that I wasn't calling Ruth with a desire for a better offer, or to see if I might play around a bit before I took vows, but rather to maintain a woman's friendship while I lived the vows. "We're not monks," I whispered self-convincingly to no one as I held the phone receiver in my hand. "Our superiors can't expect us to live this life not remaining in contact with *any* women at all."

What I told myself was half the truth. At the age of twenty-eight, I did maintain that I could live life not bereft of the presence of women but certainly not in need of a constant female companion. The experiments of retreat and mission were training me to be, as we were taught, a man for others, "in friendship and communion with all." And yet, while I moved decidedly and steadily into religious poverty, chastity, and obedience, I needed to feel as though I was loved, wanted, and desired. A man for others, yes, but also just a man. "Who doesn't want that?" Tom Stahel, the spiritual director who would guide me through philosophy studies in New York after I took those vows, said to me when I began to sort this out a few years later. An erudite and fiery southerner (who died, sadly, before his time), Tom tagged this insecurity in me immediately and then let me give voice to that need so that I could begin to ask honestly where it was I would find the love I desired: a love for the Lord, one that loved no one person and yet all persons, and received its wholeness in the constant return to prayer? Or the tactile love—voice, touch, and vision—that I might yet find in companionship with a woman? But, as it was, one year after having lived as well as any young man could expect as a Jesuit novice and still want to remain, I felt a dangerous sense of freedom and security that week at the house in Cazenovia, because outwardly I was doing everything right. Inwardly, though, there was the need of being needed that wanted to be met.

Ruth sounded surprised but happy to hear from me, though I

could hear as much hesitation in her voice as resonated in mine. I said I was calling to let her know that I was back in Syracuse and that I was doing well after my two months in the D.R. I gave a rough report, describing the world I'd witnessed there more like some freelance journalist than like the Jesuit novice who sought to draw a connection between a march of ants and the *Spiritual Exercises*.

When I changed the subject and mentioned that I was enjoying being on vacation, reading, fishing, and cooking, she asked hesitantly if I'd like to get together for dinner. "I could cook for you. Nothing fancy. I thought it might be nice to catch up."

In the back of my mind it was what I had been hoping she would ask, because I couldn't. Not cook but summon the question. Somehow, though, when she mentioned the mere act of having a meal together, it didn't seem like such a bad thing. Dinner, right? Food and talk. We were friends.

"Okay," I said, feeling illicit and elated at the same time. It was a Wednesday, so we decided on the following day, a work night.

"Since you like to fish, I'll get some salmon to broil."

"You know, I don't actually keep the fish I catch," I said, "but salmon sounds wonderful. I don't have a car, though."

"I'll drive out and pick you up after work. Let's say six thirty. It's not like rush hour's a killer around here."

"Perfect. It'll be nice to hear about an entire block of Syracuse winter I've missed."

"That'll be a long conversation," she said.

That evening, over a beer on the back porch that faced west and the lake, I mentioned to David that I was going to get together with Ruth for dinner the next day. I was feeling as though I needed to be open and nonsecretive about the whole thing so that any seemingly ulterior motives would be dispelled.

"Hmmm," he said with his characteristically vocal way of mulling a thing over. "I mean, good. If it's not yucca and egg in a dirt-floor kitchen, I'm all for it." He would be cooking that night for some Le Moyne friends, a group of three women and two other men, so I wouldn't necessarily be missed. He hesitated, and then said, "You're okay with this, though? She knows what this is all about?" There was no sweep of the hand to indicate or take in some retrievable boundary. *This* meant no one place, person, or time but the continuous effort of living and trying to define a life.

"Yeah," I said. "She knows. No one's after any forbidden fruit. I guess I mentioned it because I knew you'd want to know who the blonde in the sports car was." He raised an eyebrow and snickered. "Seriously, though, I just want to have dinner with a woman. No, I take that back. I want to have dinner with Ruth, without it looking or sounding as though that means I'm sleeping with her. 'Friends with all,' " I said, "right?"

He nodded. "Then go ahead. Have dinner, I mean."

That summer, Don sent David and me to work in opposite corners of New York, opposite from where we'd begun. I went to Buffalo. David went to Crown Heights in Brooklyn. *Agere contra.*

One of the last things Don did as my superior at St. Andrew's was drive to Buffalo to see me for spiritual direction and a check-in, standard practice for novices living in communities other than the novitiate. I taught in the Higher Achievement Program (HAP) at Canisius High School, a kind of Jesuit-run summer school for kids who needed an academic boost, as in Hunts Point. In Buffalo, though, the twelve-year-olds were much kinder than they were in the Bronx. It was good work, I said to Don when we sat down to talk, but I couldn't see myself doing it for very long.

He stared his discerning stare, and then brought up Ruth. "You told me once in the D.R. that the friendship you had struck up with her at the hospital meant a lot to you. Is this something you're pursuing?"

Coolly, I said that we were friends. In the hospital, when we had lunch together, I'd found her enjoyable and easy to be with. I left out the fact that we had gotten together for dinner. But I said in my defense (I was that consciously building a defense) that I knew no other people my age in Syracuse, so I felt fortunate to have made at least one new acquaintance in my life as a Jesuit.

"When you think of the fall, is she part of the picture? Are you looking forward to seeing her?" Don asked.

He waited for an answer, but I didn't know what he meant. If "part of the picture" meant I would see her at my apostolate, my answer was yes. But I was taking too much time.

He looked away, as though needing to think through what he had to say next. I broke the silence. "But it doesn't mean I don't want to return to the novitiate in the fall. It doesn't mean I don't want to be a Jesuit."

"I know," he said. "I know. But sometimes it's easier to say what something doesn't mean than to recognize what it does. Have you spoken to her at all since you've been here?"

"She's called me to see how I'm settling in, and I wrote her a letter describing the kids and the classes." Our phone conversation was a long one, and in her voice I could hear the questioning: What if we *had* met one year earlier? And why does that *what if* have to mean that the corner's turned with no new life possible, a life in which AJ and Ruth made a go of it? My letter did and didn't respond to this. I wrote that I admitted to feeling something beyond friendship, but if this was the case, we needed to step back, or I needed to reconsider the path I was on. What I didn't write was that I hadn't begun to consider the depth and difficulty of the latter, and I wasn't sure I could.

"You really are invested in this, aren't you?" Don asked.

Did he mean the novitiate or Ruth? I thought to myself, until it occurred to me he wasn't being ironic, but by then it was too late. I wasn't the first novice Don had ever seen. Behind my stated commitment to Jesuit life, he could tell that I anticipated Ruth's calls, enjoyed putting pen to paper to invoke her absent presence, and while I hadn't begun second-guessing my own desire to remain a celibate, I wasn't looking or sounding like a man with an undivided heart.

Less than a week later, on the same day, I got a letter from Ruth and a letter from Don. I opened Ruth's first. She used an easy and intimate tone, and after mentioning that Anne, the nurse at the hospital, had been asking about me, hoping that I was well, she segued into a strong and heartfelt response to the options I'd said in my last letter might soon be mine. In so many words, she said she would be disappointed if I didn't choose the second, in which I would give up the path of religious life I was on in order to be with her.

Then I took my Swiss Army knife to the edge of the envelope with "Gannon" scrawled above the "Demong Drive" return address and slid it across the top. The letter began with a brief line saying that Don was glad to have seen me looking and feeling well. He was writing, however, to address the serious matter of my being engaged in a particular friendship. "It has come to the point where I have reservations about allowing you to return to St. Andrew's."

The first year of the novitiate, Don wrote, tested one's desire and ability to live in a Jesuit community. The second year meant a more serious commitment to doing the work of the vows. My relationship with Ruth, it was clear to him, was an attachment whose presence would ultimately separate me emotionally from the community and interfere with my free disposal toward chastity and obedience. If I had been engaged to a woman whom I hoped to marry within the year, he offered as an analogy, I wouldn't want to be spending time alone with another woman. Where would the love, the commitment, the desire reside? So, because he had seen the work I had put into my own spiritual formation thus far, he let the decision rest with me. If I wanted to take the novitiate seriously and look forward to first vows in a year's time, I would have to agree to break off all contact of any kind with Ruth. If I couldn't agree to this, I should return to St. Andrew's immediately, collect my belongings, and leave.

My room in Buffalo looked out onto the black tar parking lot of the high school. It was afternoon—my first one off in three weeks—and the heat shimmered up and into my window. As I sat on the edge of the single bed, Don's letter, not the stifling air, made it difficult to breathe. I folded up Ruth's letter, put it back into its card-stock blue envelope, and tucked it away inside my desk. I stuffed Don's letter in my pocket and went outside. I needed to walk. I needed to move in a straight line.

When I reached the edge of Lake Erie in downtown Buffalo several hours later, I stood and stared into water the color of clear green emeralds. Nothing like its reputation in the 1970s, I remember thinking, a lake so polluted and filthy it would catch fire. A small sloop was passing the breakwater of the marina. It cut its motor, hauled up a full mainsail and unfurled the jib, then leaned to leeward in the stiffening breeze and began slicing its way into deeper water. Where? The city of Erie? Cleveland? Some port as far west as Superior? It would have to be careful if it was going beyond the reach of shore. Erie is the shallowest of the Great Lakes. Strong winds kick up its surface quickly into steep waves. If I were in that boat, I thought, I'd head for more water.

"Put out into deep water." My meditation from Luke's Gospel during the Long Retreat. I was there, Andrew, the brother, silent and dutiful in the boat. I felt the exhaustion of the labor, the exhilaration of the catch. And I heard the words that follow: "Don't be afraid."

I resented Don's ultimatum, but I knew I had invited it the day I confused my desire for a woman's friendship with sheer desire. It was selfish and had the makings of a certain recklessness. If I wanted to be a priest, and a good one, I had to learn how to accept one desire without acting on the other. And in that I had a long way yet to go. In the years to come, I would have many dinners with women whose friendships I came to cherish and rely upon, but the boundaries were clear. When they began to blur, the only thing that could be done was to walk away.

It wasn't my peripatetic prayer over Luke's Gospel that settled me, though. I needed the tilt of grace before I could see any direction clearly that day, that summer, and I felt it in the way things are sometimes made right, after you're certain you've done nothing but wrong. I didn't return to the Jesuit Residence until dinnertime and so missed the usual 5:15 liturgy. When I sat down at table with Tom, my *secundi*, who had also been sent to Canisius High School that summer, he began telling me about a frustrating afternoon of travels he had gotten caught up in. The result was that he, too, had missed Mass. Father Bill O'Leary, a large, oddly reticent and yet commanding priest who smoked Lucky Strikes and could use the F-word as every part of speech except a preposition, was sitting at our table ("Fuckin' Bill" they called him, but never to his face. He, too, has gone from this world). As though we three had planned a wayfarers' Mass of our own, he said, "Be in the chapel at seven. Can't have the novices missing out on the sacraments now, can we?"

That evening, Tom and I sat in the front row of pews in the house chapel dimly lit by a few candles and light emanating from the sacristy, where Bill moved about preparing book, water, wine, and host. He walked into our midst carrying the large lectionary in which were the readings for the day and the rite of the Mass. For a stole, the sacramental garment worn on the shoulders of every priest, he had a multicolored length of fabric woven with designs of what looked like a Native American pattern. He began solemnly, "In the name of the Father and of the Son, and of the Holy Spirit," and then sat down and said: "My brothers, welcome to this holy place." We each shared a reading, with Bill proclaiming the Gospel from his seat perched slightly higher than we were at the level of the altar, the passage from which I no longer remember. It wasn't Scripture that moved me then but Bill's own words that came after.

"Sit down for a minute," he said after the traditional closing of the Gospel. "I want to share something with you that I've been thinking and praying about a lot this summer." And what Bill went on to say, in words that might have come straight from the life of some lone Jesuit saint, was that he had once spent the happiest years of his life in the Alaskan missions, flying in and out of villages in a small single-engine plane, bringing supplies, medicine, and the "good news" to indigenous men and women who knew cold and hardship their entire lives, yet who lived with a warmth and magnanimity of spirit. Every day he wished he was back there, but he knew, too, that a false sense of desire in no way did justice to his life as a Jesuit and the *Spiritual Exercises*. "Not our will, but the Lord's." And so he worked and prayed wherever he found himself rising in the morning and going to sleep at night. Because it was the life he loved with as much depth and desire as he loved Alaska and the native Alaskans, he said, and his hand moved down the edge of his stole in a gesture of memory and affection.

"I don't have a reputation for being edifying," he said to us after a brief pause and grinned. "That's why I say these things only in prayer and privacy. But let me tell you. It's a hard but beautiful life you're starting out on, and who knows how close I am to finishing. I'll tell you that I've regretted certain days of it, but I've never regretted the whole of it. And if you can say that, now or any day, then you'll be all right."

That night I wrote back to Don, thanked him for his trust and insight, and told him that I would no longer pursue my friendship with Ruth.

To Ruth I wrote that, without wanting to, I had given her more attention than the reality of religious life allowed. But, if I had to be honest, there was much yet for me to give to and learn from this path I'd chosen. "I'll miss you. Remember when I said I felt as though I was at the beginning of a long retreat? It's time I got on with it."

In August 1991, six of the *secundi* who had preceded us at the novitiate came back to Syracuse to take their vows. Two—Nick and Tim—left during the summer, after their long experiments. I was sorry to see them both go, but their reasons for leaving are their own. Then, on a Saturday morning later in the month, with Gerry now our novice master, David and I greeted a new *primi* class of ten. Another boon, as though the years rose and fell in peaks and troughs on what is the stark sea of religious vocations. But now David and I could look on throughout the fall—throughout the faith sharing, McQuaid, the struggles to assert independence, the giving and taking, and the departure of a few for whom the life wasn't right—and let our own resolve guide us.

I didn't return to the hospital. The chair of the English Department at Le Moyne gave me two sections of Freshman Composition to teach on Tuesdays and Thursdays, and I loved being on the other side of the desk, finally, in a college classroom. If this felt like something I wanted to do with my life, the Jesuits could certainly oblige. That was the message I was receiving from my superiors. And by the end of the semester, I felt as though the life of the priestly teacher-scholar—a particularly strong Jesuit apostolate—was one I could live happily for many years.

Now, with a year and a half as Jesuit novices behind us, spring and summer left to go before taking first vows, David and I were sent on our own "long experiments" in Jesuit communities outside the novitiate, in order to test what consolation, or hesitation, was moving through us on the road to becoming members of the Society of Jesus.

In January 1992, I moved to the America House community in New York, where I would be working for two months as a chaplain at St. Clare's Hospital in old Hell's Kitchen on the West Side. Both places were new to the usual regimen of the long experiment. Traditionally, novices had gone to work at Calvary Hospital in the Bronx and lived with the Jesuits at Fordham University's old Loyola-Faber Hall. But Gerry wanted to create a wider range of options for the men on experiment, as a way not only to talk about but to demonstrate that the Jesuit's life is, if anything, a constant need to examine and respond to the question *Where is God in all of this?*

I was as open as an old book to the move. I knew the Jesuit brother who had worked at St. Clare's the summer before, and he spoke highly of the hospital and the woman in charge of pastoral care there, Sister Pascal Conforti. And America House held a certain mystique for me as a young Jesuit, because I knew it was the place where real Jesuit writers—priestly teacher-scholars in their own right—could be found.

Life at America was a welcome change from the novitiate. If part of the experiment was to experience an active Jesuit community, I was lucky to have been sent to this one. America House is, in the opinion of many, the unspoken center of the New York Province. The building itself is dark, shabby, and roach-infested, with guest rooms that are too cramped and dingy. At one time a nine-story Midtown hotel, it now sits in the shadow of fifty-story high-rises. But it has a vibrancy that comes entirely from the men who pass through its doors. It was the theologian John Courtney Murray who said, "The Jesuits bring the world to the Church, and the Church to the world," and I believe he was thinking of America House. The editors and writers on staff at the magazine *America*—a Catholic weekly that has often been criticized as being too liberal, when its intent is to bring the world to the Church—were (in my time, and I suspect still are) holy, well-read, political in the best sense, and, most of all, kind men. George Hunt, a literary man and genuine raconteur, was editor in chief.

Outside the second-floor publication offices, Jesuits from all over the world came from Kennedy Airport to the community, prayed together at Mass in the back-room chapel on the fifth floor, and then moved down the hall to the dining room that looked out on Fifty-sixth Street in Midtown. Meal and conversation took on another form of word and sacrament, as philosophers, theologians, underground priests from China and Korea, bishops from Africa and South America, Catholic writers and journalists covering contemporary issues, and occasionally a young novice like me, sat down to dinner and talked about what Jesuits were doing in education, spiritual direction, the arts, social justice, and even their own formation, in almost every corner of the globe. If I had glimpsed a possible life standing at the front of a college classroom in Syracuse, I felt as though I were living already the life I'd want to live as a Jesuit, there at America House. It wasn't so much that I knew what kind of job I wanted to do. Rather, it was this kind of community in which I wanted to live.

The Spellman Center, the part of St. Clare's to which I had been appointed, cared exclusively for people with HIV and AIDS. Men and women came to St. Clare's in the early 1990s to put off dying as long as humanly possible. They might have recently found out that they were HIV-positive, manifested the first symptoms of full-blown AIDS, begun battling their second attacks of pneumonia, or dropped off the cliff of life with oxygen masks strapped to their faces. Of course I couldn't have known this, or even seen it, when I got there. What I had to do first was dispel a host of personal and social prejudices that came with knowing someone right next to you—someone who could reach out and touch you—has AIDS.

I brought no related experience to the job or the setting, except for my few months at SUNY Hospital in Syracuse. I was neither priest nor orderly, nurse nor administrator. I was "pastoral care staff," in charge somehow of whatever soul rose out of sleep or spoke through a mask to say: "Could you read to me? I can't see so good"; or "Chaplain, huh? How 'bout a prayer? Sump'm with St. Barbara in it." And while I can say I wasn't afraid, I was certainly scared. What could I touch? Whom should I *not* touch? What about that cough from the guy in front of the TV in the rec room? How much HIV virus is in spit? And in the air lock of respiratory isolation, how long do I stay before my mask is worthless? How long should I pray while that guy (the ex-junkie) or that girl (the ex-prostitute) hacks up a lung? Christ, do I even step inside? What's to be gained by any of this?

Sister Pascal—our administrative Mother Teresa in a good suit; stern, Italian, funny, and forgiving—had seen and heard it all (my spit was more likely to kill a man with a poor immune system than his was likely to pass along HIV). She put me on a steady diet of reading, rounds with patients, some lateral spiritual direction (we'd get together for lunch once a week), and reminders to stick to my habit of Ignatian prayer. On the practical side, there are real physiological threats when working among people with HIV and AIDS. Following "universal precautions" eliminates them: masks around known TB carriers; sharps (which I never had to touch) disposed of properly in bins; gloves whenever you're in doubt; gowns if a sign on the door says wear one; thorough and frequent hand-washing. The rest was myth, blown out of proportion by ignorance and fear (thus, the late Randy Shilts's retort: Can you contract HIV from a mosquito? Sure, if you're having unprotected sex or sharing a needle with that mosquito). On the spiritual side, nothing taught me more about being in the present moment, where what has passed and what may come are either lost or uncertain, neither of any use to anyone. I used to pray often with this passage from Ignatius's *Autobiography*, when he was in Paris during a time of plague: "Finding a sick man," the would-be Jesuit touched "his sore with his hand." When he left him, "his hand began to hurt so that he thought he had the plague. He was imagining this so vividly that he couldn't overcome it until, with great force, he put his hand into his mouth, really turning it about inside, and saying, 'If you've got the plague in your hand you can have it in your mouth too.' And when he had done this the fantasy left him, and the pain in his hand as well." I did nothing so dramatic, yet I found that holding the hand of someone who knew that everyone feared his touch, skin to skin, was one of the most healing things I could do. For, once the fear left me, too, I could see the men and women in front of me as people who were sick and in need of care, which often meant wanting someone around who'd listen to them while they were locked away in more than a physical isolation.

This was all during the time when Cardinal O'Connor was in a pitched battle with the gay community in New York. The Church's stance has always been hate the sin but love the sinner. St. Clare's was the Cardinal's best, well-funded defense that the Catholic Church never stopped loving the sinner. It was the tag of "sinner" on those who had AIDS, however, that was harder to ease, if not entirely erase. Groups for gay rights like ACT UP and others saw the Church's stance on homosexuality, the use of condoms, and gay partnerships as life-threatening and hypocritical. Their members lined up for communion at St. Patrick's Cathedral, then threw the host to the floor in protest and stomped on it. Signs of that protest (visible all over the city) brought the battle into sharp either-or relief: "Curb Your Dogma" and "My Karma Ran Over Your Dogma," which I found more empty than hurtful.

I have to tell you that I never entered into a debate with anyone, gay or straight, during my work at St. Clare's about whether the lives they could save made condoms morally acceptable to use, or whether homosexuality is a sin (especially since most men and women at St. Clare's listed their risk factors as "multiple," which could mean they contracted the disease through IV drug use, prostitution, gay or straight sex—in or out of prison—or a blood transfusion. Sin? Well, here comes everyone). I'm not a geneticist or a theologian. In my opinion as a Catholic, the debate on whether homosexuality is God-created human nature or sexual aberration will go the way of the pre-Copernican model of the universe, when the earth stood still. Geneticists will discover that sexuality is hardwired into our being, and the good theologians will insist, as they always have, that Scripture is a faith narrative with a radical message of salvation: "Love one another as I have loved you."

No, I missed the finer points of that pointless debate. Instead, I set my mind on how to be with death all day, moving along West Fifty-sixth Street toward Ninth Avenue, U2's *Achtung Baby* the soundtrack in my Walkman, wanting to get to work at that hospital. There was a lot of life left in those tough souls, and I might be the last one to witness it and, if possible, do something of purpose in the present. I was (I thought to myself) like Homer's mythical Phaiakians, the sailors whose ships moved at the speed of thought, and who, after

Odysseus had told them the tale of his wanderings, took the great warrior home to Ithaca while he slept in their boat. My job was to listen and to conjure a home for those who had rarely known one. Like the day Father Jack—a priest of the New York Archdiocese whose parish was, in a sense, this hospital on the West Side where people expected to die alone—came to me and asked how my Spanish was.

"Conversational," I said.

"Good. That's better than mine. I need you to hold a one-sided conversation in Spanish with someone in a coma who refuses to die." A woman they thought would have taken her CD—Celestial Discharge—weeks ago clung tenaciously to what life remained in her. Father Jack knew her history and suspected she was afraid of dying because of a falling-out she had had years earlier with her now dead sister. Altagracia seemed to be balking at what she might have imagined superstitiously would be their final confrontation in the hereafter.

Father Jack and I walked up to the quiet ward where she lay barely breathing.

"Tell her who you are," Jack said, "and that you know how sick she is. But tell her, too, that you've spoken to Flora, and she said that she forgives you." I looked at him incredulously. He couldn't expect me to go along with all of this Latin spirit-world stuff.

"Just *do* it," he said, "and then tell her it's okay. Tell her Flora's waiting for her there with God. There's love where she's going, and everything will be all right."

I said all that in Spanish as I stood over Altagracia's wasted body, which never registered a twitch or a blink. And two hours later she was dead.

My time at St. Clare's was over in eight weeks. It had been decided earlier that the sixteen weeks of long experiment to which I was assigned would be broken up into two blocks of eight, and that I would live in two separate Jesuit communities and work in two apostolates. So, at the beginning of Lent that year, I picked up and moved again, this time to the University of Scranton in Pennsylvania, where I was about to begin an immersion into a part of the Church as mysterious and misunderstood as the dying men and women I had left at St. Clare's.

When I'd first applied to the novitiate, church documents showed that my father had been baptized in a Byzantine Catholic church in Shenandoah, Pennsylvania, which meant he was a Catholic of the Christian East. I was baptized and raised in a Roman Catholic church, but according to Canon Law at the time, the child is the rite of the father, which meant that if I went on to be ordained a priest, I could choose to be ordained in an Eastern Rite, if I showed a desire to learn and practice in that tradition. I knew that the Jesuits had a history of apostolates in the Christian East. They were the first into Russia in the seventeenth century and built the Russian College, or Russicum, in Rome for training men to work in Russia; in Rome they also ran and staffed the Pontifico Istituto Orientale, which holds the finest collection of literature and writings on Eastern Christianity in the world. And I knew men who were Jesuit priests ordained in an Eastern Rite, some of them teachers and scholars of church history and patristics, others working as parish priests in small communities of Eastern Catholics. When long experiment came up, in the second year of novitiate, there tended to be little discussion about options. You went where you were sent. But Gerry raised my canonical status as a future priest of an Eastern Catholic Rite as a question, direct but intriguing.

"Do you have any interest in learning about this part of your history? You can't say it's lost, because you've never known about it until now. But there's an interesting, almost serendipitous connection to your father's past and your being here. I guess what I'm trying to say is that you've got all the right consonants in your name. What would you say to taking the second half of experiment to explore the East?"

I said, "Yes."

Eastern Christianity is ground as formidable and tricky as it is beautiful, unearthly, and literally Byzantine in its complex historical narrative. Ronald Roberson's modest book *The Eastern Christian Churches* helped me to see, when I was trying to get a handle on the intricacy of it all, the communal and chronological groupings of what he calls the "four distinct and separate Eastern Christian communions":

> (1) the Assyrian Church of the East, which is not in communion with any other church; (2) the five Oriental Orthodox Churches, which, although each is fully independent, are in communion with one another; (3) the Orthodox Church, which is a communion of national or regional churches all of which recognize the Patriarch of Constantinople as a point of unity enjoying certain rights and privileges; and (4) the Eastern Catholic Churches, all of which are in communion with the Church of Rome and its bishop.

That's the barest outline of these "communions" of the East. Within each one there exists a vast landscape of differing peoples, places, and practices, all of which can be traced back to the earliest Christians.

I'm not able to speak for the Orthodox here, except to say that the split between what is now known as Orthodox Christianity and Catholic Christianity occurred in 1054, when the Pope in Rome and the Patriarch in Constantinople mutually excommunicated each other over the language of whether the Holy Spirit proceeds from the Father alone (position of the Eastern monks), or the Father and the Son (position of the Western theologians). Hence the Latin term in the West from this controversy, *filioque* (literally "and the Son"). But most historians agree that, on the local level, Christians of the East and the West continued to practice unaffected by this kind of maneuvering on the imperial level. That is, until the East witnessed the Crusades and saw Constantinople brutally sacked by the Latins in 1204. Then the worshiping Christians of the West and the East found themselves lining up with either the Pope or the Patriarch.

As to how Eastern *Catholic* Churches emerged from all of this, Roberson is again the most succinct:

> [After 1204], a Roman Catholic theology of the Church continued to develop which vigorously emphasized the necessity of the direct jurisdiction of the Pope over all the local

churches. This implied that churches not under the Pope's jurisdiction could be considered objects of missionary activity for the purpose of bringing them into communion with the Roman Catholic Church. At the same time, the notion of "rite" developed, according to which groups of eastern Christians who came into union with Rome would be absorbed into the single Church, but allowed to maintain their own liturgical tradition and canonical discipline.

What I found as a Catholic when I set out to rediscover my own roots in the Christian East was that most of my fellow Western Christians don't know that the Latin-based Christianity of Rome is one of six Catholic traditions, and that the Latin Rite of the West, even in translation, is one of twenty-two particular rites that various churches celebrate throughout the world. Whenever I hear arch-traditionalists longing for a return to the language of "the one true Church," I long to remind them that in this Church there exist the Egyptian Alexandrine tradition, with its Coptic and Ethiopic Rites, out of which emerged a long history of desert monasticism; the Armenian tradition (in which the Father General of the Society of Jesus, Peter-Hans Kolvenbach, is a priest), with its reserved and mournful liturgy, which some liturgists consider the most beautiful of Christian rites; the Syro-Malankarans of India, who boast a community of almost 300,000 members in Kerala State; the Byzantine tradition, which rose out of Constantinople and encompasses the rites of the Eastern Catholic churches of Bulgarians, Greeks, Hungarians, Melkites, Romanians, Ruthenians (or Rusyns), Slovaks, and Ukrainians; the East Syriac tradition of the Assyrians, Syro-Malabarese, and Chaldeans, who still worship in Iraq; and the tradition of Antioch, or West Syriacs, possibly the oldest of the Eastern Christians, to which belong two Catholic churches that have no direct counterparts anywhere in the world: the Maronites of Lebanon and the Italo-Albanians of Southern Italy and Sicily. Churches rarely heard from, if ever, though dutiful, surviving, calling themselves Catholic in some of the most restless and treacherous corners of the world.

These traditions date back to the second and third centuries of the Common Era, long before the schism of 1054, a time when Antioch in Syria and Alexandria in Egypt, each looking to Jerusalem as the Holy City, were centers of ecclesiastical life in the Eastern Roman Empire. Then, when Constantinople rose to political and spiritual prominence in the fourth and fifth centuries, Christianity spread farther east, especially among the Slavic tribes of Rusyns, Ukrainians, and Moravians.

When the Western Roman Empire fell, the Church was the sole source of cultural unity left standing, and the Latin tradition became the defining one within Catholicism. Yet the Eastern Catholic churches have always been proud of their ability to remain simultaneously faithful to and independent from Rome, especially when they found it difficult to navigate the fact that they looked like Orthodox churches inside the Catholic fold. In northeastern Pennsylvania, for instance, it's said that when Catholic priests came in the nineteenth century from places like Ruthenia and Ukraine with their wives and children, the Irish bishops made them go home, and then allowed only celibate Eastern Catholic priests into their dioceses. It was for reasons like this, too, that Roman Catholics looked upon the Eastern Catholics with suspicion and accused their own faithful in the autochthonous church of not being Catholic enough because they were not *visibly* doing what Catholics were supposed to do.

Now, of course, the deep and soulful traditions of the East tend to be the envy of the West, in its nostalgia for a past. But my father's own religious history was played out in what church historians called the "Latinization of the East." When his widowed mother and her five children moved from a Pennsylvania mining patch to some semblance of a new life in Wilkes-Barre, it was the Irish monsignor who welcomed them into Sacred Heart Catholic Church, steering them from their Eastern Catholicism, within which they had all been baptized, confirmed, and raised up to that point. It wasn't intentional, merely practical. Wilkes-Barre has no shortage of Eastern Catholic churches. But Sacred Heart was closest to the Krivaks' home on Charles Street in Plains; it had a school and was a strong community. My grandmother was a single mother who needed to worry about where she would find support and a wage to raise her kids, and Sacred Heart gave her a job cleaning at the school. What did it matter if the liturgy was in Old Slavonic or Latin, as long as she got to Mass? And eventually her children associated the rituals of the East not with nostalgia but with a time they hoped to forget.

I remember my father telling me on a Friday night during Lent after I had served benediction with Father Sammons that frankincense reminded him of being a boy and seeing his father lying in a coffin, watching his mother crying in a chair off to the side, and listening to the priest chanting the *panahida*, an Old Slavonic prayer for the dead. In that room, in winter, all of the prayers, litanies, and worship were smoke intent upon choking him. I didn't understand, then, why that time, that prayer, that memory should be so different from anything I would have known had he passed away when I was a boy. Catholics were Catholics, "the same Eucharist wherever you go," as my mother used to say, she who grew up in St. Therese's and who took us there to be raised Catholics, too, because we lived quite a ways out from the city, and because St. Therese's was the only show around.

My first experience of the Divine Liturgy was at St. George Ukrainian Catholic Church on East Seventh Street in New York, while I was in graduate school at Columbia. It was during the time Gerry was my spiritual director, and he suggested that I "check out" an Eastern Catholic church. So I went downtown one Sunday, from the West Side to the East Side. I remember the stunning, ubiquitous iconography that adorns St. George's; the pointed glow that came from candles all around the church, in spite of the fact that an arched stained-glass window to the west let in its own indirect morning light; the solemn reverence of the congregation; and the huge golden icon of the Theotokos, "Mother of God," robed in red and flanked by angels seemingly cast upon the entire back wall of the sanctuary. There was a long period of waiting in silence. A man I later learned was the deacon emerged to incense the iconstasis while the believers crossed themselves, then the first long notes of chant issued from the mouth of the now-visible priest: "Blessed is the kingdom of the Father, and of

the Son, and of the Holy Spirit . . ." It somehow all seemed to be happening in a space much darker than St. George's airy nave. Perhaps it
was because I felt as though I had walked into a cross between *The
Deer Hunter* in setting and *Ivan the Terrible* in sound, though without
the benefit of subtitles (everything was in Ukrainian). It was frighten-
ing and compelling, the constant visual and vocal reminder of our creation in the image of God, and the humble, spiritual distance each of
us seemed to hold ourselves to in the otherwise close quarters of that
church. I mention this because when I moved to my next apostolic
experiment as a Jesuit novice, I felt again something of the fear and
attraction that had stirred in me when I contemplated immersing myself in a tradition at once alien and somehow belonging to me.

The initial stage of my training at the Center for Eastern Christian
Studies at the University of Scranton was to become familiar with the
liturgical rites. I was sent to do fieldwork, in a sense. I arrived on campus on Ash Wednesday and threw myself into the Eastern Christian
communities that make northeastern Pennsylvania what one Jesuit
calls, in spite of a visibly dwindling population, "the last bastion of
Byzantium." At "the Center" I became acolyte for the morning liturgy
with Fathers John Levko and Tom Sable, two Eastern Rite Jesuits
who, like Saints John Chrysostom and Basil the Great (one stern, the
other studious), raised the notes of prayer each morning in their tiny
Byzantine chapel at 8:00. In response to those notes, a Sister of St.
Joseph, Joan Roccasalvo, was a choir of one, keeping the thread of
worship seamless. Then, like a Russian monk in the black cassock I
had to don to identify myself as a seminarian, I slipped quietly into
the great blanket of Lenten services—Matins, Vespers, the Divine
Liturgy—that covered the family of Eastern Catholic churches
throughout Scranton and neighboring Pittston: St. Mary's, St. John
the Baptist, St. Michael's, St. Joseph's, and St. Nicholas's. In my native Pennsylvania, all the liturgies were in English, with a few Old
Slavonic hymns known by the old and the young. I learned the Cyrillic alphabet (and went on to begin studies in Russian that summer),
practiced the responses to the liturgy with Sister Joan, read church

history and the Desert Fathers on my own, spent time with the Eastern Rite priests in the parishes (hospitable men who knew best how to balance the transcendent and the local), and wondered if this meant that I might be on a path back to a landscape I had years ago ceased to call my home.

As I write that, I realize how distant not only this "home" but the family in which I grew up remains in my story of religious life. Maybe those days of setting ourselves apart from the world when we entered a seminary or monastery were not so distant, and although the Jesuits taught us specifically to be religious men *of* the world, we had to retreat *from* that world in order to reenter it as religious. Or maybe it's more that Pennsylvania's Wyoming Valley always looked better to me from a romantic distance. I hadn't exactly drifted away from my family as an adult, but the choices of school, work, and travel I made meant I was something of an oddball. Not a black sheep, "tenderminded," as William James might have called me. I fared better elsewhere once I left, and so was always wary when I got too close to home. It made me slip back into what I was—a boy champing to get out—not what I hoped to become: a young man accepted by the world because I had something to offer.

My decision to join the Jesuits, though, put my wandering in perspective, at least as far as my family was concerned. Suddenly I had gained professional normalcy as a representative of the Church. I had to do more than accept this identity as my own. I had to live it as though it were what I was meant to do. And, simple as this might sound, in Scranton for those eight weeks, this living came in my daily contact with the Eastern Liturgy as a Western Jesuit. I called my parents a few times, saw them along with my brother and some aunts and uncles for dinner on a couple of occasions, but otherwise lived thirty miles north of them as though it were yet another mission three hundred or three thousand miles away.

But something bothered me, a sensation I remember distinctly having as a boy when a bit of coal ash would somehow get down my shirt as I removed the bucket of soot from the old stoker furnace we kept in our basement. It was like a dry scratch I could feel but couldn't find, until I managed to stop everything, strip off my shirt, and pick a lone cinder from my skin. A month later, on the Wednesday before Holy Week of that year, I told my father that I had to go down to Shenandoah, Pennsylvania, to check on a small detail of his baptismal status. In truth I didn't. The documents verifying his own baptism had to be made a part of my application to the Jesuits before I entered, so they were already known. But I had been thinking about driving down to that part of the state, which I hadn't been to since I was a boy. Who better to go with than the man who used to take us there to visit his uncle Joe in the town of Glen Lyon, where Matthew and I climbed on the slag heaps behind Joe's house and were rewarded for our visit with a sip of Bartels beer.

And I wanted to know something else, something I believed only my father could give me. The silence of our car ride to the novitiate the year before had convinced me that my mother embraced this life I had entered. What did my usually unreserved old man think? When the thought first came to me, I told myself it didn't matter. But it did. It did because, after all the outward resolve and certainty, saying to people, "See you later. I'm off to become a priest," I wasn't entirely sure it was the life I wanted. Even though in less than six months I would be taking my first vows as a Jesuit. I needed a ferryman to help me cross over, after he answered what I thought would be my one final question: *How do I know this is right?*

I drove down to our house in Dallas from Scranton in one of the Jesuit cars (no cassock now, just jeans, T-shirt, and sweater in the early spring weather), but my father insisted that he drive from there. So I let him. He knew the way through the forty or so miles of winding back roads from Dallas to Nanticoke that I couldn't possibly have retraced from memory. We talked, as we always did, about family and fishing, which he seemed to like most, until it got so that I would keep the conversation going with a "Yep" here, a question there, my attention fixed on his relaxed shoulders and fine silver head.

We stopped first at St. Nicholas Ukrainian Catholic Church in Glen Lyon. Monsignor Bohdan Olesh wasn't in, so we drove through town trying to reorient ourselves. Nothing, it seemed, had changed. The narrow, wood-shingled houses built close to the road looked older—paint fading, boards rotting, porches leaning, coal bins empty.

The past lived here now. We decided to stop for coffee and parked on a depleted Main Street. As we got out of the car, I saw a man in clerics walking in our direction. Maybe this is Olesh, I thought. I told my father to follow me, crossed the street, and said hello to the spry-looking priest. Before I could introduce us any further, he fixed his gaze on my father and said, "You're a Krivak." He leaned forward, his eyes narrowing. "I'm sorry to hear about your mother. Anna was a good woman." My grandmother had died peacefully two years before at the age of ninety-three, but Olesh spoke of it as though it had been last week, memory being a blessing and a curse of the Slavs.

Olesh was a short but strapping man for his age, with gray hair that looked like it could double as a wire brush (an ethnic trait, I decided). He took my father's hand as though about to shake it but held it tenderly. "Which one are you? John, Mickey, or Tommy?"

"Tom," my father said, a little embarrassed.

"Of course, the youngest. I'm Father Olesh," he said, introducing himself, then slyly, "I heard you were looking for me."

My father's bushy eyebrows arched as he roared out loud and said, "Can't hide a damn thing in this town."

Olesh mock-whispered, "Never could, and never will." Then, in spite of the difference in size between the two men, he reached up to put his arm around my father, accepting, it seemed to me, their regional brotherhood.

We went back to the rectory and told him why we had come. "A Jesuit!" he said. "And they let you delve into your Eastern past, did they? Well, you better be careful, or you'll end up wily and well-traveled, and right back here in Pennsylvania." I couldn't tell if he thought that was a good thing or a bad thing, so I smiled and said I still had a long way to go.

"Of course you do! We all do, right, Tommy?" he said, winking at my father.

"That's right, Age," my father said, blushing for me a little but warming up to Olesh's hospitality.

After coffee, we sat down in front of the parish rolls from 1894 and looked up every Krivak who had ever been inside St. Nicholas Church. My grandfather John wasn't listed, Olesh said, because he was born in 1893 and most likely baptized at St. Michael's in Shenandoah.

"Here's something, though. Did you know that John Krivak had a sister, Julianna, baptized in 1902? Aunt Julianna. Ever heard of her?" My father never had. "Must have died young. She disappears after that."

They went on like this for over an hour, a couple of Area boys digging through that past like it was some newly dynamited vein of anthracite. I had a notebook with me to record any details about persons or places I found interesting, and they would turn to me every now and then to confirm my presence and give me something to write. "What was that name, Age?" my father would ask about some other forgotten relative emerging like a ghost from those dusty rolls. Or Olesh would lean over and say with his own authority, "Better write these names and dates down there, Andy, 'cause you won't see 'em again once I close this book." I no longer thought about my own identity. I wondered if my father's memory of his father—the chant, the cold, the candle smoke and frankincense—was not so much dissipating as changing, reassociating, turning the fragments into a coherent narrative. He seemed at ease and curious as he pored over those church records, stirring up faces to go with names, finding names that never had any faces, and sifting through the past with Olesh as though they were old cronies.

After we left Glen Lyon, we drove another twenty miles south to Shenandoah, where my father was born, to see the new St. Michael's, hoping they'd retained their records from the past. Built in 1884, St. Michael's is reported to be the first Ruthenian Catholic church in the United States. But that seems late to me. The original church was destroyed in a fire in the early 1980s.

At noon, the week before Easter, the church was locked. An inhospitable cleaning woman—as though under a self-imposed house arrest—said through the glass of the front door of the rectory that the priest was out at another church and wouldn't be back for a few days. If there were any records I needed, all I had to do was write and request them. And no, we couldn't come inside. She was on her lunch break.

"Let's head into town," my father said.

Not much more than fifty years earlier, Shenandoah was a prosperous and vibrant city along a rail line, its wealth pinned to coal mining, like that of so many other once-prosperous towns in Pennsylvania. Although a smaller city than Scranton or Wilkes-Barre, Shenandoah had several theaters, which my father pointed out as he told stories of seeing the hometown boys Tommy and Jimmy Dorsey come back to play with their orchestra in the late 1940s and early 1950s. There was always something exciting and romantic about being young and on the go in Shenandoah, he said, as though it was New York or Las Vegas caught in the Blue Mountains of Pennsylvania. "I loved this place!"

We walked down West Street to the lot where once stood the boyhood home of Walter Ciszek, a Jesuit who was imprisoned in Russia for twenty-three years. Someone had put up a plaque near the demolition site identifying the boards, stone, and cinder block as the home of the priest who locals believe is a saint. In 1940, Ciszek crossed into Russia as a priest on his way to Chusovoy in the Urals. A year later he was arrested by the Soviets as a Vatican spy and sent to Lubyanka prison for six years in solitary confinement. He spent another ten years in Siberian labor camps before being released into Russian society but stripped of his American passport, so he couldn't leave. By the late 1950s, his superiors in the Maryland Province presumed he was dead. When a Russian spy was captured in the United States in the early sixties, the Soviets offered Ciszek in exchange for their operative. He returned to the United States in 1963, in the midst of Vatican II and the dismantling of the Church's efforts to send missionaries into Russia.

My father didn't know all this about the priest whose demolished house we were staring at. I gave him a bit of the history I had learned, mentioning that Ciszek was an Eastern Rite priest, which was why, or at least part of the reason, he had been in Russia. I was hoping to get my father to make the connection that I, too, might be capable of something like this someday, that is to say, travel a long way for a long time, hoping that I would and wouldn't be missed. But the plaque said enough. A Catholic boy who gave what little he had for the faith was as close to sainthood as anyone.

Then West Street came to an abrupt halt. The land dropped quickly and opened out onto a canvas of slag heaps and black dirt roads that wound through treeless hills, all outlined by the round and distant Blue Mountains. There was nowhere else to go. We looked out over the scene wrought by nearly a century of mining.

"When I was a kid, Age, I cursed those damn hills and everything they meant," my father said. "They took my father and expected me to die in them, too, I guess."

The shift in tone surprised me. "But you've had such good memories here today, haven't you?"

"That's the hell of it," he said, using his favorite expression. "During the Depression and before the war, we worked our tails off picking coal all day. After the war, it was like a different world. I could hate the hills but love the town, once I knew the hills wouldn't kill me."

I asked him if meeting Father Olesh and finding out more about the Eastern Church made him curious to return to the rite he had been baptized in, or learn the liturgy he had more of a claim to than I ever would, once he knew it wasn't trying to kill him. Maybe the two of us would find there some sort of spiritual common ground.

"What for?" he said. "It's beautiful, but it's not mine." Then he said, as though not wanting to hurt my feelings, "I'm glad you're showing this to me again, though. Now I can say I've seen it all. Mass on a footlocker in the South Pacific with guys who the next day never knew what hit 'em. And Mass with the Russians." He pronounced it "Roo-shins" because he didn't mean "people of Russia" when he referred liturgically to the "Russians." He meant Ruthenians, more properly called the Rusyns. The term is slowly being reclaimed as a greater awareness of culture and ethnicity emerges in the Church, but I heard my uncle Joe's wife, Aunt Stella, talk about the "Roo-shins" her whole life.

Then came the moment I suppose I'd been waiting for. Unprompted, my father said, "You keep at this, Age. Lots of things we lost or let go of because we had no choice in our day. But regardless of where we went to church, we never lost that faith. You heard Olesh. That was your grandmother. '*With the help of God,*' she'd always say. That's all we've got, my friend." And he put his arm around me the same way he had done on that first day of the novitiate, the day he had ferried me into religious life. The same way Olesh had embraced him not three hours earlier. Father and son, yes, but now the closest father and son might come to understanding a brotherhood, because soon I could say what it was I did. Soon I'd take my vows in the Society of Jesus, and my mother and father could say to anyone who asked, "He's a Jesuit," and they'd be right, and happy, and grateful to their God, as I was when, on the fifteenth of August, 1992, wearing a black clerical suit with white Roman collar, I knelt before the newly consecrated host that our father provincial held in the three points of thumb, middle, and index finger, and vowed to the "Heavenly and Eternal Father," as every Jesuit has since Ignatius Loyola, "perpetual chastity, poverty, and obedience" in the Society of Jesus, promising "that I shall enter that same Society in order to lead my entire life in it."

PART III

He began to feel notable changes in his soul. Sometimes he was so dejected that he found no enjoyment
in the prayers he recited, not even in attending Mass,
nor in any other form of prayer. Sometimes the exact
opposite happened to him, and so suddenly that it
seemed he had stripped away all sadness and desolation, just as one strips a cloak from another's shoulders. He was astonished at the changes, which he had
never before experienced, and said to himself: "What
kind of new life is this that we are now beginning?"

—*Autobiography of Ignatius Loyola*

PART II

I t's *pride*, in the end, that Augustine is really struggling with," Professor Deal Hudson said, summing up the three weeks we had spent on *Confessions*, his southern accent hanging on the long *i* of *pride*.

Joey from the novitiate, in his second year of philosophy studies now, expressed his skepticism that the book could be captured so singularly. He was always looking for a fight with Hudson. A losing battle in my opinion. "Six other deadly sins," Joey said too comfortably, "*deadly* being the operative word for the good bishop of Hippo." David chimed in and wondered if we weren't overshadowing the reality of God's intervention in the new Christian's life.

"All true," Hudson said, his crooked smile suggesting we had missed something. "Augustine knows firsthand those deadly sins. He knows he needs God's grace. Remember the pear tree? But in that equation you're thinking too much about *sin*, and not enough about *self*. Pride, *superbia* in the Latin, is the original and deadliest sin because it believes the source of all is, in fact, the *self*." He paused for effect. Hudson was a man as poised and intellectually confident as he was well-groomed and put together. Some students jotted in notebooks. The rest of the class waited for him to go on as he thumbed through his copy of *Confessions*.

"*Confessio*. It means praise of God, and accusation of the self. In Book Five, when he was a Manichee, Augustine writes: 'It had pleased my pride to be free from a sense of guilt, and when I had done anything wrong not to confess that it was myself who had done it, that You might heal my soul.' " Hudson put the book down and hesitated, as though in thought. "This is Peter Brown, for those of you doing the outside reading I've assigned. But it's so crucial I want to claim it here for the sake of this class. Augustine is not the convert writing a story about how he has been cured of this or that sickness, forgiven of this or that sin. He's a man who knows that he continues to convalesce. The act of *confessio*, the experience of God's grace, the self-discovery, all teach him that the journey is never so quickly and easily over. Listen to him in Book Ten." Hudson flipped a few pages, bent back the spine of his paperback, and began to read. " 'I cannot easily gather myself together so as to be more clean from this particular infection: I greatly fear my hidden parts, which Your eyes know, but not mine. Behold, I see myself in You, but whether I may be like this, I just don't know.' " He looked up. " 'I just don't *know*,' Augustine admits. *Augustine!* Of all people. Remarkable!"

Hudson had wandered down the main aisle and into our midst. As much evangelical preacher as university educator, the popular professor of philosophy at Fordham had converted to Catholicism as an adult. Hearing him read Augustine out loud, you knew there was a trail that led right back to when the man first picked up *Confessions*. He paused, bowed his head, turned, and walked back to the front of the classroom.

"When I *re*read this book," he said, taking a seat on the edge of his desk, "at this point in my life, a Christian, a scholar, a man *always* in need of God's grace, I am convinced that *Confessions* is a meditation on how the search for God is always that search for the self. Why? Because only in the *true* self—healing from the sin of *Pride*—does one find God. You Jesuits who are studying to be priests ought to know this. Isn't that removal of pride at the heart of Loyola's *Exercises*?" Again, the long *i*. "And I don't mean tamping down your ambitions to be president of this great university," he said with the same crooked lift at the edge of his mouth. "I mean the closer we come to God the closer we come to knowing who we are, and then what we can and ought to do in the presence of that God. Tell me the paths you've all been on haven't been, at their core, somehow *Confessions*-like."

The other graduate students in the class looked around at us "*Confessions*-like" men. Although we were dressed like them, they knew who we were because we talked to them, studied with some, played squash with others, and invited the more curious ones over to our community for dinner. The eight of us Jesuits, though, who were taking Hudson's course on Augustine of Hippo, said nothing. There was a time and place for faith sharing, and this didn't seem like it.

"Well, I don't want to put you on the spot. I thought we might bring Augustine into the present. Maybe it's no longer possible." He said this as though to himself. "In the meantime, everyone get started on *City of God* for the next week. I recommend y'all find time to do some lengthy reading."

Take your traditional notion of a Catholic seminary—monolithic building, men in black cassocks, silence, order and ritual the constant rule—and discard it now. As Jesuits, we never technically lived in that place Catholics imagine when they hear that you've entered "the priesthood." They exist, still, for the diocesan priests. St. Mary's in Baltimore. St. Joseph's in Yonkers. But the Jesuit, whose "house is the world," moves from one community to another, as is appropriate and necessary according to his stage and place in formation. We were, in the traditional meaning of *seminarium*, being "developed" and "nurtured" like seeds hoping to grow into stronger stalks of faith, who would in turn nurture others. But we did so locally, according to what mission was given us by our provincial superior, who answered directly to Father General in Rome (once known as "the Black Pope," because he wore a cassock and answered only to the Holy Pontiff), and always in the spirit of indifference we'd learned from the *Spiritual Exercises*.

I walked back to our house on Belmont Avenue in the Little Italy section of the Bronx with David and two new classmates from the California and New Orleans Provinces.

"I don't like getting singled out like that," Mike Taylor said. Mike had come from California to do the M.A. in philosophy at Fordham. He wanted to be a Scripture scholar, and this was where it started; this was where the philosophers and theologians were. Mike was earnest and leaned toward the conservative. His father had been killed in Vietnam when his mother was pregnant with him. She never remarried, so Mike grew up spending a lot of time with his Mexican American grandmother, whose own Catholicism became a stabilizing factor in his life as a young man.

"He missed the point," David said. "I don't think that just because we're Jesuits we're more or less '*Confessions*-like' than anyone else in that class. It seems to me that the power of the book for anyone is Augustine's constant invocation of God."

" 'You are great, Lord, and highly to be praised,' " Mike said, quoting from the first line of *Confessions*. "Sounds to me like Deal was trying to get an *Amen!* from the congregation."

"Yeah, I reckon there's Augustine and then there's Hudson. You've got to separate one mountain of *pride* from the other," Harlan Fails said. Harlan was a Texan in the New Orleans Province. He had the demeanor and mechanical abilities of Billy from our novitiate and looked (in his words) like "a cross between an Elvis impersonator and a big truck mechanic." He was from Dallas—the other Dallas—and I liked him for his wry southern understatement. He exaggerated his own long *i* in *pride*, and we all laughed at this gentle mock. "But he's got a point," Harlan went on. "We make the *Exercises* relevant to our present. Why should we leave Augustine out?"

I agreed with Elvis. Now that I was twenty-nine, my experiences of Augustine were the bookends that marked a decade. When I had studied *Confessions* for the first time as an undergraduate, I was captured by the strength of religious conviction in the unrelenting voice that dared to put "I" next to "God," even though the "I" was constantly humbled by that real presence. But reading *Confessions* as a Jesuit, now, I didn't feel it had less urgency for me. I had more time to give to it. The voice that had previously been the voice of a cautious, plaintive line of prayer sounded suddenly like the anxious prose of a man still trying to come to grips with God *and* himself. "After that utterance I will run and lay hold on you," Augustine says early in *Confessions*, addressing his soul. It was as though he had sat down and written the book over again in the course of *my* ten years between reads, because he hadn't been able to say—or lay hold of—what he wanted to say the first time.

"I don't know about the rest of you guys, but it's why *I'm* here," I said as we walked out of the back gates of campus and onto Belmont. An old Italian woman sat in a rocker on her front porch, and the litter of kittens she fed skittered from the sidewalk into tall grass along the house and fence as they sensed our approaching.

In 1992 there were four universities in the United States where young Jesuits could study philosophy: Fordham in New York, Loyola in Chicago, St. Louis University, and Gonzaga in Spokane. Of these, Fordham was the truly urban environment. While the Rose Hill campus in the Bronx remained inside the gates a beautifully mapped out expanse of Gothic buildings, leafy trees, and sweeping greens, outside was the South Bronx, loud, gritty, diverse, and dangerous. One class-mate, John, was robbed in the foyer of our residence when a mugger stealthily pushed his way in behind him, told him to keep his "fucking mouth shut," and relieved him of his wallet, which held five dollars and a student ID. (That's poverty.) And Justin was held up on Bath-gate Avenue by a man wielding a shotgun. The thief ran off with Justin's backpack, netting a cache of Latin books, the loss of which hurt the scholar more than the sight of a gun. The university was scrupulous about security yet felt its own vulnerability at times. Like when a coed was dragged into a stairwell and raped one night as she walked home late from the D train, a half mile from the campus. The police hunted for the perpetrator until a young man slinked into the Forty-eighth Precinct station house and confessed to the crime that evidence confirmed he had committed. Remorse and a change of heart? Not if you believe the story that moved quietly around the streets that week. Some of the men in this proud and tight-knit Italian neighborhood found out quickly who the rapist was and told him he'd be better off turning himself in and going to jail than letting them decide what he deserved. Of course, this was all strictly rumor.

One year before, when the provincial's formation assistant came to the novitiate and asked me where I saw myself studying philosophy, I told him I had been thinking about Chicago. It has a large population of Eastern Catholics, and I had already lived and studied in New York. But the question was a formality. David and I both would be sent to Fordham because it was in the New York Province, and New Yorkers were expected to be residents in their own houses. I felt in that first real test of discernment the sting of obedience, but at the time it didn't sting too badly. I didn't mind being sent to Fordham. I wanted the hardest philosophy program they could throw at me; Jesuits like Avery Dulles, Robert O'Connell, Gerry McCool, and Norris Clarke were active on the faculty. And I was no stranger to New York. I imagined it would be something of a homecoming.

Change is a constant character on the stage that is New York, and once I moved back after two years in Syracuse and a Jesuit novitiate, I realized I was on that stage but not of it. I could retain the props of what I once knew: the address of a favorite bar and pizza restaurant on the Upper West Side, an alumni card that let me read at the Columbia library, and the phone numbers of a few friends still around. But the city was different now, and so was I.

Home was the Bronx.

After living for a summer in Hunts Point, one of the most dangerous neighborhoods in the city, I felt my new neighborhood was trying, in its own way, to follow the script in that play about change. Italian families with money moved farther north for a bigger house in a better neighborhood. On their heels, Hispanics—increasingly Mexicans—moved in. Catholic parishes watched their Italian masses dwindle and their Spanish masses overflow. Then, in the 1990s, the Bosnian immigrants started coming, displaced by the war in the Balkans. (There had always been Albanians in the neighborhood; they ran some of the best bakeries.) With the Bosnians came Islam. By the time I moved out of the Bronx in 1995, a makeshift mosque had gone up on our corner of East 189th Street and Belmont Avenue. In our house, we thought this was somehow culturally, economically, and theologically right. But no Italian American we spoke to ever saw it as anything other than the end of an era.

In a four-floor walkup named Ciszek Hall (because Father Walter lived and died there after he returned from his imprisonment in Russia, when it was the John XXIII Center for Eastern Christian Studies), among the gardens and grapes growing below in the backyards of our neighbors, jets approaching LaGuardia Airport in the distance, car alarms, fireworks, and occasional gunshots interrupting the night (discernible by the fact that they went *pop! pop!* once or twice, unlike the running, explosive streams of fireworks), we gathered from all over the world, sixteen newly vowed Jesuits, some of us just starting out, others a year or two into it, sent by the provincials of New York, Maryland, New England, New Orleans, California, Puerto Rico, the Antilles, El Salvador, Vietnam, Nigeria, and Ghana to begin studies. We were called "scholastics" now, from the Latin that means both "schoolboys" and "an elite troop of soldiers." We placed the SJ after our names for "Society of Jesus," and took up the next stage in the long period of formation the Jesuits require for ordination to the priesthood, under the tutelage of a new triumvirate of *formators*.

Gerald J. Chojnacki—a.k.a. Jeff—was our superior. He fit the image of the fat priest: round hands, thick shoulders, big belly. But he radiated the slow, calm bearing of the most austere monk. A photograph he kept in his office showed the young Jesuit from Jersey City on his ordination day, late twenties I'd guess, collected and immaculate in his priestly vestments, full head of hair, face clean-shaven, and skinny as a rail. He was, too, for his size, a gentle man who was in no way, for as long as I knew him, weak. He took stock in tests of personality, like the Myers-Briggs and the Enneagram, believing that strength of community and faithfulness to God began with a humble knowledge of the self. In meetings he made notes unobtrusively on a yellow legal pad, keeping everything for future reference, as though our spiritual lives were a kind of *Confessions*-like book. Some of the guys called him "Big Daddy."

Raymond Swietzer was our minister. Ray was as reserved as he was efficient. He loved opera and ice hockey. He read Karl Rahner (in German) and the *New York Post*. Outside the house he taught Latin and modern romance languages at Fordham Prep. In spite or because of all this, he had an air of inflexibility about him, the surface appearance perhaps of his deeply classical mind. Yet, once when a scholastic asked in community meeting why we had season tickets to the symphony and not the New York Rangers, Ray stood up and said in his reasoned tone: "We have symphony tickets because they were a gift subscription to the house from a very generous donor." There were groans from the hockey fans. "But, it seems to me," Ray continued unfazed, "that William has a point. We should offer the scholastics both, or nothing."

Charlie Mutenot, our third priest and guide, was an adjunct professor of theology at Fordham. Charlie was one of those intensely direct Jesuits who cultivated his own irreverent sense of humor. When Mike mentioned a few weeks into the semester that he had more work to do than he could possibly handle, Charlie, who'd done a tour of Vietnam as a chopper pilot, said: "As my old flight instructor used to say, 'Step into this chopper, son, and you'll be busier than a one-legged man in an ass-kicking contest.' So buckle up." His Ph.D. was in liberation theology. Out of graduate school now, he was working on "apostolic analysis," a kind of cross between practical theology and social science, assessing the material as well as spiritual needs of a community, then organizing people to meet those needs. He likened the renovation of a crack house or the installation of a stop sign on a corner (where two kids had already been hit by cars) to the biblical feeding of the five thousand.

Anyone who wants to be ordained a priest in the Catholic Church has to study a certain amount of philosophy before his training in theology and divinity. It's the tradition of Holy Orders, whether you're a Franciscan, Dominican, Marist, or diocesan priest. Because we were Jesuits, though, philosophy was considered our first *mission*, which is to say we were *sent* to studies, in the same way that Avery Dulles was sent to Fordham to teach theology, or Matteo Ricci (long ago) was sent to China.

So, much like other graduate students, those of us who were directed to the Bronx applied to and enrolled in the master's program at Fordham. We took survey courses on Plato and Aristotle, Aquinas and Augustine, Nietzsche and Kierkegaard, and seminars on political philosophy and the role of the public intellectual. We considered the philosophy of art from the medievals to the modernists, and delved into the postmodernism of contemporary thinkers like Levinas, Derrida, and Rorty. Ethics, too, had to be part of the training, and so we studied a range of positions from natural law to the emotivists and the new virtue theorists. Then, at the end of three years, we were given a two-hour oral examination on questions from any period or problem in the history of philosophy, which we were expected to pass.

To keep track of our progress, a Jesuit on the faculty was appointed our program director (although we studied with non-Jesuits as well). He made sure we took a precise set of courses to suit not our but the Church's needs and led a philosophical integration seminar in our last year, which gave us practice in the discourse. That sounds as though we sat around a table and memorized rote answers to expectedly contentious questions that required doctrinally correct positions (abortion, birth control, divorce, women's ordination . . . You get the picture). But no. We discussed philosophy as a discipline, extant and relevant in our lives as men wanting to be priests. And all this at a time when it seemed aberrant, if not madness. What is the freedom of responsibility? What constitutes an informed conscience? Does God stand aloof from our suffering? Is there, in the end, something rather than nothing? There was, of course, an obedience to orthodoxy at work here. But so, too, was there wisdom and desire. "The fear of the Lord is the beginning of knowledge; wisdom and instruction fools despise," Proverbs says. And no one seemed to despise fools more than the Jesuits.

"You're studying to be a priest and they let you read Nietzsche?" a friend of mine asked when I called to tell him I had moved to the Bronx. I had studied Nietzsche as an undergraduate. Religious life hadn't imposed amnesia upon me. We were supposed to be modern men ministering in a modern world—where a maelstrom of social, ethical, and theological opinions swirled—so ideally there should be nothing we did not know. John Henry Newman thought the same in the nineteenth century: "Whatever the risk of corruption from intercourse with the world around, such a risk must be encountered if a great idea is fully to be understood and much more if it is to be fully exhibited." Or, as an old Jesuit, whose own philosophical formation came at the hands of some of the Church's greatest intellectuals, once said: "The mind unfettered finds its way to God."

We understood this responsibility to form our minds and our consciences. We had come here for something far greater than a great idea. Yet, to be given this mission meant also that we were trusted in our faith and in our prayer to accomplish what was required of us. If those "long and exacting tests" of the novitiate had done anything, it was to turn us into men who could return from a course on Nietzsche's thought week after week, immersed in the pull as well as the problems of the mind that wrote *Zarathustra*, and gather at liturgy as brothers and a community of believers, right there in the Bronx, because, no, God was not dead, not if we were somehow to be living proof of that.

Proof, though, seems always to be the sticking point in a philosophy that's meant to be, as Clement of Alexandria said two hundred years before Augustine, "a handmaid to theology." Never mind philosophical atheism. How are we, or any philosopher who professes to be a Christian, supposed to believe rationally in the existence of God when human reason—corrupted by the Fall that the Christ was said to redeem—can never stand on the same plain as faith?

It's an ongoing question. Some, like Immanuel Kant, answered that reason has no place in faith, and so kept philosophy separated from faith. Others, like Kierkegaard and Karl Barth, said that faith outstrips reason in the running, and preached their inspired theology accordingly. But the Catholic Church has always refused to let the two separate, because both are part of what's considered the "not yet" and the "already" of human salvation. Can we know God entirely in this life? No. And so faith keeps us moving toward that promise. But is it, then, useless to say that we can know God at all on the journey? The First Vatican Council (1869–1870, famous for its pronouncement on the infallibility of the Pope, who was Pius IX at the time) didn't think so. We *can* know God through reason, the cardinals all assented. "Even though faith is above reason, there can never be any real disagreement between faith and reason, since it is the same God who reveals the mysteries and infuses faith, and who has endowed the human mind with the light of reason." Leo XIII's encyclical on the restoration of Christian philosophy, *Aeterni Patris*, in 1879, shored up the same. And in 1998, John Paul II's encyclical *Fides et Ratio* reminded Catholics of the late twentieth century (in case there was any doubt) that the relationship between faith and reason extends back to the ancients themselves, and their own search to "Know Thyself." The journey to "engage truth more and more deeply" is a journey (that indefatigable Pope wrote) "which has unfolded—as it must—within the horizon of personal self-consciousness: the more human beings know reality and the world, the more they know themselves in their uniqueness, with the question of the meaning of things and their very existence becoming ever more pressing. This is why all that is the object of our knowledge becomes a part of our life."

So it became as well for us. We scholastics knew that Anselm's proof for God's existence is of "a being than which no greater can be conceived." That Thomas Aquinas's Five Ways argue for an immovable, originating, noncontingent, perfect, and governing God. And that René Descartes suggested that the idea of a perfect being in his mind could not exist as something unreal or as a deception. Others found their own subtle and ingenious ways to assert or shore up belief. Yet this "reason," these "proofs" in Christian philosophy are not like the elements of Euclidean geometry, which rest within a hermetically sealed world of two dimensions and can be worked through elegantly to their final Q.E.D. The two are more like an interactive map of the created world. We need it to get home, and the maker of this map *wants* us to get home. That's the thing, because, along the way, if the traveler were to study it closely enough, it would become clear that no one, no being, has been left out of its design and influence. This isn't the Deist who creates and sits by. This is the kind of Mapmaker who goes out on the road with the traveler. And when the traveler is curious, lost, tired, or all three, somehow (as though the Maker has seen to it) someone arrives or emerges along a similar path, pulls up a rock, and tells the traveler a story of another who had passed through this same way and eventually gotten home. Then, when both are rested and certain that this is, without doubt, the road to be on, they give their blessings and part, because there's a ways yet to go.

Are these "proofs" of where and from whom this seemingly endless source of detail originates (and then resides in fellow pilgrims and innkeepers on the way) true? Does God exist? Find God in them and as a result of them, and God exists. The answer, as with so much else, emerges in the pressing on. There's *something rather than nothing* when there's searching rather than standing still.

What we *learned* was that as public servants and vowed religious we were being given the responsibility to be guides on the path of what the Church understands as its earthly pilgrimage. Map readers in the service of the great Maker. "Salvation comes from God alone," the Catholic catechism asserts. "We believe the Church as the mother of our new birth, and not *in* the Church as if she were the author of our salvation." What would be the use of faith—its life, its proofs, its landscapes, its ongoing narrative—if there were no element of what St. Paul calls "the substance of things hoped for"? Faith is *certain*, in its way. "Ten thousand difficulties do not make one doubt," Newman wrote. Yet the catechism also asserts that "faith *seeks* understanding" and cites Augustine: "I believe in order to understand; and I understand the better to believe." Faith as both *certain* and *seeker* is no paradox. It's the nature of belief, and the way in which we studied our philosophy.

Formation as constant trial continued. We had our primary mission: studies now. Yet, because we were Jesuits, when we weren't reading, eating, cleaning, or praying, we set out in twos to do whatever we could with ten hours a week allotted to us for apostolic work outside the community. Mike and a Californian named Scott ran the youth choir at the parish of St. Anthony of Padua. David, Rocco, and two men from Africa, Chuks and Greg, got involved in Campus Ministry's retreat program at Fordham. Justin and Sean taught a Wednesday-night confirmation class to sixteen-year-olds at St. Martin of Tours. Anh and another student at the university ran a youth group for Vietnamese teenagers. Harlan and Charlie (with my help sometimes) taught a group of students from the neighborhood how to put out a newsletter they called *The Bronx Tale*. I went to St. Barnabas Hospital with Tom and worked again as a chaplain for patients with HIV and AIDS.

We weren't proselytizing Catholics scouring the Bronx for helpless souls. It's hard to imagine that we could have been so confident, accomplished, or, at the end of the day, energetic. But no Mormons or Jehovah's Witnesses we, looking to convert the masses or warn of impending apocalypse. Our hope was to take care of those who needed some taking care of, which we knew from our formation was as much a tradition of the Order as its scholars. "Our main aim (to God's greater glory) during this undertaking at Trent," Ignatius told his theologians en route to the reforming council in 1546, "is to put into practice (as a group that lives together in one appropriate place) preaching, confessions and readings, teaching children, giving good example, visiting the poor in the hospitals, exhorting those around us, each of us according to the different talents he may happen to have."

St. Barnabas Hospital in the Bronx wasn't St. Clare's. The pastoral care staff was small: a shy, bantam priest from the New York Archdiocese, Father McGary, and a nun from the Sparkill Dominicans, Sister Miriam. The hospital then hadn't the concentrated care for patients with HIV that St. Clare's had nearly perfected. I was given a list of patients that Father McGary had compiled and then sent out on my rounds. Charts somewhere recorded details for the benefit of doctors, nurses, and caregivers, but not for me. So I had to go looking among the myriad of convalescents for those who might be in need of a little healing.

One day (not long after we had begun *City of God* with Hudson) I walked into a room where a young black man—early twenties, Haitian, French surname—was lying in bed. He was thin and in the kind of pain that looks as though it's become a constant companion. I introduced myself. He said hello. His name was Laurent. He looked somewhat puzzled when he saw me, and I asked him if there was anything he needed.

"I called the nurse for some water," he said weakly, "but she's busy this morning." I filled his cup and found a straw. After he finished drinking he said, "There's probably nothing else you can do."

"Okay, well, have a good day. I'll be certain to keep you in my prayers." It was my standard leaving. Nothing forced.

I started for the door and, just as I was about to walk out, heard him say behind me, "You can't do that, can you?"

I turned around. "What do you mean?" I asked. "Of course I'll keep you in my prayers."

"But I'm, you know, sick," he said, his eyes, argent and hollow, fixed on me.

I was puzzled myself. "That's why you're in the hospital, Laurent. That's why I'm visiting you as a chaplain."

"But I'm sick because . . . I've sinned."

I realized then what he was getting at, or rather, what he had been going through. I had rarely gotten this from patients at St. Clare's. It was as though pasts had passed and were forgotten once you entered that full, dissident city block of hospital in Hell's Kitchen, and the acceptance of death made the future assurance of heaven—where or whatever that might be—for everyone a consoling reality. Rather, I heard it more from others who called themselves Catholics and Christians, and who believed that AIDS was a punishment for homosexuals. "As far as I know, theologically," I would say, trying to hold back my anger, "we're all held accountable for sin, just as we're all entitled to forgiveness. As for what I know about epidemiology, HIV is a virus, one that I'm certain doesn't give a good goddamn about what you believe."

Caught among these righteous, no doubt, Laurent had become his own punisher as well as the punished.

"I thought that, as a priest, you would know this," he said.

So that was it. The collar. I'd never worn one at St. Clare's. And we never wore them now to class or around the house. But we put our "clerics" on for the apostolate. I was ambivalent, I have to confess, about this detail of religious identity. My vows as a Jesuit were spoken from the heart, not written in white across my neck. Yet there was something defining about wearing the collar. As I approached the age of thirty, I wanted those other laborers and professionals around me to know that I, too, was engaged with work in this world. It happened to be a different kind of work. So, most days, I was glad to walk down Arthur Avenue and over to St. Barnabas with the white tab showing through my black overcoat, especially when it evoked a friendly "Morning, Father!" from someone at a market stall or leaving a café.

I sat down in the chair by Laurent's bedside. "I know why you're here," I said. "You've got AIDS. How you got it, I don't know. I don't care. What I'm supposed to care about is your spiritual well-being in this hospital. For what little time I'm allowed, that's what I try to do, for everyone. The collar means nothing in that respect." I took the plastic strip out of my black shirt and undid the top button. "I'm just a guy trying to do a good thing for someone who's stuck here and not feeling so well." I could see him relax.

"But if this collar makes you think you're being punished for something you did in the past, something so horrible you can't be forgiven, then let me tell you, with this collar on"—and I slid it back into position—"God doesn't condemn us out of vengeance for any sin. That's the truth. Our sorrow is His. You're sick because of a virus, not because God won't forgive you. Do you understand?" He nodded. "That's official, my friend." I tapped the white tab showing again at the base of my neck. "Don't let anyone tell you otherwise. Right now, you need to try to get well. God will forgive you anything if it's what you want."

He seemed changed now. His smile widened. "Thank you, Father," he said.

I didn't have the heart to tell him that I wasn't a priest yet. It'll complicate a complicated situation, I thought. I made a mental note to tell Father McGary, in case there was something else Laurent felt he wanted to say.

"Get some sleep," I said, refilled his cup, pushed the chair back into the corner of the room, and walked out.

"The great mistake," Hudson said to us, "is to equate the younger man of *Confessions* with the older, quite worldly man writing *City of God*."

Like some unknowing prophet sent to remind us that things never unfold the way we plan them, Hudson—plowing through the Bishop of Hippo's massive apologetic tome with only a few weeks to go before our first four months of life as vowed Jesuits in philosophy studies came to their natural close—would not let go in class that day of this one point: Augustine's notion of the *civitas peregrina* in Book 18: "I undertook to write about the origin, the development, and the destined ends of the two cities. One of these is the City of God, the other the city of this world; and God's City lives in this world's city, as far as its human element is concerned; but it lives here as an alien sojourner."

"We're not engaged in wholesale condemnation or flight from the so-called city of men," Hudson said from the edge of his desk. "We have to live here. A better translation of this *sojourner*, as Brown suggests, is *resident stranger*, someone grateful for the city, working in it, improving on its good, yet condemning and walking away from its evil." He lowered his head, deep in thought no doubt, then gazed out over us all again, smiled, and said, "It's quite simple in the end. We belong and we don't belong."

Hudson had long ago stopped asking us *Confessions*-like men if we found our lives similar in any way to the Christian philosopher's. We did and we didn't.

By now I knew what to do in any Eastern Catholic church I entered: the prayers and responses of the liturgy, when and how to cross myself (right shoulder first, thumb, middle finger, and forefinger together), the chaste kiss of veneration to the surfaces of icons, Holy Communion of bread soaked in wine received on a spoon. I wasn't mimicking the faithful; I had taken the time to watch, learn, and pray. Now I felt like something of a lost son returned among them, one in search of a community to which he might once—a long time ago—have belonged.

So, Sunday mornings during my first year of studies in the Bronx, I left Ciszek Hall at 9:00, took the D train into Manhattan, got out at the Broadway-Lafayette stop in SoHo, and walked over to St. Michael's Russian Catholic Church for the Divine Liturgy at 11:00.

St. Michael's is an inconspicuous chapel next to Old St. Patrick's Cathedral where tiny Jersey Street dead-ends into Mulberry. It looks more like a shabby grammar school than a church. Inside, though, there is no mistaking it for anything other than a place of worship. The nave is small but open. Indirect sun barely passes through clouded windows, each decorated with a single stained-glass cross (remnants of the church's Western past). The walls are adorned with icons recognizable (Mother of God, Cross of Christ) and obscure (Blessed Father Leontios Federov). Clusters of candle stands flank the deacon doors of the icon screen, on which are painted from left to right the images of John the Baptist, St. Andrew, Mary and Child, Christ, a young St. Stephen, and St. Michael the Archangel. The Annunciation and the four Evangelists mark the Royal Doors, and above the entire screen sweep smaller panels of the life of Christ. All about the sacred space is that lingering, palpable smell of frankincense and gardenia, rising, it seems, from the floor, which is wood and feels more forgiving than most. Everyone inside, with a few exceptions made for older parishioners, stands.

The church was founded in 1936 by Father Andrew Rogosh for Russian Catholic émigrés at the time when the Vatican believed it had to combat the atheism of the Communists in Russia. The Russicum College in Rome was set up at that time by Pope Pius XI for priests who wanted to study Russian culture, liturgy, and theology in order to be a part of this mission. Catholics argued that their spiritual presence had always been a part of Russia, as far back as the tenth century conversion of Kievan Rus, and so they deserved—in spite of their long expulsion from the country—to minister to those Catholics who remained there. The Orthodox and the Soviets thought any Catholic coming to Russia was a Vatican spy.

Priests who attempted to get inside Russia during the years of Communism knew that if they succeeded, the result was most likely a death sentence. Those who were caught—like Walter Ciszek—were either executed or sent to prisons in Siberia, where they starved or succumbed to disease. When the Church rethought its mission to Russia in the light of Vatican II, it didn't give up on serving the millions of Catholics who already lived in Russia, most of them in Siberia because of the camps. There were others, too, spread out now around the world. It was these to whom St. Michael's wanted to minister.

But an actual Russian Catholic of the Eastern Rite is a rare bird, usually a transplant from another Eastern or some Roman Catholic church who has discovered a home among those who make up the local community. Ciszek (a Polish American) came to the liturgies on Mulberry when he lived in the Bronx in later life. The church also attracted Dorothy Day, Catherine de Hueck Doherty, and Thomas Merton (who, the church historian says, came here "on occasion in his younger years"). St. Michael's was that kind of place. Founded for the Russians who never arrived, it has become a way station for searchers, a deeper window of tradition within Catholic tradition, small, on the fringe, and holy. It's a place for those who fit and don't quite fit.

I came to St. Michael's as one of the searchers. My philosophy studies were going well. Who wouldn't want to stop what he was doing at the age of twenty-nine and read Plato, Augustine, and Nietzsche again? What I found myself resisting as I moved along in this next stage of Jesuit life, though, was the scholastic's usual apostolates and identity. The youth groups and retreat work and campus ministry activities were important to do and maintain as part of any Catholic college, but I'd never been a student at a Catholic college before, let alone a vowed Jesuit. I needed something else, something that nurtured as well as challenged me, something that was a little bit different and on the fringe, because I fit and I didn't fit. I had my work at the hospital, but I wanted something else that pointed more toward the challenge of a possible future as a priest. That was, after all, what I was being trained for. So I turned to what I had begun in my long experiment and gravitated to St. Michael's with that ongoing desire for solitude and communion.

Once there, I watched and waited, admiring the harmony and determination of the choir of ten among the congregation (which rarely exceeded twenty-five), staying afterward occasionally for coffee with the regulars. I introduced myself to Father Solles and Chris, the permanent deacon, who had seen me at liturgies and was glad finally to find out about this stranger among them. Then I began trading English for Russian lessons with a woman from Moscow who lived in Brooklyn and took the train to St. Michael's every Sunday as I did; she had been a practicing Orthodox in Moscow but now said to me, in the spirit of the eleventh century, "Orthodox. Catholic. What does it matter?" I expressed interest in the process of becoming a lector and had a few brief lessons toward that ministry. The church, it turned out, was a very active community, spurred on by Father Solles, who himself was a prison chaplain at Rikers Island. Mostly, though, it was the liturgy that continued to attract me, immersing myself in its mystical sublime each Sunday after I had been engaged in logic, reason, and argument all week. When I was at St. Michael's I never felt like a Jesuit scholastic. I was a Catholic standing among believers, my eyes following the gallery of holy images, my voice responding to the seamless liturgical chant, my mind and heart putting aside "all earthly cares" as prayers were lifted up "like incense" and we all asked to be kept holy for one more day. "You keep at this, Age," I heard my father say, and so brought myself to do that.

When I walked into St. Michael's for the first time, woven into its tapestry was a pained yet soulful-looking older gentleman sitting on a fold-out chair off to the side reading a prayer book. During the liturgy he stood for the great entrance of the holy gifts (when the congregation sings, "Let us who mystically represent the cherubim . . .") and I saw a cane slide down the back of his seat.

Tom Mason was an old New Yorker who still had a trace of his Irish brogue. There was nothing overly pious or self-conscious about him. Like spies who know the second verse of the national anthem, people new to the Eastern Rites tend to overdo in public the many possible ways of showing reverence in a church. But Tom, I learned later, when we had the chance to talk, had been coming to St. Michael's for longer than he could remember, which hardly seemed to matter anymore. He was retired from advertising. His wife gone, his children moved away, he kept to a small circle of friends, his New York apartment, and liturgies on Sunday.

I'm sure he would never have said more than hello to me. But when he found out that I was a Jesuit studying philosophy at Fordham, he told me that he had gone to Regis, the Jesuit high school in New York, and remembered a childhood friend who was a priest in the New York Province.

"Do you know Father Hinfey?" he asked. I did. "He's a good man. Africa, last I heard."

"He's back now," I said. "I'll send along your greetings when I see him."

Tom said he would be grateful, then asked me why it was I had come to St. Michael's. When I told him of my Rusyn background and that I was in search of an Eastern Catholic community, he said, "You Jesuits have a funny history with the East, don'tcha? All that puffed-up piety and *for the greater glory of Loyola*. As though, if the Russians would take a minute and listen, they'd suddenly admit they've been wrong to accuse you of anything but loving your brothers."

This is where I would have said, "I suppose you're right," turned, and found a less confrontational believer to talk to. But there was something disarming about the same old Jesuit clichés coming out in the brogue of an Irish "Eastern" Catholic who had gone to Regis. I said, "No one believes that anymore," and he seemed to take that as the response that proved I was not one of the zealous.

Because I could never time the D train right on Sundays, I was always early to liturgies, but never earlier than Tom. So it seemed as though my conversations with him were always before the service, outside on Mulberry Street if the weather was nice, upstairs in the church as it got colder. Sometimes we would go to a café around the corner on Prince Street. He was well-read in the Church Fathers, and he had a way of connecting points of change and departure in his life with what he had come to read, discover, and believe in his self-taught vocation as patristic theologian.

There was more, though, to my reason for abandoning the Bronx for Manhattan on a Sunday morning. As my semester wore on into November and December, so did the community at Ciszek Hall. Three years in now, and in spite of this new stage, a community of like minds and hearts also brings with it habits and personal quirks that die hard. Men with the loftiest ideals in common are tough to live with. I was complaining to Tom over coffee one Sunday about the wildly varying levels of housecleaning that one could expect from any given brother on a given Saturday. "Tell me why you would think that mold in a shower stall should be left alone, as though it were being cultivated like vegetables." I was behind in the work I had to do for a Russian reading tutorial, which I had taken along with my philosophy courses, hoping to maintain what I had learned in an intensive language course in New Haven that summer. The truth is, although I loved the chance to return to philosophy studies, I saw it as a utilitarian end to what I hoped would be future work in the Christian East. Russian and Russia, I told Tom, were what I wanted most to be engaged with, and the sooner the better.

He listened as he stirred his coffee, then cut in. "It's your man, Taft, the Jesuit, who makes the brilliant distinction between the moral aspect of Western Christianity and the notion of transfiguration in the East." It was a cold, dry, and bright New York morning in December. Tom looked at me for a moment, as if to say, "May I proceed?" and then continued. "You see, the problem in the West is that we're on this path to the final reward that will be determined by merit. How much good, how much bad? How often to communion, how many sinful thoughts? Basic stuff. You're in or you're out. Right?" He drew breath and shifted. His deteriorating legs and back put him in constant pain. "But in the East, they see humanity as . . . what does Taft say, 'an imperfect similitude of God which grace perfects,' or something like that. What you do or what you don't do are not in some race at the end of which—priest or layman—you'll either win or lose. Rather, we're constantly, in our own *imperfection*, seeking to be a more perfect image of Christ. Yes? Seeing, as it were, the beauty of the present moment."

There I was, complaining about having to spend my days studying philosophy and cleaning bathrooms with men whose histories were sometimes not to be believed, while others longed to spend "one hour reading those books again," as Tom had said to me on another occasion. And now he had me, long before he sprang the trap of his rhetorical "Yes?"

I said, "Not bad for an Irishman."

"It's impossible, of course, perfection I mean, and often living in the present moment." He went on, ignoring my comment, shifting and wincing again. "But that's the beauty of it. Look at the icons we keep and revere in the church," he said and seemed to peer through the wall of the café, as though speaking of them meant having to acknowledge where the icons lived. "Good God, they're beautiful, even the poorest of 'em! Imperfect perfection. Our momentary glimpse of heaven on this temporal earth. What was it John of Damascus said: 'I do not venerate matter, but I venerate the creator of matter, who became matter for my sake.' That, lad, is powerful stuff."

Taken down and built back up, and with what graciousness, I thought. Powerful stuff indeed. Then, wanting to respond in some meaningful way, I told Tom that, with what little time I could find, I had been balancing out the required Augustine readings with Gregory of Nyssa's *Life of Moses*.

"Ah, yes, the Gregories," he said, referring to both Nyssa and Nazianzus. "And?"

"Well, I've been wondering why, if Augustine's strength of will and sense of self led him to the autobiographical *Confessions*, Gregory of Nyssa chose to write a biography of Moses, a meditation on the journey to the Promised Land. It's a completely different landscape and model, a man of silence and the desert, God appearing on high from a cleft in the rock. And yet who understands his God more, or is so close to Him day after day, than Moses? Listen to this." I still carried a notebook with me, writing down things I had read that I wanted to save. I fished it out of my backpack and opened to my latest entry. "Gregory puts these words to Moses in God's mouth: *'Because you are straining with so great a desire for that which is before you and there is no weariness in your progress, know that the spaces around you are so vast you will never reach the end of your journey.'*"

When I was introduced as a novice to the Eastern Rites in Scranton, I was more engaged with understanding the roles of being a son to my parents and a brother to the Jesuits than with the Christian East. But as I began my philosophy studies, parallels between my own spiritual journey and Byzantine theology became more apparent to me. The Patristic writers of the East are a forgotten panoply of poets and philosophers whose voices and views emerged ahead of their time. Athanasius wrote the life of the desert monk Anthony the Great, a figure who drew Thomas Merton to the works of the Desert Fathers. John Cassian's and John Climacus's works on monasticism in the East are on a par with Benedict's *Rule* in the West. The fiery John Chrysostom and the towering Basil the Great are as well-known for composing the sublime liturgies sung in the Eastern churches as they are for their theological prowess. Of them all, though, Gregory of Nyssa, a direct contemporary of Augustine's (and living in Cappadocia, modern-day Turkey), was the writer to whom I was most drawn. He seemed to come into his own sense of holiness over time. He was not a convert but a tepid Christian as a young man in the fourth century, chose oratory over the priesthood, and married. But in his twenties, relics of the Forty Martyrs of Sebaste—soldiers of Licinius who refused to renounce Christianity and so were sent naked in a boat out to the middle of a frozen lake, where they died—shook him from his torpor and moved him to a place not unlike what Augustine found: his heart restless. Where did I find an affinity? I wondered as I read more and more of Gregory. And I began to sense that it was with this Moses-like life of retreat and journey.

Gregory took a view of God's grace that was different from Augustine's radical conversion. He understood the Christian life to be as much a journey toward perfection as it was a desire for salvation. Like most theologians of the East, he believed salvation was guaranteed, as it were, by virtue of God's love. This is the *apokatastasis*, literally the "restoration" of every person, and all creation, to the original, perfect state of God's intention. St. Matthew uses the same word when Jesus says, *"Elijah does come, and he is to restore all things; but I tell you that Elijah has already come."* Rather, the path we are called to walk—our labor as Christians—is one of striving constantly to *become* perfect, as God *is* perfect, even as we face those things that tend to get us in trouble, the task of both our bodily and our spiritual lives, in this world and the next. For this we are in need of grace. "Christian perfection has but one limit," Gregory writes in *Life of Moses*, "that of having none."

"Not bad for a Jesuit," Tom said when I had finished reading. "But what do you cling to that passage for? You seem overly fond of it. Are you?"

"I'm overly fond of every story where the hero can't sit still."

He guffawed. "That's a good one, lad! I can't decide if it'll stand you in good stead or destroy you in Loyola's army."

I said, "Let's hope," not sure myself of which one would prove to be true in time, then added, "but good companions to have on the search anyway," and tucked the notebook back into my pack.

"Ah, so you see," he continued, "give your brothers a break, as I know you're wont. They're called to their own, even the less than perfect ones." He winked. "You don't have to become them, but you have to become someone. Let's go." He got up slowly from the table, put on his coat, wrapped a scarf around his neck, and pushed the chair in with his cane. "We don't want to be late for church."

For all of the theological breadth Tom had, his capacity for inclusion was as fickle as the expressions on his face. As we took the corner and walked up Mulberry, he saw a new crowd out in front of the church and lit into what he considered the fake posturing of the newcomers. "More smells-and-bells people who wish there never was a Vatican Two comin' over here to get their fix! Lord bless us and save us."

Then he leaned heavily on his cane for more speed.

How simple it should have all been. The Spirit calls, the man says yes, and the life that's lived is a fine one, austere, yet somehow heroic. It has its up and downs, the poignant tests—a lover not taken, the faith crisis that has everything to do with death, the hard acceptance that what you envisioned doing in later life has been erased forever by one superior's behest—but anyone in any life could say as much.

What I can say is that as a Jesuit scholastic in December 1992—sometime after Tom Mason, dead ten years now, and I had discussed the finer points of Eastern Christian theology's human path of spiritual progress and then filed into St. Michael's for the Divine Liturgy—I began to experience what I can only call a *turning*, although it seemed to me at first to be a disastrous turning away. I retraced my steps to Belmont Avenue, pressed the key inside the lock on the door of Ciszek Hall, walked four flights up the back stairs to my room, and sat down at my desk to translate some Akhmatova poetry that I had been given by my Russian teacher, I supposed to push me to a place of discovery, discovery of how much there was yet to learn.

When I had passed through papers, exams, Christmas, a gathering over New Year's of all the scholastics from Maryland and New York at Jogues Retreat House in Wernersville, and returned to another semester of studies, I felt as though I'd been tossed into a prison, locked in an exile, not as punishment, though, but rather as a cruel twist of freedom. I had decided my fate. And now, the headiness of having taken "perpetual" vows fading, the spiritual honeymoon over, the books I picked up became lead weights, the men I turned to for companionship preoccupied drones instead of engaged interlocutors (they would, I know, have said the same of me, for we were all working out our own salvation). The prayerful consolation I had experienced during the months surrounding my decision to take first vows seemed to dry up like a drop of water on a hot stone. But what could I do? I saw my spiritual director, Tom Stahel, every six weeks at America House. I felt better in his presence, an equal, a brother. He was a man who thought clearly and could cut through any encroaching self-pity or doubt. And I felt comforted as well surrounded by the kinds of books—fiction, poetry, classics—he kept on his shelves, which seemed to lighten in some way the gloom of the back room he lived in. As in the library I dreamed of having in my own house, I needed to be surrounded by books. My appointments for spiritual direction were also chances to get into Manhattan for a movie or a drink with some former Columbia friends, who seemed to think that there was a certain attraction to my life now that I had been at it for more than two years. Then back to the Bronx, where I'd throw myself into studies, chores, and the hospital. If I kept my head down, my prayer up, and did the work, whatever I'd once felt had to return eventually.

Mystics speak of the spiritual path as an ascent, sometimes a slog through dense undergrowth at its driest moments, other times the dizzyingly sublime reach of some great height. The latter is the goal, and the hope. Abraham's faith was rewarded with God's blessing in the place he named "Yahweh-yireh; hence people now say, 'On the mountain the Lord will see.'" Moses, called by the Lord, "went up the mountain to God," on Sinai. And before Gregory of Nyssa warns that "you will never reach the end of your journey," he reminds his reader that the "knowledge of God is a mountain steep indeed," yet difficult to climb. "The majority of people scarcely reach its base."

I, too, believed I had chosen the path of a limitless *upward* journey toward perfection, until it began to turn into a spiraling fall. From a distance, the events sound prosaic, though most likely because I can remember little of the pain and numbness of spirit that deadened the blackness I was living in. All I can say is that, like others, somewhere in the middle *I found myself in a dark wood.*

There was no single event I can point to that triggered any of this. Rather, it was *events* that belonged as much to the day-to-day as any you or I would encounter. Perhaps this is what made them all the more dangerous. "A commander and leader of an army will encamp, explore the fortifications and defenses of the stronghold, and attack at the weakest point," Ignatius writes in his Rules for Discernment of Spirits. "In the same way, the enemy of our human nature investigates from every side all our virtues." And then what?

The spring semester, our classes were monotonous lectures taught by junior faculty. I wanted to opt out of basic Aristotle and Aquinas—work I had already done—and take a literature seminar, but the philosophical course was set out for a reason. We had to follow it regardless. All of the rhetoric about Wisdom was now reduced to "Do as I say, not as I do."

In midwinter, my room on the fourth floor got the bulk of the old furnace's heat. Below, each floor ran increasingly cold. When Ray, who lived on the second floor, turned up the thermostat to level out the temperature, my room got hotter. The rest of the house remained the same. I slept with my windows wide open, even during a week-long subzero cold snap. An L.L.Bean thermometer I kept on the zipper of a sweater recorded a steady eighty-two degrees indoors.

I say "slept," but that was in the day, an hour or two at most, slumped over a book I read to no purpose. Then all night I'd lie awake in a stultifying imbalance of heat, exhaustion, and indifference. I literally begged for something to be done about the furnace, but in his capacity as minister, Ray said it was impossible to correct.

Frustration became edginess, especially with the load of four full graduate courses placed upon us. We were, in general, a generous and forgiving bunch at Ciszek Hall. But one night, with a string of papers due, I snapped at Harlan in our computer room for not having fixed a terminal that was down. He was in charge of repairs. I wasn't beadle in this house. I needed to write like everyone else, and all of the other

computers were taken except one, on which Mike was playing soli-
taire. It never occurred to me to tell him to give it up and go watch TV
if he had no other work to do. Instead I heard myself say to Harlan, as
I poked angrily at the keyboard that wouldn't respond in turn, "You're
supposed to be in charge of this."

He looked at me without a hint of reaction registering on his face,
declared flatly, "I guess Ray will have to buy another," and then
walked away.

I looked around for someone, anyone, to berate.

"Take this one, AJ," David said, standing up and gathering his
books. He had been watching me. "You okay?" he asked when I sat
down.

"Trying to get some goddamn work done in this place," I said, hoping Mike, who stayed glued to his screen, would hear my disdain.

My house job was to buy produce at the market on Arthur Avenue
with Greg, a scholastic from Ghana, who never seemed to show up
when it was time to go shopping. We were given two hundred dollars
every two weeks to spend on fruit and vegetables for the house, but
even going twice a week I managed to spend about fifty dollars per
shop. There was always something left over. So, usually alone on my
outings, I would stop in Madonia's bakery and buy a few pounds of
biscotti and cookies, which I'd place on the counter in the dining
room where we had an espresso machine.

"That's not produce," Ray said to me with the barest hint of accusation behind a suspicious smile one afternoon while I was unloading
my shopping cart. He was pointing to the box wrapped in twine like it
was Christmastime.

I chucked a bunch of bananas into a basket and said, "Yes it is. It
produces goodwill in this house, something we could all use a few
pounds of." He raised his eyebrows, I'm sure, at the irony to which I
at that time was blind, but he never challenged my purchase of baked
produce again.

Something else, though, fed on the heat, annoyance, and irritation
that made me feel as if I was caught in a room from which I couldn't
escape: the smell of the sick and weak that was too close for comfort.

Chuks Afiawari from Nigeria lived in the room across the narrow hallway from me. He was part of our formation class but not studying in the degree program. He would take a wider swathe of graduate and undergraduate liberal arts courses, then return to Africa to continue his studies for the priesthood. A great-souled man with a glinting smile and strong laugh, he lived, moved, and breathed with an optimism and cheer that was never forced and never wavered. When I first met him, I was reminded of how disparate in our companionship this vocation to the Jesuits called us to be. I enjoyed being around him for his curiosity and sense of humor. The first few months of the semester, he, a Californian named Sean (who looked like he used to surf Steamer Lane in Santa Cruz, though I don't know if he had ever been on a board), and I occupied the back wing of the fourth floor, known as the monks' corner, as much for its good spirit as for its quiet.

In November, Chuks came down with a relapse of malaria he had contracted in Africa some time before. At first the symptoms oscillated and looked like flu. But then he was unable to get out of bed, the headaches, fever, sweating, diarrhea, and abdominal pain having settled in for another round of what he himself knew from experience was the disease.

For a week he lived on liquids. The Jesuits' physician—who knew well all of the men who had been to Africa and gotten malaria—checked in daily. Someone was always with Chuks. He wasn't in any danger of dying, so, aside from moral support, there was little the rest of us could do.

After his fever subsided, I stopped in to ask if he needed anything, or to update him on minor details of the house. Gradually the crease in his forehead that came with the pain disappeared. He began to smile again and make attempts at the odd joke. But I noticed something else about the room. It had taken on the pungent odor of more than sweat. It was the efflux from a body working to reclaim its liver and blood from an insidious parasite. Even though sheets once soaked with sweat had been washed, every organic surface—walls, floors, clothes, papers, books, the door—smelled as though it had attempted to rid itself of whatever plasmodia had made its home in Chuks. Each time I found myself walking to or away from my room, the smell of one man's malaria became for me the scent of . . . what? A thing over which I had no control, regardless of how close it lived and breathed. With it came a fear that, in my decision to become a Jesuit, I hadn't fully reckoned the extent of the cost it would in time exact on me. For all of my good discernment, I had an equally bad record of seeing costs when I thought I had found a certain peace necessary to survive and carry on in this life.

My own spiritual malady might have gone unobserved, but the effects never could. In my meetings with Jeff, he asked about each of the areas of the house in which my commitment was either shored up hard or crumbling: studies, community, apostolate, prayer. I wasn't sure then if I was the model of the typical or the atypical scholastic, but he sat and recorded my responses—curt if they were truthful, veiled if I thought the question was impossible to answer—into his yellow pad with a pencil, as though he were applying brush to canvas and painting a portrait of the Jesuit as a young man.

There is an old joke among scholastics that goes something like this: A group of men in formation are sitting on the steps in front of their house, talking. They see Father Superior approaching in the distance.

"Here he comes," one says.

"Yep," says another, "always checking up on us."

"Like we're a bunch of kids he can't trust to do anything," says a third.

As the older priest approaches the house, he touches his hat to the men gathered, then walks past without saying another word.

"Typical," the first one says when the older priest is out of earshot.

"Doesn't give a damn about us," says the other.

"Like we never existed," says the third.

Because Jeff held me, as he did all of us, to the ideal of achieving a balance between spiritual health, community engagement, and academic performance as we tried to do what the Society asked of us, I blamed him for the workload, the heat, the pettiness, and the exhaustion, those things no one in that house had any real control over.

I knew at the time that a fight was brewing. What I didn't expect was all of the magnanimity and insight of the *Spiritual Exercises* to vanish in an instant while I threw a tantrum over something as small as a bicycle.

I see it now as an obvious desire to flee the confines, real and constructed, of the house. Having spent one summer in New Haven as a student, and expecting to spend another, I asked if I could, prorating my own stipend (seventy-five dollars a month), purchase a bike to use for the eight weeks of Russian studies I was again looking forward to in the following summer. Jeff asked if I meant the bicycle to be a community or a personal one. I said both. When the language program at Yale was over, I'd leave the bike at Ciszek Hall for anyone to use, should he want to. Jeff agreed, although remaining unconvinced, it seemed to me.

The conflict came when, because I'm tall, I had to order a larger frame than the shop had in stock. That meant an unrefundable fifty-dollar deposit. I went ahead with the purchase, and I knew what I was doing. In theory it would be a community bike, but only one other guy in the house was my size, and he ran marathons. So, in fact, it would be by default mine. And the whiff of *mine* coming from a scholastic new to the vow of communal poverty can be detected by a Jesuit superior of a formation community.

I didn't remember then, but I'd gone through this same scenario before. When I lived in Santa Fe, I wanted to buy a motorcycle and return east by way of a cross-country chautauqua. I had just read Robert Pirsig's *Zen and the Art of Motorcycle Maintenance.*

"Which one of your friends has some piece of junk he's trying to unload?" my parents asked me when I called to consult them (ask permission) about the purchase.

"These would be the friends you've never met and know nothing about, right?" I said, miffed that they could jump to conclusion and judgment all at once. "Never mind who," I said. "The money is mine. I made it waiting tables. Remember?"

"And my money pays your tuition," my father shot back over the phone. "Remember? So you make your decision as to which motorcycle you'd like to ride."

I flew home to Pennsylvania on United Airlines. But I never forgave my parents for questioning not my choice of vehicles but my choice of friends, although friends had nothing to do with who was buying or selling the bike.

When Jeff heard about the custom frame and the fact that I had put money down for it without consulting him again, he jumped to his own conclusions.

"This has poor discernment written all over it," he said. "Have you taken any of this decision into prayer?"

"Have I agonized over whether I should accept a twenty-one-inch frame and not order a twenty-three-inch frame?" I said, my anger rising now to the unbearable temperature of my room. "No. Have I considered how the purchase fits into poverty? Yes. I thought we had both talked about this."

"We've talked about it," he said. "But I don't think you've really prayed about it."

If there was one thing I was clinging to like a drowning man clinging to a raft, it was prayer. In those same Rules where Ignatius lays out the stratagem of "the Enemy," he insists upon "more prayer, meditation, and examination of ourselves." Each day at 4:00, no matter what I had to do, I took to the eastern-facing chair in my room, gazed at the icon of a poor yet powerful Christ, under whose banner of humility I had decided to spend my life, and prayed until it was time for Mass at 5:15. This hour, coupled with the liturgy, continued to sustain me, to keep me focused on what mattered in community, and to have it questioned, as though I couldn't be trusted to keep myself alive, was too much.

"Fuck it," I said to the man who held my future as a Jesuit in his hands. "I'll walk to my Russian classes." And he said nothing as I left the room.

I never wondered then if I was in danger of leaving or being dismissed from the Order. I'm sure childish outbursts masked as righteousness weren't unknown in that house. I, for my part, wanted to live this life, and in spite of what fears conspired to weaken my defenses, I trusted the work of the past two years that had led to my religious vows. What I began to wonder, though, was if I could keep my own fever at bay long enough to finish philosophy studies and move on to what I was increasingly hopeful would mean an apostolate somewhere in the Christian East.

Shortly after this scene, Jeff called me into his office and told me he wanted me to rethink my plans for the summer. "I'm not sure more studies for you are a good idea."

I could see it coming, but on this one I was standing firm. "I want to study Russian again. I want to move forward with *one* thing I've already begun, rather than dropping it and getting nothing out of it. I want to do more than dabble." He gave no response, so I went on, though convinced I could say nothing convincing. "The parish in New Haven where I stay is a good balance. The pastor makes me preach at least three Sundays to give the other priests a break. Last year he joked about having the bishop come in from Hartford to ordain me so that he could take the summer off and go sailing."

Jeff flashed a quick grin and then said more ominously, "I'm worried about you, AJ. I don't know what it is. On the surface you've got it together. And you've got a way of drawing the fringe of a community into the center. Or at least you had. Now you don't seem able to draw the fringe of yourself into your own center, as though you're not entirely sure about what you want."

He was finding words for something I was already aware of. I had convinced myself that the tenacity I was showing here was a reflection of my inner spirit and desire to persevere. But that, too, began to look and feel as though it were breaking down, like when you're sick for a long time and you begin to wonder if you'll ever know what it is to be healthy again. I was losing my memory of what spiritual consolation I had fed on in the not-so-distant past. "What do you do when it feels as though it's a battle being lost one pawn at a time?" I asked in a tone that hinted at my surrender. "Not something you're standing over and working through in a give-and-take of gain and sacrifice, but a realization that you may not be up for the fight?"

He shifted his girth slowly in the big chair. "To be truthful," he said, "I'm afraid you're going to have a nervous breakdown."

At that I felt anger rising again but checked it, knowing that Jeff was trying to help. "I wouldn't give anyone the satisfaction of seeing me break down," I said. "Sometimes I'm amazed there isn't more of it, the way we're pushed and examined, the way we live so closely and yet know so little about each other. Sure, there's faith sharing and spiritual direction. But it's not madness I'm feeling. It's frustration. Not like I want to get laid or anything like that. It's . . ." And I was caught not knowing what "it" was.

"It's true," Jeff said, as though I had finished. "There are times when I wonder more about the ones who get through formation seemingly without a care. And hearing you articulate it that way, I wonder if you're as weak as you say you are. But you're in some place of restlessness, AJ, that doesn't seem at all healthy or helpful. What is it?" he asked.

We always seemed to have these meetings in the afternoon, when Jeff, whose room was on the other side of the house, drew his blinds at a slight angle to keep out the glare of the sun. I liked the feeling of rest that came over me sitting there before him. Well into April, spring, and standard time, I could see how much longer the days had gotten since I'd been there last, sometime in February.

"Do you know what it is?" I said after a long silence. "There's no beauty in any of this."

"What do you mean by beauty?" he asked.

"I mean there's no wonder, no care. If this life were a woman, would I cherish her? A child, nurture him? Instead, we jump through hoops. We lock our windows. We eat our food. We read our books. And we say we pray so that we might live more like Christ. But where is Christ? Every time I try to look for what is Christ-like, I hear: *Do this! Don't do that! Don't get too comfortable there!* The reason I make that trek down to St. Michael's every Sunday is because I feel like I'm *grasping* something beautiful, cherishing and nurturing it." I leaned forward. "Is it always going to be like this?"

He didn't shake his head or even move. He just said, "I don't know."

Once when I was twelve or thirteen—I'm not sure exactly, I remember the feeling of having a newfound confidence in my physical strength—I was helping my father cut and split logs in our backyard for the wood-burning stove we kept in the basement. It was early fall, the air crisp. He had on a watch cap and a red and gray flannel shirt opened at the neck, but no coat. Because he worked powerfully but steadily, he never seemed to sweat. Yet a tremendous amount of heat poured from his body. In winter he wore a loosely buttoned wool coat over the same open-necked flannel shirt. That day, he had a new chain saw. We were beginning to stack up fuel for the winter.

For every two logs I split into stove-size quarters, my father produced an exponentially larger pile to work on, slicing away at the pin oak and maple we had culled from the trees that bordered our property. I was slow but effective with the splitting wedge, and my mother's strong tea and blueberry pancakes had given me an extra boost of energy that morning. I believed that if I persisted and swung hard enough, I could split any amount of wood my father carved up.

After what might have been half a cord of wood was spread out on the ground of our backyard, my father put down the saw, picked up another ax, and joined me. Sight, swing, *Tok!* Sight, swing, *Tok!* A bit faster, more powerfully, he seemed to say as stumps exploded beneath the impact of his falling blade. I picked up the pace and matched him, blow for blow. He smiled, saying once out loud when I found the seam of an oak and cleaved it in two with what felt to me like the surgical ease of a diamond cutter, "That's it, Age!"

We rested when he thought there was enough wood to cover the bottom of the old coal bin we still had in our basement. (We had switched to a new electric furnace the year before.) He wanted to do the bulk of the work before noon. He sat down on a large stump we were saving for last and lit his pipe. His hands trembled slightly, and he saw that I was watching.

"Damn saw," he said, laughing. "Shakes the shit out of you." He put the pack of matches back into his pocket and began to brush dust from his pants. The air was swirling with the clean scent of morning and the slightly bluish taste of exhaust from a two-stroke engine. I looked over at the newly baptized chain saw sitting on the ground, flawless red paint on its round body, black brushed steel handle, REMINGTON stamped on the eighteen-inch elliptical blade already smoothed away in places by the wood it had been devouring. Everything about that day seemed perfect.

Dr. Bauer had stopped taking notes when I began telling the story. Now she peered across the room at me.

She was plain-featured but elegant, older—not much older than I, though she seemed it. I could hear the white-noise machine humming away outside the door. Traffic stopped and started at the light on Park Avenue. Before I'd stepped into the building at five minutes to seven in the evening, I thought about how much I loved fall, even in the city.

"Did you chop wood with him often?" she asked.

"After fishing? It was my favorite thing to do. But it wasn't the wood that day, it was the saw. I wanted to learn how to use it, and he said that I couldn't. 'You don't know how,' he said. So I asked him to show me. 'It'll rip your leg off!' he said. 'You need more meat on your bones.' That's what he always used to say. Every one of my brothers no fatter than a flagpole and it's 'You need more meat on your bones.' "

"Was there another time when he might not have felt so rushed and taken the effort to show you how to use a chain saw?"

"He never offered. And I never asked again. That's how we were."

"I see. But if you wanted to learn," she went on, "why didn't you press your father to teach you at another time?"

I suddenly felt uncomfortable, as though I didn't know what to do with my hands. "He got angry. No, not angry. Frustrated, you know? He's got things he wants to do, and life intrudes." Somehow, though, that didn't sound entirely fair. I swept my memory. "I guess when I was younger I helped him out with work around the house, like holding a two-by-four in place when he was refinishing our basement, or holding a flashlight when he was fixing an appliance. Then he taught me how to do things, like find a stud in the wall, test a socket, or make a chalk line." She never moves, I thought to myself. Is she as uncomfortable here as I am?

"He taught you some things but not everything," Dr. Bauer said, more declarative than a question.

"My father was a city kid who married into the country. His father-in-law was a carpenter. His brother-in-law was a carpenter. When he wanted to buy the house my mother grew up in from his own mother-in-law, she said no, because he wouldn't be able to maintain it the way she thought it ought to be maintained. So the house went to renters who drove it into the ground so badly my grandmother cried for days when she saw it after they moved out." That memory was a bitter one even to me. "I think my father learned to do all of the things he takes pride in knowing how to do out of spite."

"That's interesting."

I was quiet as I realized onto what ground I had wandered. "Well, I'd have done it differently," I said finally.

"Past tense?"

"I guess we're talking about a different kind of fatherhood. I lost the chance of becoming a real one a while ago."

"Lost it, or opted out?"

"Both," I said and told her about Pen.

When Jeff recommended that I begin therapy after I returned from my second summer of Russian language studies, I resisted, thinking that he suspected there was something wrong with me and it was only a matter of time before it was confirmed. But I relented when he came up to New Haven for a visit and said, "It's a good place to start, knowing who you are. And it'll serve you well when you're a superior with the care of others on your mind. You will be, you know."

I was surprised as much by his level of candor as by his concern. "So it's not because you think I'm crazy."

"Not crazy," he said, "but you need to be careful." I could tell that he didn't want to say or suggest too much.

In deference to Jeff's insistence that I should do something besides study for the summer, I relaxed my Russian schedule, preached a few more Sundays at the church, made friends with some other summer school students, and took advantage of New Haven's Concerts on the Green. I don't think those things were all what Jeff had in mind, but I did what I could. I was trying to strike that balance between the real and the ideal, erring on the side of the real. And when I got back to Fordham, I refused to let course work consume more than its fair share of my Jesuit identity and time. I saw Professor Balestra after our final exam in Classical Modern Philosophy, and he said, graciously, that he was sorry not to have been able to give me the A he thought I should have gotten for the course. "Your treatment of Spinoza on the exam in the key question of his ethics came up short. What happened?" he asked. And what could I say? That I read Spinoza on the subway after visiting my shrink every Monday night before our Tuesday morning class?

"I guess I thought I knew more than I was able to write in the end," I said and left it at that.

Over the course of the winter, Dr. Bauer and I returned to what we jointly referred to as "the chain saw analogy." Sometime in mid-January, though, I confessed that I had been afraid throughout these sessions that she was going to discover something pathologically wrong, and everyone but me would know about it. She seemed taken aback and then said, as professionally as she was able, that I had nothing to worry about. "You're quite sane, Andrew. You came to me for help with understanding how you fit in with and relate to individuals and communities. I think we're getting somewhere."

My relief that night, riding back to the Bronx on the 4 train, was palpable. "I'm sane," I said to a panhandler who had gotten on at the Grand Concourse. I figured the quarter I had fished out of my pocket and dropped into his ratty paper coffee cup (one of the blue and white ones with the Greek design around the brim) could buy me this single anonymous assertion.

"Fuck you, buddy," he snarled. "It ain't so easy on this side."

I don't come from a family of cheerleaders. We carry the Eastern European curse. Brooding, moody, constant swings between generosity and meanness. The scare of what I had experienced as a spiraling fall the winter before, and what had led Jeff to suggest that I get some professional help, sent me to do my own research into depression. I didn't know what I would find, but I didn't expect to discover so clinically that it is—when all of its romance as well as stigma is stripped away—a disease. Not a platform for poets or the reason why there are artists like van Gogh and saints like John of the Cross. It's an insidious condition that finds its way into a mind with a neurological affinity and does its thing, sometimes letting you live with it in a kind of careful détente, sometimes slowly ratcheting up its stake to deadly effect.

When I spoke to my mother about my "concerns" one day, she told me—to my surprise—that she had suffered a disturbing bout of depression after my younger brother had been born. That would have made me almost three. It was winter, a bad one, and she said she couldn't even look at the breakfast dishes, after my father had gone to work and everyone else to school, without bursting into tears. I must have stared out unknowingly from whatever chair she had put me into, waiting, wondering why both she and my baby brother were crying.

"But one day in the spring," she said, "and I'll never forget this, that *sadness* left me as quickly as it had come on. Or at least that's how it seemed. I remembered that we were supposed to have a coal shipment that day from Tommy Reese, the coal man. We had the stoker furnace then, remember?" How could I forget, I who at the age of ten was put in charge of taking out the ashes? "Well, when Tommy came, he set up the coal chute from the truck into the bin, let it go with that constant *hiss* it used to make, then came inside for a cup of coffee as he always did. And we started talking. You were chewing away at the pages of a *National Geographic*, and Matthew had stopped crying, or maybe he was taking a nap, so there was nothing to do but sit and talk. I don't remember what we talked about, but he was the nicest old man, Mr. Reese. You used to light up whenever you saw that truck arrive. And after he was gone, I felt as though I was cured of some long illness, because I took a half hour out of my day for another person."

While I'm sure that it took more than one morning of conversation for my mother to climb out of her own form of depression there in Pennsylvania's early days of what we all knew, before reading T. S. Eliot, was a cruel April, I understood what she meant. My mother had discovered the talking cure. And sometimes that's all it takes.

William Styron's account in *Darkness Visible* of a depression so severe it nearly took his life was sobering when I discovered it. Never was I close to the despair that his lifelong illness had brought him to. I received no medication that year for anything more than a sinus infection. Therapy—the talking cure—worked to give me a way into the door of discovering how I ticked. And sometimes I think knowing *that* I ticked gave me a renewed sense of self-control and regained purpose. That, and the chance to talk to someone, cooled me down once I had heard that I was "quite sane."

But in my own search for what had triggered my spiral, Styron's account became epiphanic when he discussed the origins of depression in *loss*, at a time when I was suddenly aware again of what I had lost myself. Although I had been spared from having a loved one die when I was a child, as a young man I provided stoic cover for a loss of my own making. And an adult's loss of a child can be as searing as any child's loss of an adult. It's this event that brings on what Styron calls the "incomplete mourning" that can precipitate depression in a variety of forms, nagging, debilitating, and sometimes deadly. I will tell you right now that life never dangled me over the "deadly" cliff, as it has so many others. On the contrary, I was fortunate to discover—perhaps before it was too late—that while some details of my life had put me on the path toward priesthood, others remained to be discovered about the deeper path that, like an underground spring, runs beneath all others: the search for God that is the search for the self.

Loss is a fact for those men and women who choose as their vocation Catholic religious life. Few people understand this because most think so strictly of something "lost" in the corporeal sense. Yet a radical move from contemporary culture into a counterculture of Catholic spirituality—as monk, priest, brother, or nun—bears with it the loss of those things we have been told our entire lives will be given to us: a primary partner; the physical and emotional nourishment of sex; procreation; some semblance of wealth if we work hard enough (certainly not poverty); an opportunity to make our voices heard in the world, which is to say, exert our independence; and the promise that we'll be remembered by someone who loved us in the end. But after kneeling and promising to live a life of "poverty, chastity, and obedience," we stand up to find that all of those other promises must now be ignored, no matter how often or hard they knock at our door. Our backs are turned.

Yes, it's a choice one freely makes, and I don't believe that the choice itself is a sickness, as some suggest. Far more men and women have led good religious lives than poor ones. There are a number of things religious life gives one that might otherwise be lacking in a secular life, if one is inclined toward them: the spiritual support of a community and a daily *ordo* that provides time for prayer; the freedom within that community to worry less about one's specific needs; an intellectual tradition beyond compare (there was no one standing over us censoring what we read); a singular and life-giving friendship with the person of the risen Jesus; and the inexplicable suggestion that somehow this life is, in a profound way, a beautiful thing. But when a man in my situation begins to see, in a delayed response, how tactile the loss of what he once knew—not carnal pleasures but admittedly normal human needs—can be, the finality of his decision can come upon him with a darkness and emptiness as chilling as death.

I had come to a certain peace with regard to my actions as a young man over the years, and especially now as a Jesuit. But as I made this order of celibate men my commitment and my home, I was aware, too, that the *fact* of physical loss—a child I had fathered—was something more to me than the abstract truth most of these men seemed to have accepted about not having children. I don't mean that as a criticism. I mean that as a statement of the complex reality of experiences that lead a man to believe he has a vocation to live vows of poverty, chastity, and obedience. He has to accept that desire will always be like a kind of hoarfrost, dissipating before it can be touched or become something real at the end of the day, all the while knowing that it will be there again in some form tomorrow, and every day thereafter. Some men made the choice not to marry and raise a family knowing full well the ache of what they were leaving behind. Others might have known and felt desire but didn't feel the pull toward a particular intimate relationship. Other men happily remained virgins, turning after a while to a love accessed through contemplation and prayer rather than the physical intimacy that would also provide them with families. And, despite what the Church has asserted recently in an attempt to distance itself from this issue within the priesthood, it has to be said that some men understood their own homosexuality as a part of who they were created by God to become. They admitted, in their own psychological well-being, a physical desire for male companionship, but without the crushing urge to consummate that desire with sex. They, too, turned to the love and labor of prayer and gave their desire to God, happier, perhaps, in this state for being able to remain in the company of men. What I mean to say, for myself and for those I once knew, is that the last thing anyone should expect a priest or religious to be is *asexual*. Loyal to the vows? Yes. But without knowledge of himself? No.

Dr. Bauer and I spent surprisingly little time on my role in the choice against becoming a biological father. "Have you forgiven yourself?" she asked me, one or two sessions after I brought it up, sounding like a good confessor. I wasn't quick but content with my answer. "Yes." And when we moved on from there, I had a new respect for her, as though between sessions she was going home and reading Ignatius Loyola's *Spiritual Exercises*. For all I know, she might have been.

The rest of the time we spent on the loss of *expectations* I had of a different fatherhood. Chain saws, travel, and conversations inside cars made me realize that my father couldn't teach me everything I wanted and expected to know of the world. Others—men willing to say to a man in whatever stage of his formation: "Here's how you do this, and why"—had to become my teachers and fathers. How to rig a sailboat. How to balance a line of prose. How to choose the greater of two loves. How to continue to grapple and climb in a life that you yourself have chosen in that solitary search for the self. And through all of this, my own father watched from the distance of what he had given and what he had not, to say, "That's it, Age."

One day when I was climbing the stairs to my room in Ciszek Hall, distracted by some thought or another, I realized that I had kept climbing right to the door that allowed access to the roof. I jiggled the handle, and the door swung open.

It was nearing the end of what had been a long winter, and the air had that grip of unremitting chill. I stepped out onto the flat tar summit with such a childish delight that the door blew shut behind me before I had the chance to make sure it wasn't locked. I stood, frozen, five floors up, staring at a jet on its slow descent. If I'm locked out, I thought, panicking now won't do any good. I'll enjoy the view for a while and worry about getting back in later. It can't be that hard around here.

I walked out to the two-foot lip that separated the rooftop from the side of the building and peered down onto the empty street below. I looked across at antennae and church steeples, high above the occasional automatons that ducked in and out of doors with erratic and faceless moves, while a river of cars and buses jerked and slipped up Fordham Road. To the south I could see the top of the Chrysler Building. To the west a span of the George Washington Bridge.

Then I saw the racing pigeons, released for exercise from their lofts.

I had missed the keeper as he climbed out of his own stairway two streets over. But when he raised a flag and I saw the flock—maybe fifty pigeons in all—rocketing skyward, I was transfixed by this sign of life.

When you see pigeons released for the first time, you expect the crowded moment of flight to be their last act of conforming before each breaks away and disappears to nest alone on some urban ledge. Watch, though, and you see not chaos but a beauty in their gathering. They come together in a formation of one bird following another, following another, so that the entire flock moves in what appears to be an exact, premeditated pattern but is actually a series of fifty split-second lags, like the lights that spell out names and illuminate moving images by blinking at the right time. As they reel in sync, a few birds peel away from the pack, their own flight now looking like a carpet's frayed edge, then fall back into the warp and woof again, letting others break out and come back into the order-chaos-order of the flock.

After almost an hour, the flag comes down and they return to their keeper and their coop.

I started going up to the roof regularly through the rest of the winter (I wasn't locked out) and into the spring, the same time, 4:00, always on a Friday before Mass. It became an extension of the prayer I clung to, like a half hour of Vespers, or office of readings from the Psalms, which I didn't recite but watched from the perch of my chapel in the Bronx.

In March during Lent, I had been on the roof a few minutes, preparing myself for the clockwork release of the pigeons that was becoming another kind of cure for me, when I heard the door open and saw David walk out of the stairway.

"I thought this was where you were. I saw you disappear up the stairs." He was winded from the climb.

"Come over here. You've got to see this." I pointed in the direction of the rooftop lofts as the keeper was emerging like a priest from his sacristy.

"Who's that?"

"I don't know. I call him Santo."

"Santo?"

"You'll see."

The gates flung open, a flag went up, and the flock ascended as one body into the sky. The pigeons rose, arced, dived, rose again, floated intermittently on the draft, and bolted off in a new direction. At times they would appear to tire and look as though they wanted to land, but then at the last minute they'd weave, accelerate, and veer off. For nearly an hour they danced their aerial dance until the keeper took down his flag and they returned to the roof.

I didn't know if he was prepared to sit and watch for so long, but David never said a word, as though instantly he understood the holiness of this flight. When they were done, he just said, "Santo."

We walked back down the stairs and into the chapel in time for Mass. After dinner we asked Mike and Harlan if they wanted to go over to An Beal Bocht in Riverdale with us for a pint. In spite of what I described earlier, seen through the veneer of a weakness I was unable to counter, the four of us had eked out something of a friendship there in the Bronx, so much so that I missed Mike and Harlan when they went back to their provinces at the end of philosophy studies. And I think of them fondly to this day, wondering where they, too, have gotten in their searches. In that pub better known by the translation of its name, "The Poor Mouth," on a chilly night in early spring, the four of us seemed to forget the difficulties of the year we had shared together and apart, and spoke of the private hopes we had for the future, as vowed Jesuits and as men, not knowing what it would hold for any of us but grateful at least on that day that we were in it together.

And as though I should be taught again to see where grace is as well as the beautiful, in early June of that year my father and I drove into central Pennsylvania to go fishing together for what would be the last time in our lives. Having begun to put behind me some of what had almost strangled me a year earlier, I was happy to be released from the confines of the city and find myself at home in the countryside. That week we bypassed some great Pennsylvania waters in the remote counties of the Endless Mountains—the Western Branch of the Susquehanna, Pine Creek, and Kettle Creek—to fish for perch and smallmouth bass at state parks whose names I have forgotten. It didn't matter to me, though. These lesser places were where my father wanted to go and stay put. Sometimes we fished separately. Most times we found a grassy bank near to each other. We rarely talked, except when we agreed it was time to knock off for lunch or supper.

"You will savor the paradox that wilderness and paradise are the same place," a Scotsman by the name of William B. Currie wrote the year before in his book *The River Within: A Life of Fly-fishing*. And so I did, on the last day, while I stood looking at the chiseled profile of my father in his van Gogh–like straw hat, deep blue denim shirt, well-worn Carhartts, and leather boots. Still as seemingly powerful as ever, he tossed a filament of line into the water and, when it came to rest inside ripples where we had seen a fish rise, glanced over to see if I had witnessed his well-placed cast.

"That's it!" I said.

W ith the fall of Communism and the Iron Curtain in 1989, there was renewed interest in creating a viable Jesuit presence in Russia, which had always had a mixed reaction to the subjects of Loyola. A few Jesuits now lived in two converted apartments on Trofimova near the Avtozavodskaya metro stop in the southeast corner of Moscow. An English scholastic had helped to establish the community; a Polish Jesuit was appointed superior; and I knew that an American scholastic had been living there since 1993. After two summers in the Russian language course at Yale, I requested to spend the following summer with the Jesuit community in Moscow. When I got permission from the provincial's office to inquire about available space in the community, I sent off a letter immediately and received a fax that said: "Come."

The first Jesuits in Russia arrived in 1687 and opened a school and residence in Moscow with the help of Leopold I, Holy Roman Emperor. Two years later they were expelled from Moscow by Peter the Great, seventeen years old at the time and out from under the thumb of his half sister Sophia, who had attempted to exert power from inside Novodevichy Convent.

Under the "reforms" of Peter, the Jesuits returned in 1691 to minister in the new church built by the few Catholics who lived in Moscow. They managed to hang on for almost thirty years before they were thrown out again. This time, though, all Western religious were leaving Moscow and St. Petersburg. Franciscans, Capuchins, Jesuits. Everyone.

By the mid-eighteenth century, the Jesuits were active on every continent except Australia and Antarctica. They charted rivers, mapped stars, learned languages, designed cathedrals, and were welcomed by kings, a group founded in order to set out and discover—with no guarantee of return—all for the greater glory of God. In the sixteenth century, Ignatius Loyola wrote more letters in Latin and Spanish to his subjects scattered around the world than any writer, in any language, at the time. Then, in 1773, Pope Clement XIV, under pressure from the Bourbon courts in France, who feared and resented the Order's growing reach, suppressed the Society of Jesus. Twenty-three thousand religious priests and brothers no longer had an identity, and for forty-one years the Church and all Catholic nations would lay claim to no one, or no thing, Jesuit.

Except Catherine the Great, who envisioned a cultural revival of Russia in the late eighteenth century. She was impressed with the Jesuits' reputation for running colleges and universities, and invited them back to White Russia and St. Petersburg. She rejected the Pope's authority and forbade the promulgation of *Dominus ac Redemptor*, the bull that had officially erased the Society of Jesus. In 1786, the Jesuits had six colleges and 178 members in Russia. In 1801, there were 347. Rome was no longer home to one of the Church's most influential religious orders. St. Petersburg was. Before reestablishing the Jesuits throughout the world in 1814, Pope Pius VII promulgated a brief in 1801 that reestablished the Society of Jesus first in Russia.

Then, under the reign of Czar Alexander I, it all collapsed. Alexander was amenable at first to the presence of Catholics in Russia and supported the building and maintenance of schools. But with the invasion of Napoléon came a hardened internal resistance in Russia to the influences of the Catholic West, at the forefront of which were thought to be the Jesuits. In 1815 they were expelled from St. Petersburg and Moscow. In 1820 they were exiled from Russia entirely.

Until June 1992, when Jesuits who had already been in Russia since 1990 officially registered as the Russian Independent Region of the Society of Jesus.

Zbigniew Szala was a slight but taut man. His blue eyes had steely gray centers that warned he was anything but soft or deferential. His moves suggested—in spite of the cigarettes he chain-smoked—that he had been an athlete in his native Poland. Certainly he played soccer, probably as a striker, and he must have been a skier. Like most Jesuit superiors, he held who he was, and who he had been called to be, in a discerning balance between charity and indifference.

I had learned of Father Szala from what I had read about the Jesuits' activities in Russia. I knew he had written the block Cyrillic script on the official letter that invited me to the Russian Federation. He seemed to maintain a distance as practiced as the language itself. He picked me up at Sheremetyevo Airport in Moscow and drove to the flat on Trofimova without ever saying a word.

In a room that doubled in the apartment as his office (not in the airport, where, in those days, it was said that Mafia thugs roamed and eavesdropped for information about imports, money, whatever you might have that they wanted), he sat me down over coffee and wanted to know about my flight, how I was feeling, how my studies were going back in America. We spoke Russian. He knew little English. I was tired. But in that place of exhilaration that comes before physical collapse, like a surge of heat before hypothermia, my mind seemed at home with the alien answers it was giving. Answers that Szala, too, seemed to think were good ones. Still, as though waiting for me to finish reciting my lines, he cautioned, "You cannot do anything here, Andrei, until you *know* the language and understand the culture." He put out one cigarette and lit another in a single motion, dragged deep on the new one, and exhaled the smoke as he added, "And neither will be as easy as you think."

I told him that I had been studying Russian for two years now. It was difficult, but I was making progress. He smiled and spoke more slowly, as though I hadn't understood. "Everything is difficult in Russia, Andrei. *Vsyo!* Everything!" he repeated with the exhaled emphasis of more smoke. "I'm glad you've studied. There's much more to study. And that's why you're here. Your work is studies." The Russian word he used for "difficult" and for "work" was *trud*, a word I would see every day I spent in Moscow. For, where the escalator rose out of the deep metro to street level, a mural of men and women caught in iconic displays of farming, steelmaking, nuclear engineering, communications, education, and sport was etched onto the station's ceiling, capturing the once ideal ethic of the Soviet state, a reminder to all those returning home from work that night of what they would be working for tomorrow: *Mir*—peace, *Svoboda*—freedom, *Ravenstvo*—equality, *Bratstvo*—brotherhood, *Schastye*—happiness, and *Trud*—labor. I, too, was happy to work for such unattainable ideals. As though I were rising out of my own depths on an escalator of promise, I felt purpose, mission, and desire with every step I took in the new Russia.

Three other men lived in the apartment that summer.

Aleks was a native Muscovite who had converted to Catholicism during his time at Moscow State University. He spoke flawless English *and* Russian in a deliberate, measured monotone that he had adopted as a means to cure a stutter. He was an artist and a scholar, an iconographer who studied Hebrew and aspired to do graduate work in Semitic languages.

Alfonso was from Mexico. He had come to Russia after his philosophy studies three years prior. A melancholy Latin, he, too, had felt adrift during those years after first vows and found a new kind of spiritual home among the Russians. Szala saw his determination and rewarded it with encouragement. Alfonso's Russian improved rapidly. He spent the next period of formation in Moscow as Szala's assistant. After that he requested to transfer to the Russian Province. In two years he would be ordained a priest.

And Richard was the American scholastic who had been in Moscow all year. He had petitioned Father General in Rome to be sent to Russia after his philosophy studies. His provincial had already said no to the request. Abroad, Szala implied the same when he wanted to know why a scholastic who knew no Russian should be sent to him. But Richard never let up, and his zeal eventually prevailed. The door was opening wide for the Jesuits in this place that had for centuries coaxed and confounded them. Russia had priority. If you wanted to go, all you had to do was keep asking.

Richard had taken care of the details necessary for my stay with the community. By fax, phone, and e-mail he told me what to do, when to do it, and what not to do before I ever set foot on Russian soil. When I called in the spring to tell him that I had received my visa from the embassy, he seemed excited that an American would be joining him for the summer. It was harder than he had expected, he confessed, to work up to a functioning level in the language. His ability to do anything outside daily chores and reading was limited by the extent to which he could grasp Russian, and the bleak Moscow winter had taken its toll on him. "I'll tell Nadia my tutor that she's got another student for the summer," he said to me. "It'll be a welcome change to have an American Jesuit around here."

In the beginning, the spare, narrow apartment that had once been two family flats was a comfort to me. Its quotidian needs—cleaning, dishes, laundry, cooking—I could approach and accomplish in the course of a day. I saw it as a kind of novitiate all over again. I had enough space. I kept my clothes in the bottom of a china cabinet in the living room, where I slept on a couch that folded out into a bed. I used the dining room and the kitchen table for studying. When I wanted to pray, I went down the hall and into the other half of the flat, where we had a small house chapel.

But outside, on the streets, was the *stránnaya straná*, the "strange land," of Russia, where an accent over first and last vowels separates the word for "strangeness" and "journey" from the word for "home." I learned where to shop among the many fruit sellers that in those days lined Trofimova, what to ask for, and how to do math in Russian in my head. What I had yet to learn was some humility.

Every day, from 9:00 in the morning to 1:00 in the afternoon, I studied with Nadia. She was a willowy and fashionably turned out woman in her mid-forties, a single mother whose eighteen-year-old son had begun his military service. She wondered out loud when he would be sent south to Chechnya and his death. She never spoke about the father.

Nadia had lived in Moscow her whole life and witnessed the rapid decline of Communism, after believing that the system was as near to perfection as was possible in this world. And although she now approached life with a resigned mixture of savvy and sadness, Nadia held on—sometimes endearingly, sometimes maddeningly—to the Russian triumphalism she must have been taught as a girl. When she employed the word *Russia*, the qualifier *great* either preceded it or was not far behind. The Russian writers were the greatest. There were no greater museums or greater paintings than the Russian museums and the Russian painters. The root of Russia's present evils was the preponderance of non-Russians in society, who had no cultural sense of *greatness*, especially the people from the Caucasus.

Much of Moscow harbored deep-seated racism toward Chechens, Kazakhs, Tajiks, anyone who was *chornyi*, or black. "They don't understand us, they can't be trusted," Nadia said to me one day when I told her that I had made friends with the family of Kazakhs who sold fruits and vegetables on the street outside our apartment.

"They are willing to talk to me," I said. "They taught me the word for eggplant. *Baklazhan*."

She was horrified. "*Ostorozhno*, Andrei. Be careful," she said, looking at me sideways as though I were either joking or naïve. "I don't mean that they should be mistrusted or persecuted because they are dark," she said. "People who do that are ignorant. But you should know that they hate Russians, and for *that* reason can't be trusted. *Ostorozhno*," she said again, the same command given on the Moscow metro before the doors slam shut.

Nadia always arrived forty-five minutes to an hour late in the morning, took a thirty-minute break for tea, spoke—or rather whispered—to someone on the phone for fifteen minutes after, and accepted her eight dollars U.S. an hour for a full twenty-hour week with that same mixture of savvy and sadness.

Some days, though, Nadia would say, "Andrei, this afternoon we are going to a place I want you to see." It was all part of my lesson, and here was where I saw Moscow. We went to Chekhov's house, Moscow State University, Novodevichy Convent, the Pushkin Fine Arts Museum, Tretyakov Gallery (where I saw Rublev's sublime and broken icon of Christ), and once an underground theater group's contemporary rendition of *Jesus Christ Superstar*, complete with Judas in leather and a motorcycle onstage. One Saturday we went with Alfonso to the revered and crowded with pilgrims Trinity Monastery of Saint Sergius in Zagorsk. On another, Nadia, her son, two friends, Richard, and I took a train to the more rustic New Jerusalem Monastery outside Moscow. There we hired a severe and handsome woman guide who spoke Russian in deep, rapid tones and never smiled.

"Will you go more slowly, please?" Nadia asked curtly when we stopped briefly to wait for some stragglers on the tour. "My students are not all Russian."

Hawklike, the woman's eyes seized on Nadia, as though sensing weakness in the request. She said, "If they've paid as Russians, I will speak as a Russian," and went on with what I could at least gather was a nationalistic recounting of the bombing of the monastery "by the Fascist heathens of Nazi Germany" during the Second World War. I did pay Russian prices, which weren't even close to what they charged tourists. Because I had grown a beard again and wore jeans and T-shirts, I easily passed as a Russian, if I kept my mouth shut.

I knew that Szala asked Nadia about my progress. Pleased with me, he would be pleased with her. I was in the end getting my money's worth of language and culture. Szala was getting to see how committed, or noncommitted, another eager Jesuit might be. And Nadia? I don't know what she got, aside from payment in a stable currency. I suppose we respected the constant struggles in which stranger and citizen were both engaged: What did it mean, this desire to be a priest, a Jesuit? she would ask. And why Russia? What will you do when the army takes your son, I countered, and your city can offer you no means of employment? I feigned the indifference and determination of Szala, hoping she would recognize a united front. But I needed her, too, and came to appreciate what we both got out of each other that summer: we were loners at home in and yet in search of some community to which we might belong. I don't know where she found hers, but I discovered soon enough that I wasn't going to find mine here.

Richard surprised me when I met him. Having come to this country not knowing any Russian, he spoke well enough after a year to work as a volunteer at the Catholic aid group Caritas and sustain a small group of Russian friends. He wasn't reading Pushkin, but he got along with little help. By June, the difficulties of the winter he had alluded to on the phone seemed themselves to have melted away. The first week I was in Moscow he said he wanted to orient me as best he could because he would be traveling to Novosibirsk, a city in central Siberia, to visit the Jesuits there and to make a retreat. Orientation meant registering my visa with the fickle bureaucrats at UVIR (Upravlenia Viz i Registratsii), getting a student discount for a monthly metro pass, taking me to Mass at Eglise St. Louis de Française on Maly Lubyanka behind the former KGB prison in the center of Moscow (where Ciszek was held), and showing me a Western ice-cream store near the Hotel Metropol where I could buy milk shakes, Richard insisted with a knowing grin, "better than the ones at McDonald's."

When he returned to Moscow in mid-July, though, Richard was mean as a snake.

"Cook and clean toilets. That's what he wants me to do," he fumed under his breath one afternoon after storming out of a meeting with Szala. "That's what I did all winter. And then he says I can't speak Russian! What does he think we had our conversation in? Mandarin?"

The rift should have been clearer to me. Richard, a young man whose tragic flaw was believing that *he* always knew best (didn't we all?), never fit into the community Szala envisioned for the Russian Province: hardworking, team-playing, "mortified" Jesuits. There wasn't room for Americans who seemingly always got what they wanted. Culture and language was Szala's Ignatian *laborare est orare* for the Jesuits in Russia. In his mind, the single year Richard had given to studies only scratched the surface.

But I began to suspect that Richard was suffering his own kind of loss. He believed that he was ready to do the work of the region, helping parish communities, giving retreats, coordinating assistance. Jumping into an imposing task, however prematurely, had the added benefit of creating more desire to do the greater work of staying put in this country.

"Send me to Novosibirsk," he had said to Szala.

Szala's response: "You're not ready."

I felt for Richard, and I didn't. He'd come here against the advice of his superiors. The deck of formation, you quickly learn in the Society of Jesus, can be a deck of few cards. Play one as strong as Russia, and you were close to exhausting every other possibility of where you might go. And when the dealers folded up the table and left town, you'd have to get used to the strange land's dangerous vagaries and numbing distance. That doesn't sound much like the spirit of Ignatian indifference, I know. But there's the ideal, and then there's the real.

Richard's animosity split the apartment down the middle. I couldn't remain a neutral bystander, no matter how closely I kept to my own daily tasks. I was an American, and I hadn't yet the command of Russian to stand behind. That meant I knew nothing of what was *trud*. When Szala and Alfonso saw Richard and me talking, they must have believed I was sympathetic to his complaints, because Szala never engaged me in even the simplest conversation for the next month and a half that I was there.

Except for a moment when we had by chance been sitting at the kitchen table together for a cup of tea one afternoon. Wanting to make conversation, I asked Szala if he could explain to me the correct usage of the subjunctive in a particular phrase I had heard. He told me, but did so in a dismissive tone, as though it made no difference anyway.

"So you're still studying your Russian?" he asked.

The question surprised me. "Of course," I said.

"You're not tired of it yet? You seem tired of it."

"I'm not tired, no," I said, uncertain about the line of questioning.

"It's easy when you're tired to speak your own language. To give up."

I knew, then, on what side of the divide I stood in Szala's mind. Not his. "I haven't given up."

"That's good," he said as he stubbed out his cigarette and got up from the table. "Keep speaking Russian, if you can."

"If you can," I repeated. "But in this house, with whom?"

Szala shrugged.

Alfonso also said little to me, and what he did was frequently in Spanish, again suggesting my Russian would never be as good as his. I wondered, though, when I heard him switch into his own native tongue, the ease and delight of expression obvious in the lift of his mood, if he, too, didn't get a little tired here sometimes.

Aleks, the native Russian in the house, wanted to speak English. He had been sent to London for his studies and insisted, whenever we engaged in conversation, that he needed to practice his English in Moscow. Rather than avoid him (he was too interesting to avoid), I suggested we trade off, fifteen minutes English, fifteen minutes Russian. It worked, if I could get him to commit to the full half hour.

Yet Richard, the one who could have done the most to bridge the cultural and linguistic gaps in the community, seemed determined for some reason to poison what time I had left in Moscow. Perhaps since his was unbearable already.

He became arrogant in his insistence that we speak nothing but English to each other, regardless of where we were, as though I had become his American ear and confidant, a role, once I saw how it was interpreted, I wanted no part of. When I asked him if he could try to help me by speaking Russian every now and then, he said, "I speak Russian all day and I'm tired of it. Besides, you don't know the language well enough to have a conversation with me." Then he would mumble something quickly and incomprehensibly, look to me for a response, and smirk. "See? You'll never be here long enough." Or, on the days when we had a community meal after Mass and I wanted to describe my day to Szala, Richard would pounce on the first grammatical mistake I made, then interrupt to explain to everyone what I was trying to say. Szala made no response to Richard's insolence or my fatigue.

By August, I could feel that familiar gloom, frustration, and sadness coming on. This time, I barely summoned the effort to pray. At most, I'd whisper the first few lines of Psalm 42, from the Divine Office, somehow appropriate here. "Like the deer that yearns for running streams, so my soul is yearning for you my God . . . the God of my life." Yearning—and with it a desire to run—pounded down on me like sun on parched grass. I remembered a famous letter Dostoyevsky had written from prison to a woman named Natalia Dmitrievna Fonvizina: "I shall tell you that at such a time one thirsts for faith as 'the withered grass' thirsts for water, and one actually finds it, because in misfortune the truth shines through." It wasn't faith, though, that I longed for. It was a conviction of where I might put my faith to work. Was this how I was to live out my call in the end, in a dry land that tempts with its visions of emptiness? Walter Ciszek lived here, starved and imprisoned, thirsting for freedom, but remaining faithful to the end. I wanted so badly to drink in this same place, yet could feel the unslakable thirst of being in a strange land, too far away from anything or anyone I might love, no truth shining, only the fear of affliction.

On the days when Nadia left after lunch, I would find a place on my map of Moscow where I hadn't yet been, locate the nearest metro, and explore. Artists' stalls in Gorky Park, the cafés and buskers along the Arbat, Izmailovsky Park on the weekends, or some days a church or monastery where I could slip in to hear part of a liturgy or Vespers in Old Slavonic. If there were historic sites, I would photograph them. If there were shops or merchants around, I would suss out who might be willing to talk about what they were selling. If they were terse, I moved on. If they gave me their time, and their Russian (fifteen minutes was my average lesson), I would ask questions, answer questions about myself, and in the end spend the few hundred rubles on whatever it was they were trying to sell. I acquired quite a stash of samizdat poetry and small icons this way.

During my last week in Moscow, torrential rains soaked the city. At first I resisted them and made my afternoon jaunts in spite of the floods, returning to the apartment just in time for Mass, soaked through but defiant. After a few days, though, I stayed inside, believing that it couldn't rain forever. I was nearly mad with restlessness and the desire to get out of that place when I awoke after lunch one afternoon to find the sun shining through the drapes.

Instead of venturing to a new stop along Moscow's Ring, I walked out of the apartment and down to where the involuted Moskva River turned back on itself, creating a kind of stagnant bay. Families from our building and others surrounding it had emerged from their own gloom to do the same.

Where the weeds cleared along the road and the water came into view, I saw what looked like a replica of a Mississippi riverboat. White with red trim along the top of its smokestack and sides, it was named the *Kiev* and lay half sunk but tied to its dock as though it were going out that evening for a charter. When I raised my camera to take a photograph, three men emerged from the listing interior and started waving to me. They didn't look as though they were about to invite me inside.

"*Nyet!*" they yelled. "*Nye nado! Von ot cyuda!*" "Don't do that! Get out of here!" Gangsters, I decided, and moved on.

The week before, in the midst of the rains, I had gone to visit the Moscow home of Lev Tolstoy in Khamovniki, a borough in the southwest corner of the city settled in the late seventeenth century by merchants, along with the aristocratic families who financed them. The old estate of Ivan Arnautov was where Tolstoy wrote many of his works of social and religious philosophy, such as *What I Believe In, What Shall We Do, The Kingdom of God Is Within Us*, and his final piece, responding to his excommunication from the Orthodox Church, "My Answer to the Synod." The pamphlet you can buy in lieu of a tour presents this as a place of industry and happiness for the Tolstoy family. It wasn't.

The count and his wife had come here so that the children could attend school. The two of them rarely spoke to each other. Tolstoy wished, in spite of the work he accomplished in Moscow, that he'd never had to leave his inspirational birthplace of Yasnaya Polyana in Tula, some one hundred miles south of Moscow, where he could scythe his own wheat, like Levin in *Anna Karenina*, and strive, as he wrote in his diary, "to be self-sufficient, and to give more than I take." Every diary entry that records his return to Yasnaya Polyana after the family moved to Moscow for the winters contains the word *home*.

The house in Moscow was something of a compromise between

the writer and his wife, who was a self-professed city lady. "I wasn't made for solitude," the vibrant Sophia wrote in her own diary about life in the country. "It crushed my soul." When the family first came to Moscow, in the summer of 1881, they lived in the city center, in a rented property at number 3 Denezhny Lane (now Maly Lyovshinsky Lane). "A month has passed—the most agonizing of my life," Tolstoy wrote on October 5, 1881. "The move to Moscow. They are still settling down. When will they start to live? It's not in order to live, but to do as other people do. Unhappy people! They have no life."

When he found the estate in Khamovniki for sale in the spring of 1882, Tolstoy must have realized that this neighborhood of factories and forests was the closest retreat to country life he would find in the Moscow environs. He added a wing and another floor to the estate house, redecorated the interior, moved in new furniture, beds and a piano, and made a workroom where he could pursue his love for manual labor. This was the house where he famously learned to make his own shoes. Outside, he kept a horse, rode a bicycle, and in the winter flooded the garden to make a skating rink for the children. By January 1883, Tolstoy had settled into a productive routine of shoemaking, room tidying, and writing, noting, "As soon as I wake up, I often have thoughts and clear ideas about what was previously confused, so that I rejoice and feel that progress has been made."

I stayed at the museum long into the afternoon, reading on a garden bench in full view of the old writer's study, and left when a pensioner, who took tickets and hushed noisy tourists, shuffled over to me in her felt booties and whispered in a tender, diminutive Russian: "Young man, I am sorry, please, but it is nearly time to go."

I thought of the house of Lev Tolstoy as I walked along the reedy bend in the river, letting my exhaustion catch up to me in one fell swoop of emotion, and said to no one: "What am I going to do?" All I could think of was how utterly alone and increasingly despondent I had become, regardless of the fact that I would be leaving soon. Where, amidst the frustration of community and language, was the talking cure now? In his maliciousness, Richard was right when he said I'd never be here long enough. Three months was barely an introduction.

The larger question for me in Moscow was whether a place like Russia was where I wanted to live my life as a Jesuit. Was it the beginning of the question: Did I want to live my life as a Jesuit at all? Each scholastic moves through formation with some ideal in mind of what he wants to do with his life. I had asked to come to Russia because I dreamed of playing a role in the dialogue between religion and culture in the Christian East. For all of their bad history with the Russians, the Jesuits still have the best men and resources to bridge the differences between East and West. And for me, it seemed an almost providential opportunity to fuse my family's past with an unfolding future.

But perhaps what I was facing now was another facet or deeper realization of loss within the gain of religious life. If I could point to a gain. I came to realize quickly that I would never fit in this country or community. The Church, if it was to stay here, needed priests on the ground, in Siberia and in far corners of the Caucasus. I would have withered at some parish in Krasnoyarsk or Dushanbe as I was withering in Moscow from loneliness after only three months. Besides, I had discovered quickly that my interest in the Eastern Christian churches would have been viewed by both Catholics and Orthodox as counterproductive, if not hostile. The Eastern Catholics were considered by the Russian Orthodox to be the greatest stumbling block to ecumenism. Catholics were Latin. End of discussion. No, if I asked to come back here to live and work, I thought, I would become a man like Richard. And that I refused to do.

Does there have to be an equivalent or recognizable gain to balance out a loss, though? St. Ignatius would say that I should be happy to lose *all* for the sake of Christ's love. If I wasn't prepared for that, what was I prepared for? Most Jesuits I knew would freely admit to not wanting the kind of hard, severe life a mission like Russia promised. I couldn't say yet. That was what I'd come here to find out. Perhaps I really wanted to be like Tolstoy. Not for what the man produced but for what he pursued. Build the study, draw the curtains, shorten the legs of your chair if you have to, but sit down and *work*. In his retreat from distractions, in his love for labor, and in his writing,

Tolstoy had been in search of one thing, it seemed: the creativity that would lead him to beauty. If I was to remain a Jesuit—or at heart a Catholic and a Christian—I decided, regardless of where I lived or what I did, it would have to be a vocation of creativity and love, not blind obedience to a duty, which led in the end to thirst and emptiness.

As I followed the path into a clearing, I saw two fishermen casting hooks with hunks of pork on them into the river. I asked if they had caught anything. They said they hadn't, but I should bring my fishing pole and join them.

"I don't have one," I said.

"What! You're a Russian and you don't fish?"

When I told them that I wasn't a Russian, that I was from New York and living in their neighborhood for the summer, they were surprised and delighted to have met their first American.

"Excellent, excellent," one said with a laugh, his eyes squinting as he smiled, gold teeth (what was left of them) flashing in his mouth. "Journalist?" he asked, when he saw that it was a camera I had slung around my back.

I hesitated. "Student."

"Where did you learn to speak Russian?" the other one asked.

"Here," I said. "*Nu, mne trudno.* Though it's difficult for me."

"Then you've learned well."

"*Pochemu?* Why?" I asked.

"Because Russians love difficulty."

"*Eto pravda,*" his friend said as he worked another slice of pork onto a fishhook and tossed it into the water. He sat down on a bucket and took a swig from a bottle of vodka.

"Well," I said again, "I'm not a Russian." But I said it quietly, and I don't think they heard me.

"Well," the other said, as though he *had* heard me and was conscious of the echo, "*Ne bespokoites.* Don't worry." And it occurred to me then that this phrase in Russian literally means "Don't be without peace." Then he added, "If we had another pole, we'd invite you to join us." Accepted sooner by two fishermen than by my fellow Jesuits in this place. Ah, but whose fault was that? The fishermen were being polite. Eventually they, too, would pull in their lines and head for home.

"*Spasibo*. Thank you," I said, conscious now of the theological conversation Russians carry on whenever they speak. *Spasi* from "to save," and *Bog*, "God," together means "God save you." "I have to go," I said. "Good luck . . . with the fish."

"Yes, yes," they sang together as though a choir. "*S Bogom.*" "Go with God," and they crossed themselves there in the grass on the riverbank, Fathers, Sons, and Holy Ghosts. I turned away so they wouldn't see, and did the same.

PART IV

Consider well, then, your calling, so that on the one hand you can give great thanks to God who has given you something so great, and on the other so that you can ask God for a special favor in order to be able to respond to it.

—Ignatius Loyola, letter to the students in Coimbra,
May 7, 1547

At the end of my philosophy studies, I made my annual retreat at Linwood, the Society of St. Ursula's retreat house in Rhinebeck, New York, overlooking an open expanse of the Hudson River. Along with daily prayer, community life, and work, the annual retreat is a necessary brick in the bulwark of a Jesuit's vocation. It lasts for eight days and is placed either within a period of transition or at a time of rest. I had been coming to Linwood with my scholastic community for our entire three years of studies, in May, the day after exams were done, with the same director, writing in the same marble-covered composition book that tracked my reflections, thoughts, and prayer. It wasn't as though questions and concerns were stored up or put on hold throughout the year. Spiritual direction was ongoing. Rather, retreat represented a different kind of time and space through which to move forward, a "withdrawal," as Ignatius says, "from all worldly cares," while seeking to "approach and be united" with the Lord in that continual desire for companionship. I had come to look forward to my annual retreats as times in which, in the words of the priest's prayer after the Our Father, I felt "protected from all anxiety" as I sifted—sometimes with more than a little doubt—through where I might find God in all of this. And I can say that I always left those retreats "with joyful hope," as that same prayer says.

When I woke in the cool Hudson Valley morning on the first day, I dressed and walked outside to an Adirondack chair covered in dew where I sat anyway and wrote down a dream I had had the night before. Then I got some breakfast and settled into a corner pew in the chapel. The sun was fully up, light streaming through the tall, thin windows. The chill was lessening. An hour later I walked into my spiritual director's tiny meeting room and recapped the year, laying open my heart to where my prayer might take me over the next eight days.

Father Joseph Constantino, SJ, perfected the art of being casually well-groomed. That day he sat in a chair beneath a good watercolor of the lighthouse at a bend in the river that you could see from the grounds of Linwood. In his late forties, with salt-and-pepper hair, and dressed (even at this hour, in this place) in a blue oxford shirt unbuttoned at the top, Joe was more at home on the Upper East Side than on the banks of the Hudson. But he was no arch-traditionalist. A philosopher who had stepped out of academia to rethink the priorities of his own spiritual journey, Joe believed the Church and the Society had to move forward to embrace the genuine cultural shifts that Catholics, and Catholic men entering the Jesuits, encountered in their deepest faith searches. "This so-called pluralism is not some great crisis we have to stamp out before we're destroyed," he had said on many occasions when the chance to talk about philosophy emerged. "The relativist's cry to 'do what you want, there is no truth' is nothing new. The thirteenth century dealt with as much pluralism among thinkers and believers as we do now, if not more, and it produced Thomas Aquinas." Returning to some golden age of discipline and order was not the answer, Joe believed. Discipline and order are cultivated in the man. If a Jesuit understands the *Exercises*, he'll see Ignatius's genius for understanding and responding to the contemporary *and* the eternal. Reaction is not tradition. Reaction is nostalgia, and nostalgia is false memory. With Joe I always agreed.

I described to him my dream, one I had been having intermittently over the past year: "I am in a large house, sitting in a small room, naked, wiping droplets of water off a brass bowl. A woman walks into the room. She is older than I am, a widow, I think for some reason, or a mother who has lost a son. She's dressed in red and appears elegant. I cover myself up poorly with the small towel I am using and apologize out loud for my nakedness. She smiles and seems unabashed or unconcerned. There is a brief exchange of playful words that I cannot remember except in tone, something to the effect that in the past she might have taken advantage of the situation, but now she wants to show me these. She puts two pair of earrings in my hand. Then she turns to face a large mirror. I pick out the pair I like best, a silver material in the shape of a cross. I want to hold them up to her ears and say, 'These would look beautiful on you,' but I can't. I don't have the nerve to touch her, or to say the words."

He listened and asked me about my prayer.

I felt tired, a fatigue beyond the physical. "You know me," I said indifferently. "It'll take two days before I settle in, focus on the same old questions of community and intimacy, and then decide that life's no better anywhere else."

A look, then, of dismissal from this man whose own settled and yet searching foundation I looked forward to returning to for eight days each year. "Doesn't sound like you at all, actually. But if that's where you are, then bag the retreat, go back to the Bronx or wherever it is you're going, and save yourself the time and work."

I thought of the passage I had starred in the opening pages of my copy of the *Exercises* and read with a beginner's mind each time I came here: "It will be profitable for the one who is to go through the Exercises to enter upon them with magnanimity and generosity . . . with his entire will and liberty." My smart-alecky attitude was all off. I apologized to Joe and said he was right. He grinned to regain the good rapport we had built up over the past three years and said, "Don't apologize to me!" as though there were someone else in the room about whom I had forgotten, someone I might have offended more.

"The truth is," I said, "I feel as though I am at something of a crossroads. Or, do you know how hot water seems to swirl randomly before it settles into a boil? I feel like that right now. Not boiling but swirling, and it's not a comfortable place."

"But you've just been given a fantastic regency assignment."

"I know. On the outside, there's nothing to complain about."

"What is it, then?"

"I've been thinking about where I fit or, rather, where I *will* fit. Sometimes I wonder if I'm on a path of least resistance, and one day I'll wake up wondering what I gained by not speaking up for myself or my desires. It's a question of calling, I guess," I said, and backtracked over the past nine months.

My last year at Ciszek Hall, Jeff Chojnacki, a man I will forever credit with saving my life, made me the beadle, and a new class arrived for their three years of studies in the Bronx. Ray was a good minister to work with. I sometimes had the feeling that he thought I wasn't the best choice for the job (what are ministers for?), but after I proved I could be as meticulous about detail as I was depressive in my moods, he granted me his own brand of insider status and started referring a few complaints and concerns to me. With what time was left at our community on Belmont, I prepared for my philosophy exams and took a course in American poetry. It wasn't any kind of permission I needed to do this, just an open slot in my class schedule, which I had never had before.

It was time also to begin talking to the provincial and his formation assistant about my assignment for the period of teaching we called "regency." I wanted to go to a college English department. I'd done well (I was told) at Le Moyne as an adjunct during the fall of my second year in the novitiate. I had begun publishing essays—reflections on literature in a contemporary context—in *America* magazine. And I was finally getting some poetry published in literary journals, poetry I managed to scratch out during half-hour writing blocks I set aside in the mornings or occasionally during my afternoon prayer, where I clung tightly to something Gerry Blaszczak once said to me, that poetry is, at the right time, a kind of prayer. The first poem I got accepted in a small Michigan journal was a short lyric called "The Osprey," in which I re-created a landscape of solitude and communion from what I remembered of my time on Cape Cod, and what I searched for as a Jesuit in the Bronx: some form of beauty.

Jesuits in Jesuit colleges were increasingly few and far between and so were sought-after commodities, often hired under guidelines similar to affirmative action. When the Jesuit president (formerly of Le Moyne) at Loyola College in Baltimore informed his English Department that I was "on the market," I got an offer to teach creative writing full-time for two years. Could I be that lucky? I told the provincial and the formation assistant that this was what I wanted to do.

But Loyola College was in the Maryland Province. If I moved there, a community in the New York Province would be out a scholastic, and the Jesuit community at Le Moyne had a tradition of receiving scholastic regents. The superior made it clear he wanted to keep that tradition alive.

In the early spring, I received my letter from the provincial.

Dear Andrew: Peace of Christ.

I know that in recent months you have been working closely with the Assistant for Formation to discern your regency assignment. From our very recent correspondence, I am aware that, although the discernment process has not been the most satisfying for you, you realize and accept the Provincial's stated apostolic priorities.

I was assigned formally to teach in the English and Philosophy Departments at Le Moyne College in Syracuse for the fall. Two part-time positions cobbled together to make me a full-time college instructor. After a few specifics on dates for a required workshop and procedural details for my next move, the letter finished with the hope that I

will do great things for the Lord at Le Moyne. We trust that you will find and give great support in the Jesuit community there, and, moved with zeal to minister the Gospel to God's people, you will find yourself confirmed in your call to priesthood in the Society. Keep the faith and the joyful hope that goes with it.

The unsatisfying discernment process that the provincial alluded to had been my initial frustration at seeing the personal fit of teaching creative writing at Loyola Baltimore trumped by the provincial need of maintaining a young Jesuit presence at Le Moyne, the "stated apostolic priorities." But that was only pride talking, the old desire to be desired. Shaking that off, I knew I was about to enter the stage in formation where a scholastic could finally do something, for the province as well as for himself. Placed between philosophy studies and our training in theology, regency was meant to be a time of apprenticeship, not unlike learning a trade in a boatyard after four years of college. You need to know that you're capable of more than contemplation, that there's something regenerative as well as obedient in what Virgil called *labor impobus*: damn hard work.

So I did what I was asked to do. I trusted that my *formators* and superiors would listen to my request to be sent to one place. They trusted that I knew why I was being sent to another. That was obedience, and I had taken a vow to obey.

All that led to what I said to Joe on that first day of retreat. "I entered the Jesuits believing that I was called to live out the prayer of the *Exercises*: 'Take, Lord, and receive my entire will. Your grace is enough.' But since then, I feel as though I've been passing through some narrow passage where the velocity of everything has increased, and I'm about to emerge into a broader, deeper course. The rub is that I'm not sure whether this course will take me further into, or away from, the Jesuits."

He inclined his head but maintained the director's silence, and so I went on. "There's something about that dream. The feeling not of freedom in the nakedness but of paralysis. For all of the open-minded desire to seek that I entered religious life with, I'm paralyzed by the fear that I've lost the other parts of the search. The certainty, and the beauty."

"But you haven't even begun," he said finally. "The vows, the formation, the *certainty* that you're doing something you love. These aren't a question of calling but the tasks of a lifetime. Let me ask you something. Can you point to any Jesuits who you think are happy?"

"Sure." I went through a list. Don, Gerry, Charlie, Ray. "You," I said. "Unless I'm mistaken."

"You're not. What about your peers?"

"Well, David, Tom, Rocco, Peter. Some guys who have gone on to theology studies, though I don't know them all that well."

"And do you think they've all been sailing through this without ever wondering, Why am I doing this?" I shook my head. This I knew, of course, from the practice of faith sharing we kept to throughout our philosophy studies, a powerful reminder each month that these men living and working right next to you ask themselves "Why?" too. But I needed this human context, and humbling, both of which marked Joe's genius as a director. "Everyone, Jesuit or not, has to face the fact that, in the end, our desires may not add up to much," he said. "Don't you see? You're like the rich young man. *What must I do?* Do what you're supposed to do. Believe and trust."

Belief I'd always known. Trust I had built up along the way. But both were no small part of the consolation I felt at the end of these yearly retreats, knowing that there were entire communities of men who had taken the same vows I had and gave of themselves out of the same witness to belief and desire to trust. That's why the vows are made in public and not private. So there was that much to consider.

Then Joe said something that he must have known I was thinking, because it shocked me for its directness, yet relieved a certain anxiety I had begun to feel. "I am willing to accept that God may be calling you to leave the Society, AJ. But it has to be God, not anyone, or anything, else. God and good discernment brought you here. God and good discernment are the voices that are going to direct you, in or out."

As I got up to go, he said, "Try to rest. Don't rush the prayer. You've just finished a tough three years."

In a section of the *Exercises* called Rules for Discernment of Spirits II, Ignatius continues to discuss what he identifies as "the different movements produced in the soul" and offers this classic test of whether our souls are progressing or stuck. "In souls that are progressing to great perfection, the action of the good angel is delicate, gentle, delightful. It may be compared to a drop of water penetrating a sponge. The action of the evil spirit upon such souls is violent, noisy, and disturbing. It may be compared to a drop of water falling upon a stone." It's an Ignatian metaphor that always stayed with me because it may be the only water image the saint employs in the landscape of the *Exercises*. I had read it as long ago as the Long Retreat, sometimes substituting for the image of water on stone (which also could seem like a delight to me when I was fishing) Dostoyevsky's own metaphor of desolation as "withered grass." That's how it felt, too, at times, as disturbed as ground that should be alive and yielding but is rootless dust, yearning, thirsting, and out of reach of any stream or raindrops that might soothe a longing.

Joe gave me some latitude during those eight days to take advantage of being out of the Bronx. So I fished for a few hours every afternoon on the Roeliff Jansen Kill, a trout stream north of Rhinebeck. I returned for meals, Mass, my periods of prayer and spiritual direction refreshed and focused.

After a few days I was wracked with severe migraines and back pain. I checked my body for tick bites and found nothing. When I wasn't asleep or lying in bed, I would move to the large sitting room that overlooked the Hudson and search for some semblance of prayer in the pain. The paralysis was real now. For as much as I wanted to examine the questions Joe had put to me, I was in the grip of something that kept them at bay.

Two days before the end of the retreat I went for a walk after supper. There was a path that led along the edge of the property, through a hollow, and out onto the railroad tracks where trains to Albany screamed by night and day. Ibuprofen had eased my back pain. I'd found a regular pattern of waking and sleeping. But I had lost—or perhaps never had—the magnanimity and desire Joe reminded me I was missing. I was, in the words of the prophet, neither hot nor cold, and at risk of being spat out.

I walked down this hollow all the time. I liked the feeling of limitless arriving and departing that rose up when I emerged from the woods and stared north or south along the tracks, waiting for a train to appear silently from nowhere around the bend, then the danger of the place sinking in as that train swept by in a sudden rush. At ground level the threat moved faster than its warning. Only a slinky, metallic sound that rattled like silver chains through the iron gauge let you know the bullet was coming.

Once the train had passed, it was the water that drew me. The depth and strong currents of the Hudson make it ocean and river. It's as fast and volatile on a slack tide as it is at ebb or flood. In the flats that drained and filled every six hours or so, I saw shorebirds, snapping turtles, water snakes, once the thrash of striped bass following bait fish. On the bluffs above, there were men and women at prayer, temporary hermits in their temporary cells. In this other, riparian world, there was the permanence of not the things but the passage of creation, brackish, swift, and unforgiving.

That evening I had walked almost as far north as the Rhinebeck station along the track bed and riverbank when I saw it would be getting dark soon and so turned around to go back. I took one last look at the surface of the water from close up before tucking into the woods and trudging up to the retreat house. I felt impatient and resentful that I had to spend another two days at work on this retreat when there was little more that I thought could be gained from it. If I was going to remain a Jesuit, I had to go where I was told, and keep moving. Sticking with it has gotten me this far, I thought to myself as I bounded along the creosote ties that kept the marriage tight between ground and track. But suddenly I felt a skeptical powerlessness in the resignation of this head-down, stay-the-course tack. "How can it be of God," I remember saying clearly to myself, "when it's men who decide what can and cannot be withstood?"

"Of God" seemed to echo in my head when I stepped from what bits of daylight remained on the water's edge into the dense and dark hollow, and brushed the branch of a sapling away from my face. The air was warm, the weather unusually humid. But as I walked past a desiccated carcass of a deer that—in its head-down silence at track level—had been hit by a train and thrown clear into the brush, a blast of cold wind rushed through the woods and chilled me. "It's not of God," I heard a voice say, confident and declarative, and yet seeming to deride. Was there someone in the woods? I stopped walking and looked around quickly, more startled than afraid. Another rush of cold and the voice again, "Don't you see? What God? Fuck 'em!" This time mocking, unrecognizable. I had the urge to run, like I did when I was a boy and, walking home at night from my grandmother's house at the top of our dead-end street, I would stare into the blackness of the woods and imagine what lay in wait for me there.

Something held me fast, though, a thin, strong desire to stay put, to stand my ground, regardless of how weak or powerless I was. "God and good discernment brought you here." "That's it, Age." The air warmed again, and I walked back up to the top of the hill, out onto the grass at Linwood. I was shaken and thirsty, and I remember feeling this, with the clarity of an entire eight days of retreat: a deep and stark aloneness. Then, like the deer that yearns for running streams, I went into the chapel, knelt down, and prayed.

The first night I spent on the campus of Le Moyne College as a Jesuit scholastic was in an empty all-men's dormitory, Nelligan Hall. A soccer camp had moved out, and the residential life staff hadn't yet begun to get rooms ready for the first day of classes, which would be in a few weeks. I was going to be Nelligan's resident chaplain.

I went to sleep on a mattress on the carpeted floor of my concrete suite. I liberated a sheet and a blanket from a linen closet in the Jesuit Residence, but I didn't use the blanket. The air was stuffy, so I left the windows wide open while straight, torrential rains fell all night. In those spare and empty surroundings, I felt the presence of some new beginning.

I woke in the morning to the sound of lovemaking. I had just fallen back to sleep when I heard a slow crescendo of breathing coming into my room on clear morning air, steady and strong at first, then accentuated by low moans and short gasps that quickly rose to a cry and trailed off.

"Not alone after all," I said to myself and felt the pang of not having that lover. I blamed it on the proximity of fantasy and told myself that this life, too, had its intimacy, deepened by prayer. Then I went back to sleep. And yet, when I looked around the dorm the next morning, expecting to surprise the two rogue R.A.'s who had conveniently decided to arrive early for the school year, I found no one. The place was abandoned.

I had never been an R.A. myself in college, and in spite of my newfound understanding of how authority worked and was managed, I believed that intellectual and moral education came by leaving young men and women to do what they would in the absence of authority. If you're a philosopher, as Socrates tried to convince the Athenians, you do the Good because it's good, not because you're afraid you'll otherwise be punished.

The Office of Residential Life didn't see it that way. They wanted both the presence and the appearance of intellectual and moral authority to play a role in the formation of undergraduates away from home for the first time. A sign on my door read: A. J. KRIVAK, S.J. CHAPLAIN.

Le Moyne College was established in Syracuse in 1947 by the Jesuits of the New York Province for men coming home from the war, because Syracuse University tended not to admit Catholics in those days (or maybe Catholics didn't want to go there). Armed with the G.I. Bill, and facing the landscape of an America vastly different from the Depression they couldn't forget, former soldiers from Europe and the South Pacific wanted to study philosophy, biology, and history so that they could become teachers, doctors, and lawyers. The Jesuits obliged.

When I was sent there to teach almost fifty years later, Le Moyne was a coeducational school of roughly fifteen hundred students. Some of the original faculty members—who were scholastics like me when they arrived, or newly ordained priests—were retired and living in the Jesuit Residence on campus. Father Ted Clarkson used to remind me every time I sat down at his table for lunch that he, too, had been a chaplain in Nelligan Hall.

"That was nineteen fifty. Nelligan was new, and the students were a lot older. They had been to Iwo Jima." He said this with great deliberation, the name of the island a pronounced and slow "EEE-wo GEE-ma." Then he'd let out a conspiratorial chuckle as he stared down at his soup through thick, horn-rimmed glasses. "Goddamn guys sure knew how to cause trouble then, heh, heh, heh. But goddamn smart, too." Clarkson's heart was as big as his own reputation for causing trouble.

Forget the elite of Georgetown, who have educated presidents, statesmen, and third-world dictators. Forget the former athletic glory of Fordham, where Vince Lombardi was a student, and Marquette, which sends its fair share of players to the NBA. Le Moyne has a mission all its own. A liberal arts college among the likes of Hamilton, Colgate, and SU, it doesn't have the ranking of those three schools in Upstate New York, but that's not what it's there for. The tradition of the Jesuits at Le Moyne has always been to give central New York's Catholic working class a college education. It was there for the men who had returned from Guadalcanal and the Battle of the Bulge, first-timers in college among entire families, who now watched their grandsons and granddaughters go there, Catholic, working-class students possessing the brilliance at times of Hopkins's "immortal diamond," "all at once what Christ is, since he was what I am . . . / Jack, joke, poor potsherd, patch, matchwood." The kind of student who comes into your office concerned with why you wrote not the paragraph of comments on the last page that suggested a promising argument for the entire essay but a note to avoid a sentence fragment on the third. That's when you discover a life of fragments, of *potsherd, patch, matchwood.*

"I don't know what you *mean* by a fragment," an earnest but upset first-year student named Melinda said to me while she sat on the edge of a chair next to the desk in my office. It was early in the fall semester. (I was getting used to things like having my own office.) On that day Mel appeared more than concerned. She spoke as though she was in pain.

"It means the sentence is missing either a subject or a verb," I said. She looked back at me with a blank stare. "In this case, 'Proving a connection to illegal trafficking in human organs' has no subject." Students always wrote about heady front-line debates, wanting to prove one side or another, as though obscurity of topic translated into clarity of analysis. The best paper I ever received was an essay that argued, based on personal statistics, team performance, and media perception before and after his death, that Thurman Munson's leadership qualities had had a quantifiable effect on the performance of the New York Yankees during the years in the 1970s when he was captain, at the time the only named captain of the Yankees since Lou Gehrig. The paper was poised in that triangular balance of original thought, good writing, and enough supporting facts.

Melinda sighed. "Why?" she said. "Why do you have to do that? I stayed up until two in the morning writing this paper. My mother's sick and my sister had a baby. Her idiot boyfriend knocked her up and now he's living in Utica with some other bitch! I go home for one day and it's someone yelling here, someone crying there." She looked down at the paper and shook her head. "I just . . . I just . . . What's the use?" she said and started to cry.

I grabbed a box of tissues on my desk ("Essential!" the department chair had told me when I first arrived) and handed it to her. "Mel, the fragment's not a judgment. It's a fragment. You fix it, and you go on." I pointed out how putting "Jones's comment suggests" in place of "proving" made it a sentence. She seemed to think it was too easy a solution but accepted it nevertheless.

"Maybe the problem here is in the *proving*," I said. "You've got that word hanging out there as if your entire paper rests on making this one point. So you mistook it for the subject." I was speaking a language, though, of which she understood little. I tried again. "There are two places I've seen an attempt at proving anything: geometry, with things like the equal sides of an isosceles triangle, and theology, with the existence of God. I have to put my money on the theologians," I said, "or they'll fire me. But the point is we're not talking about mathematicians and theologians. We're talking about having a good idea, and making it a better one."

She wiped her glasses with another tissue and said, still somewhat frustrated, "But isn't that what we're supposed to be doing, *proving* that what we have to say is *right*?"

"Well, Dr. Taylor might take me to task on this in his logic course, but for right now, I don't expect you to prove anything. Or at least I'm not asking you to. What we're supposed to be thinking about is how best to express the ideas we're beginning to formulate. If you and another student were having a conversation about, say, stronger child support laws, or the importance of understanding an unwed mother's emotional as well as economic well-being, you would decide how best to present the strongest argument, present it, then suggest why your views are worth serious consideration. Because you care about them, right? If you were to write up that conversation, I would consider whether your views came from good sources, were presented with good reasoning, and sounded as though you cared about them."

She was sitting up in the chair now. "I like that emotional and economic thing," she said. "My sister's so screwed up, and I end up giving her money that I need for school. I could write about that?"

"Sure. You should probably leave your sister out of it, but the details would make for a fantastic research topic. It might help you to understand some things. You know, get a different perspective, without feeling as though there's something you have to prove."

"I can prove there's a jerk-off living in Utica," she said.

"I'm sure you could, but that would be too easy, wouldn't it?"

This was why I came to love teaching at Le Moyne.

After my having left the world as an adult, then spending five years as a novice and a "schoolboy," the return to adulthood in this sixth year—teaching, being respected by colleagues, having an identity— gave me a boost of happiness and resolve, in spite of conflicting feelings I had about how bad or ineffectual I would be as a full-time college instructor, which had beset me ever since I got the letter from the provincial making my assignment official. But once I stood in front of those classes, myself a version of Hopkins's "matchwood" dressed in a clerical collar (for the first few weeks) and looking far younger than my thirty-two years, I stopped wondering if I had found the right community or call. I was happy doing what I was doing for the first time in a long time.

Even though I was split half-time between philosophy and English, each department got its side of the bargain. I taught a full load of four courses in the fall semester and three in the spring. Fall consisted of two sections of English Composition (twenty students per section with an essay due every Friday) and two sections of Introduction to Western Thought (forty students per section, with two essays, a midterm, and a final exam. Remember that flight instructor?).

The composition courses were labor intensive but enjoyable in a problem-solving sort of way. Although I was a merciless stickler on things like fragments, agreement, proper use of the semicolon, I was so because I knew that most students hadn't gone through that novitiate of English grammar on their own. If I didn't say, "This is a run-on," or "This is a fragment," someone else would have to. And when it came time for a job cover letter? The Jesuits at least, I thought to myself, should oblige. But I had also remembered Robert Pirsig in the classroom in *Zen and the Art of Motorcycle Maintenance*. The problems aren't necessarily solved by reciting the rules. There has to be some conviction that you can teach *quality*, or what I had been calling "beauty." It came to me one Saturday morning, three weeks into the semester, when a large, native brown trout, dappled with black spots across a background of autumn red and bronze, rose and took the fly I had drifted above it in a pool on Chittenango Creek. There has to be some *beauty* in it for these students, I thought, knowing that I would spend the entire evening and all day Sunday commenting on their poorly conceived compositions. If there isn't, they'll find nothing in this stripping down and building back up of their own language but resentment, infantilism, and loss. I released the fish back into its Syracuse waters and went home to think about how I could make English 101 a beautiful thing.

Which, in the end, I don't believe for a minute I ever succeeded in doing. My classes were a curiosity to some (reading Rebecca West and the prologue to *Black Lamb and Grey Falcon*, Hopkins's poetry next to sections of the *Spiritual Exercises*, a Tobias Wolff short story and a passage from *This Boy's Life*, all writing that I admired) and a required annoyance to others. After the poor attendance, the plagiarisms, and the office cries of "I don't *get* it," few gathered up their fragments and laid them out to make sense of what rules, order, and beauty lay therein. But, if for only a few, I decided, all right then.

Teaching philosophy was yet a greater challenge. I tried to make it my own by relying on the seminar style of learning I had experienced at St. John's College. A reading was assigned, students were expected to complete it (at St. John's we seemed to spend more time reading than breathing), and then the class sat around a table and set off on a conversation that began with one opening question. Something like this: "What is *justice?*"

At Le Moyne, with close to forty students in a class that sped through work from Plato to Descartes in four months, it was hard to maintain any semblance of a discussion atmosphere. I did what I could, covering the chalkboard with key words, diagrams of Socrates' arguments throughout various chapters, and (anathema at St. John's) the purpose of the Allegory of the Cave. The students did their best to follow, and the tenacity of the examined life prevailed. I spent most of the time on Plato's *Republic*, believing that if you had this text under your belt, you could honestly say you had been introduced to philosophy. But we also puzzled over Aristotle's *Ethics*. We considered Aquinas's five proofs for the existence of God on our own terms (atheism and conservatism slugging it out among those freshmen who, for the first time in their lives, didn't have their parents telling them what to believe). And Descartes stumped everyone who thought *Meditations* meant we'd be studying Buddhism. But the thread of the questions was clear, if the answers were not: Who are we? What ought we to do with this life? Is there something rather than nothing? And why, in the end, should it even matter? If only those students knew, then, that I was as wracked to find the answers for myself as they were to find the answers for the exam. Because I was approaching the most difficult final exam of my life. I knew I could pass it. What I didn't know was if I wanted to take it.

I always hoped that from the steady population of slightly older undergraduates at Le Moyne, who had come to college after some time "out in the world" (a noble trademark of the school), a handful would sign up for my philosophy sections. And they came. Like hybrids of the Holy Spirit and the gadfly, they came, sitting up front, answering questions because they had something to say, asking questions because they wanted something *more* to say, and in the end making me hope I never told them anything that wasn't true. I needed them because I needed to know that the questions mattered, and that sometimes you had to accept that what you once thought whole was a fragment. So the only thing to do was go back to square one and make sense of a new direction.

Like Michelle and Lisa, who showed up on the first day of class that fall and stared suspiciously at the awkward and too-serious-looking young man dressed in priestly clerics in front of thirty-eight other first-year students.

I, too, was pigeonholing them. Fit, good-looking women wearing designer tees and snug jeans that sat below bare midriffs, long hair tucked underneath baseball caps, their voices identifiably Syracusan from the learned flat *a*. What could they have to say? Yet all semester they questioned and prodded, wrote and worked out answers. Lisa was intimidating without being overbearing to the other students in the class, and, I'll admit, I encouraged it. She works too hard not to be allowed a voice, I thought. Michelle was quieter, although the better writer. She spoke when I asked her a question directly, and then everyone listened.

At midterm and the end of the semester before the final, I held a series of question-and-answer study groups. Students could ask in an informal setting anything they wanted about what we had gone over during the semester. It was a Socratic way of answering the all-consuming philosophical question: What's going to be on the exam?

Michelle and Lisa came for the last session; they both worked and could afford only one night off. Michelle wanted to ask about the composition of souls in Plato's *Republic*. Gold for the philosophers, silver for their auxiliaries, and bronze for the guardians. She took notes quietly and then asked why, in the Allegory of the Cave, Socrates says the philosopher faces genuine danger.

"Because Plato believed philosophy was a matter of life and death," I said. "He had witnessed the trial that condemned Socrates." If she was asking this much, the difficulty of the exam was not an issue for her. I threw this out hoping it might spark a discussion. Michelle looked down and kept on writing. Someone else asked, "Do we have to know all five ways of proving there is a God? I mean, like, why do we need to know more than one? I'm a Catholic, not some tree worshiper."

As we were leaving the library for the evening, and I wished the students luck in all their exams, Lisa thanked me for making the course tough for them. "I knew from the first day that we were in for it. You looked like one mean Jesuit."

"If only you knew," I said.

Michelle asked me how long I'd be at Le Moyne and where I would go after that. I explained what I could about the process. "Didn't you both tell me during an office visit that you were getting married over the holidays?" I asked, turning the conversation away from what I wasn't doing.

"I am!" Lisa said. "The Saturday before Christmas." I congratulated her. Michelle looked as though she was hoping I wouldn't pursue the question with her. But I did.

"Well," she said. "I kind of had to call it off." Lisa, who had known all about it, put her arm around Michelle and whispered, "It's okay, babe."

"I'm sorry. The two of you seemed happy to be planning your weddings so close together."

"We were, but it's for the better," Michelle said with a stoic front. "I've learned a few things in the past few months. And the toughest was that my boyfriend's soul isn't gold or silver, or bronze." She looked over at Lisa and smiled. "It's tin." She wasn't gloating. She didn't look sad. Then they both wished me a Merry Christmas, and I told them not to be strangers.

Cura personalis, care of the whole person, wasn't something the Jesuits had a monopoly on as teachers. I had learned it from my teachers, and I'd never stepped foot in a Catholic school until I entered a religious order. Such care was more universally that constant search for narratives and their elements—fragmented and unfinished—that might somehow be useful and wonderful.

What made it my own as a Jesuit was the turn from the nuts and bolts of English and philosophy to the "composition of place." After six years in religious life, I had settled on this habit of prayer: I would retreat at 4:15 every afternoon to the privacy of the chapel in the Jesuit Residence, where I remained until the loyal band of daily Mass goers arrived for liturgy at 5:15. I found my desire for contemplation in the overlapping hours of the private and the communal (a habit of religious life I maintain to this day). During that time I continued to practice the prayer of the names. I always had papers or my briefcase with me. Rather than drop everything outside the chapel and enter into a forced silence, I took in whatever I was carrying, which inevitably meant all the students I was teaching that semester. There I would compose some likeness of person after person, questions and comments, searching and silent, my prayer turning into one of gratitude that I had found such worthy companions in my own ongoing formation. I had hopes for what I would become, fears of what the future might bring, but their hopes and fears seemed as interesting, pressing, and God-filled as mine. Sometimes the harder I prayed for them, the more I found peace in myself.

In spite of my happiness and enthusiasm, though, I caught a glimpse of some of the burdens that would come not just with teaching but with being a priest holding all of the names in an attitude of work and prayer as a man for others in communion with all. Not every name and its story is an attractive one, though it, too, wants to be wanted and cared for as much, if not more.

Midway into that semester, one of my philosophy students came into my office to ask about her failing grade on the first paper. Beth was the kind of student who was all but invisible in class, overweight, sullen, seemingly disengaged from everyone and everything around. Her paper was poorly reasoned and poorly written, a patchwork of the obvious. One of Hopkins's immortal diamonds, certainly, but I had given some guidelines on form and content, and she followed none of them.

Angry and upset because she had never been given a grade so low in her life, she tried to argue that she had written a fine paper. "Okay, a C maybe, but not failing!"

"The grade is more than fair." I stood my ground. "You need to work on clarifying your ideas, then bringing them together. Studying philosophy for the first time is difficult, Beth. Forget about the grade for now and start thinking about what Plato means by the Good, or why the Myth of Gyges is a catalyst to the argument of the *Republic*. Talk in class. Don't get mad, get curious."

Then I heard the fragments come crashing down. In a rush of tears she told me that because she wasn't thin and attractive, she lived a lonely, friendless life. She hated home, where she could never seem to shake off the role of ugly duckling, and had come to college thinking things would be different. They weren't. Her roommates ignored or made fun of her. She couldn't study. And now her grade in my class made her afraid that she might fail out.

I assured her that rough starts were to be expected, and that there was plenty of time to make this grade nothing more than a growing pain.

"I probably try too hard," she said, wiping away another flood of tears. "I want some friends. Is that too much to ask?"

I told her to keep up with the reading and try talking to other students in class. "If you're still struggling on your next paper, make an appointment to see me during office hours before you write it." In the meantime, I told her, if she felt increasingly ill at ease with her roommates or college life, there were people here trained to help her through things like that.

Visibly calmer, she thanked me and said, "I *am* going to get a good grade in this class."

The next week she came in with questions about a quiz. The day after that she came in again with her notes from class, asked if women could be philosopher kings (a question someone else had brought up), and then began to talk about her roommates.

"They hate me. One said I'm *fat*."

"You should go talk to someone about this," I advised. "Students shouldn't be harassing you like that."

"Oh, I'll be okay. I'm feeling better now that you've said I can come see you."

"Beth, I teach philosophy. I can't do anything about your roommates. You need to go see someone whose job it is to sort these things out for students."

"You're a Jesuit, aren't you?"

"Yes, but I'm not a professional counselor."

"But I felt so much better after I talked to you yesterday and last week. You were the first person who seemed to understand what I was going through. Can't you help me? I'd rather have you than someone else."

I felt a spooky tinge of fear. "If you have a question about philosophy, we can talk about it. Otherwise I can't be of any help."

"Well, I'll make it sound philosophical," she said.

I looked up at the clock. It was almost noon. "Listen, I have to be back at the Jesuit Residence for a special lunch today," I lied. I got up and started to collect my papers. She sat in her chair and watched. "So I'm going to have to leave." She got up grudgingly and walked out. I locked the door to my office and headed in the opposite direction.

That afternoon I called the counseling center myself and told them about a hypothetical student whose sense of boundaries might be a little unclear.

"What are you afraid of, Mr. Krivak?" the receptionist on the other end of the line asked.

"I don't know. I'm afraid she wants to get a little too close." So much for the hypothetical. "Not sexually. I mean, well, emotionally."

"Okay then. Keep your door open, keep a record of all her visits and what she says to you, and keep doing what you're doing."

"It's probably nothing," I said, feeling guilty about making a big deal out of some undergrad's own enthusiasm, "but I want to be sure."

"Of course you do," the receptionist said. It sounded patronizing to me.

"One more thing," I said. Never mind the guilt. I'm covering my bases. "What can I do if she acts more . . . odd?"

"Call security."

Beth came by Monday morning of the following week. She walked slowly up the hall and then appeared, as though framed, in the open door. "Hi. It's Philosophy. Can I come in?" After a simple question, she started to talk about her roommates. I stopped her in midsentence, reminded her of what I had told her last week, and said it might be better if she left. I asked colleagues in the offices to the right and left of me if they would be especially alert.

When Beth returned the next day, I got up to leave.

"Where are you going?" she asked, disappointment in her voice.

"Meeting."

Wednesday of that week I canceled my office hours. I went back in the afternoon but kept the door closed. The phone rang and rang, but I never answered.

On Friday afternoon, Beth called from her dorm room. This time I picked it up thinking it was a colleague with whom I was planning to go fishing. "Mr. Krivak? I came by to see you this morning, but you weren't in. I need to talk to you. It's the weekend. I'm feeling depressed and I don't know what to do."

"Beth, listen to me. If you have an issue with your roommates, you need to call the counseling center. I've talked to them already about what students having problems should do. They'll make an appointment as soon as possible and sort through things with you."

"I called them and went in to see someone already," she said. "Because you told me to, remember? And it was this mean old lady. Same questions. Home, school. I can't stand it. You *know* me. You *listen* to me. They don't. I want you to help. I need to see *you*."

Fear and anger rose in me like bile. Fear of what a person might do. Anger at having been dragged into something I wanted no part of. I tried to keep my cool. "I can't," I said.

"But you have to. I don't know if I can make it through the weekend without you. Can I call you?"

Without me? Where was this coming from? I thought, now in a panic. "No! I'm going away for the weekend."

I was about to hang up when she said, "I think I might kill myself."

The silence lingered. This was either great manipulation or the truth that she and I both feared. "Beth, I can call someone and have her come over to you right now if you're in trouble."

"Oh, you don't *want* to help," she screamed into the phone. "Just like all the others. I'm not pretty and so you won't help!" Then she slammed down the receiver.

Beth turned out to be all right, sort of. She wasn't suicidal, she wanted attention, this time from me. In the past, the same threat had worked on others. Yes, she was lonely, unattractive, and antisocial, but her roommates avoided her because she never said anything to them. They had never harassed her; they ignored her, not wanting to get dragged into something difficult. In the end, the school psychologist got her calmed her down enough to finish her classes.

And about a month later Beth poked her head into my office one last time. I tensed up, thinking to myself, Not again. But looking shy and sounding sincere, she said, "I wanted to tell you that Philosophy's doing better now." Then she set off down the hall, in care of her own person I supposed, leaving me with the humility of what the desire for that care meant. "Accounted as worthless and a fool . . . , rather than to be esteemed as wise and prudent in this world," Ignatius writes. "So Christ was treated before me."

In the spring, the English Department asked me to teach a seminar called Contemporary American Poetry. I greeted a new round of students in Philosophy 101. The workload slackened, slightly, and I began to feel as though I was accepted by my colleagues. Not that I hadn't felt accepted previously. It was, rather, as though they got used to the idea that I would be around them for two years. I remembered when I'd started to work at the boatyard on Cape Cod, after I had moved north from South Carolina. None of the other guys in the yard, outside the rigging loft, said anything to me the entire summer and fall. It wasn't until I was standing in front of the coffeemaker two days into the new year that one of the haulers asked me how my Christmas was. I wasn't sure he was talking to me until I realized there was no one else in the room.

"Quiet," I said.

"Yup. Just the way I like it. See ya 'round."

That was it, "See ya 'round," but it meant that he knew I wasn't some kid who'd work for a few months, then be gone forever. I'd be around.

It was like that at Le Moyne. And when my colleagues there went home to houses, families, partners, bills, worries about tenure, and the fallout of department politics, I went home to the Jesuits: Mass, a drink before dinner, a chef-prepared menu in the dining room of the residence, my suite in Nelligan, where I kept a CD player along with my guitar and slept on a futon, and my office, where, as Paul Simon used to sing, "I have my books and my poetry to protect me." I requested money for expenses from Father Minister. And I showed up for my benign check-ins with the superior. He told me once to ease up on my phone calls because my bill was so high. I pointed out that all the calls were to David, who had been sent to teach in Buffalo.

"I've got to stay connected to guys my age," I said. "What's the alternative? Spend the money on booze?"

"No, I understand," he said. "Just, uh, try to keep the calls a little shorter."

I saw David three times that year. Once in Buffalo, once in Syracuse, once at the halfway point in Rochester to ski. We were both buried under the workload of teaching, yet finding in it something creative, we told each other, that we felt we had lost in studies. But I could also see that this was going to be part of our "careers" as Jesuits. We'd no longer be in the same place at the same time, friends as well as brothers. Better to get used to that and move on.

There was one thing I did, though, that I insisted I would keep as my own. Every morning from six o'clock to nine I ignored everything academic and spiritual and sat down to write. No English Department, no philosophy, no office hours, no students, no Jesuit Residence, no Society of Jesus. Just a desk, a pad, a pencil, and a laptop. For three hours a day, every day. That's all I wanted it to be.

After I had gotten the news about "The Osprey," I began writing more. I separated the time from my prayer and looked for points during the day when I'd have a free hour or two to work on a poem with the intention of finishing it. I began reading regularly again. James Wright. Seamus Heaney. Les Murray. I had never stopped reading poetry, but now I was reading as I had when I was in the writing program at Columbia: to see the poem on the page as the poet saw the page. What is *this*, and why this form, these words set out in this way, rather than some line of prose? How might I make something beautiful?

As in the house of Lev Tolstoy, I wanted writing to be a part of my Jesuit apostolate. But I had already been turned away from the teaching position in Baltimore. When I asked if I could take some time during the summer to focus solely on writing, I was looked at suspiciously. The only apostolic work I had done with my summers since having entered the Jesuits was teach in the Higher Achievement Program in Buffalo. All of the others were taken up with study or travel.

"You want to write?" Jeff asked with some surprise the spring before I was to start at Le Moyne.

"I was thinking of going up to Cornwall on Hudson for the summer and staying at the retreat house."

"Here's what I recommend. Stay in the Bronx. Find an apostolate here. I'll ask the sister who runs St. Rita's Asian Center if she needs any teachers. And you can go up to Cornwall on the weekends."

Same old story, I thought. If you're not visibly engaged with a traditional apostolate, then you're not really working. Jeff did say to me later, as though to explain his decision, "You will write, AJ. One day. The Society has a great tradition of that, and I see it in you. But this is the time of formation." He was right. If I were out in the world, I'd be teaching all day and writing on weekends, if that, anyway. When summer came around, I spent weekdays teaching fourth-grade Vietnamese kids how to do fractions. On the weekends there was no car available to get to Cornwall. Just as well. The time spent on the road would have been time better spent at a desk right there in the Bronx. I discovered the ordinary problems of an ordinary person who wants to be an artist but can't seem to find a room of his own. I moved to Syracuse resigned that it was not likely the Jesuits would ever offer me the space to be creative. So I would have to build it myself. "Your obligation / is not discharged by any common rite," Seamus Heaney's father-as-Virgil intones in *Station Island*. "What you do you must do on your own." That's why I cast my mornings in stone and clung to the privacy of a room that was nothing more than a cell in a dormitory. It worked well, and I worked, too.

To this end. Back when I was a chaplain at St. Clare's Hospital in New York, I'd gone to hear Robert Fagles read from his new translation of the *Iliad*. Listening to him reminded me of poring over Homer in a sophomore Greek tutorial at St. John's, a place and time when I first understood what poetry could do. One of the poems I wrote in Syracuse that winter was meant to be an imitation of Keats's "On First Looking into Chapman's Homer." I sent it out with the title "On

Hearing Fagles's Homer." Months later, Rosemary Deen at *Common-weal* wrote back to me and said, "Why, it's *your* Homer, not Fagles's. I'll publish your poem if you say as much." I sent it back to her as "Reading Homer," and I heard what others have described as a call within the call, what I decided, regardless of how or where I lived my life of belief and trust, would be a call to "say as much."

With a month of classes left in the school year, I went to see a therapist again. I sent myself this time. Throughout the spring, all I could think about were the two magnetic poles of creativity and absence. I wasn't depressed or stuck. After a year of teaching, I remained consoled and content. I trusted that feeling, even if I wasn't exactly sure of its source. I wanted to go on with *this*. But I wasn't certain any longer what *this* was: the Jesuits, academia, solitude, community? All I could say was that something sounded disconnected when I tried to tell myself they could both come together as one identity. Could they? What I wanted to know, or hear myself say, was where I belonged.

Dr. Anthony Siena had been recommended to me by a friend teaching in the Psychology Department at Le Moyne. His area of expertise was marriage and family counseling. When I called him to set up an appointment, he sounded more like a spiritual director than a psychoanalyst. He knew the Jesuits. He was a Catholic himself and seemed to have a good sense of what I was hoping to discern.

I drove to his office on the edge of town for a 4:00 appointment in the middle of May. The empty gravel drive and prefabricated building had a feel more of public services than of private practice. I began to wonder if I had gotten the day wrong when a minivan pulled in behind me.

"Sorry I'm late," a thin, middle-aged Little League coach graying at the temples called through an open driver-side window. "Had to drop the kids."

Inside his office, there was no attempt at décor of any kind. We sat in solid wood chairs across from each other. The vision of the man now reminded me as much of spiritual direction as the voice.

He began with a recap from our phone conversation, emphasizing that I didn't feel any crises in my life, actual or impending, spiritual or otherwise.

I said, "I want to talk about a few things, and ask if you think you hear anything that sounds hollow. Anything that sounds as if I'm engaged with one while longing for another. Anything that doesn't sound . . . right."

"I see. You mean engaged with religious life, longing for . . ."

"Another."

He asked what I was thinking. "Another kind of life?"

"Why is it that I'm not sure I know anymore?"

I saw Tony (never Dr. Siena) for five sessions. We talked about my year, my studies in the Bronx that had preceded it, the feelings of depression—loss and what I referred to in front of him, too, as the lack of beauty—that had led me to counseling before, the intermittent thud of loneliness that I had come to accept as a Jesuit, the faith that kept me trying to live my vows, and the hope for what the future might bring.

"I bound out of bed every morning here," I told him one day, "the way I remember bounding out of bed when I worked in the boatyard, or when I was living in New York City, because I can't wait to see what the work will bring. How a poem might look or sound once I finish it. What a student will ask. What a colleague will say. What kind of peace or uncertainty I'll feel at the end of the day when I examine it. And then, there's the emptiness. The feeling that I'm not becoming what I had hoped for."

For four weeks Tony watched and listened, relaxed and attentive, like a veteran shortstop in front of a consistent right-handed hitter. He threw all of my questions back at me. "What do you do with that?" he'd ask. "We all have hopes that one day disappoint us. Why is this any different, do you think? Your life's quite blessed, it seems to me. Why do you feel as though you don't belong? Don't you want to belong?"

All good questions for any man to take a level swing at. I had little patience for the Jesuit who complained—sometimes bitterly—about life in the Society yet went along for the ride on a path of least resistance. It was fullness I wanted to live with, yet not necessarily the fullness of the many if that was what it came down to. *Better a dry crust with peace than a house full of feasting with strife,* Proverbs says. And so I listened to myself, wanting to be sure that it was my voice speaking, asking, prodding, and wondering—wondering, yes, why my life should be any different now after my having embraced the difference of these past six years and preparing now to begin a seventh.

On the fifth week, Tony let me go. To the question "Where do I belong?" he said that, in his experience, the answer is as much in the making as it is in the discovery. To my question "How much of the hope will remain?" he said, "There's no way to know." To my question "What do you hear?" he said, "I hear the honest search of an honest man. I think you should get on with it. Let me know how it all turns out."

When I'd left Moscow in 1994, I hadn't returned directly to New York. I made a stop in Prague, then backtracked into Slovakia, to the eastern town of Prešov and the village of Vit'az, where my mother's parents had grown up before the First World War. The journey is a chapter incidental to this story, except to say that, without the Jesuits, I never would have come to relate that distant past to my own present. If Russia held a place for me in my Jesuit future, it would have to be by way of another return to that country, in some capacity I was unable to imagine. But I believed that I hadn't turned east for nothing. So two years later I asked to spend a summer in Bratislava, to study Slovak, witness the rebirth of an Eastern Catholicism on its own ancient soil, and see how another community of Jesuits lived out their vocations at a time when I was questioning my own. It was the superior of the Le Moyne community at the time, Father Blake, who obliged. "Why don't you go do something for the summer that your formation assistant would never let you do on his own dime?" he said.

In June 1996, the Jesuit Residence in Prague buzzed with the kind of activity that made it seem like any other community at work. Two years prior, the city of Kafka, Kundera, and Havel really did have an unbearable lightness of being to it. A priest named František and two scholastics named Vaclav and Tomás, in a spirit of Jesuit as well as

Slav camaraderie, took me to the Konvikt Pub in Old Town, where we talked about the newly split Czechoslovakia, they wondering if there'd ever been such a country in anything more than name. The dark, heady beer we drank glass after glass of made me loopy with a wistful pride that I could call myself brother to these men after having been so quickly dismissed by others in Russia. I looked for them again when I arrived at the residence attached to the Church of St. Ignatius Loyola on Ječná in Prague's New Town. But František now ran a large parish in Moravia. Vaclav was studying theology in Paris, where he would be ordained soon. And Tomás was working at a Catholic publication for his regency.

I didn't stay long in Prague. The next day, jet-lagged but energized by the momentum of the trek ahead, I boarded the 11:39 train for Bratislava. I slept fitfully and woke near the town of Brno. From the windows of the train, the city (I had read) that was once proposed as a provincial capital because of its location midway between the Czech lands and Slovakia looked as though it was struggling with its own newfound growth and freedom. I mentioned this to a Czech passenger in the car with me, and he said he had heard that the downtown was experiencing a great deal of new development, but he wasn't sure if this was true. After twenty minutes we pulled away.

The countryside of Moravia, as it slips from the Czech Republic and into Slovakia, is simply beautiful, and I use the word *simply* as it ought to be used. Nothing dramatic, demanding, or sublime. Farms, a few castle-studded hills, patches of forest and the flash of creeks and small rivers, the stuff of a God-created order nurtured by human hands. After Brno, the Czech border guards changed places with the Slovaks, uniforms of steely blue with black trim giving way to olive drab and red. There was a quick passport check in the Slovak town of Kuty, and then the train ducked into the woods, emerged at the foot of the Maly Tatras, and followed the southeasterly drop of the Danube River basin into Bratislava, the stunted, poor cousin to Prague.

I had missed Bratislava when I visited eastern Slovakia in '94, so I didn't know what to expect. I feared that my summer would turn out the way it had in Moscow, cut off, struggling to fit into a community of brothers who wanted little if anything to do with me. But somehow, too, I was able to reject that as not likely, for the Slovak Jesuits—as well as the Czechs—had worked defiantly and secretly during the years of Communism. These men weren't outsiders setting up something new in an inhospitable place. They were leaders within a community of faith in their own land, believers who now could show their faith with impunity.

I had thought a lot about Slovakia since I had been here last. During the Velvet Revolution, everyone had cheered on a country that they understood largely to be Czech. And it was. After the split, Slovakia was an unknown quantity in the West, if it was any quantity at all. When the war in the Balkans blew up, in 1993, friends of mine in New York wanted to know if I'd ever thought of going there to fight for my fellow Slovenians. Jesuits I knew who had studied history thought I was going to the former Yugoslavia for the summer. And I'd still come across the occasional article, often in a major newspaper, in which the writer referred to "Czechoslovakia" without the qualifier *former*. Slovaks had emerged from World War II with a battered image for their support of Hitler, who'd made Slovakia a puppet state run by a priest, Father Josef Tiso, and their nearly entire deportation of Slovak Jews. Living in the middle of Europe and remaining essentially invisible explains in part, however, some of the more nationalistic sins of the Slovaks, especially in the twentieth century. But the country and its people—five and a half million, 60 percent of whom are Catholic—now seemed to want to accept their past as something at best less than glorious, at worst downright barbaric, and move on as a country within a continent that's no stranger to barbarism. The Slovaks know (like any Slav) that memory can be a powerful sword wielded in the name of nationalism. As Christians, they also know that forgiveness has to come with another's willingness to forget a past by changing the present.

The Jesuit Institute of St. Aloysius Gonzaga in Bratislava sits across from the president's palace and adjacent to a museum in the Old Town square. Here traffic is excluded. None of the buildings seem newer than the early nineteenth century. This was real estate any European would be envious of, and yet it seemed like everyday Slovakia. Few people were recognizably tourists. Most dressed and looked like Slovaks—men in browns and grays; women wearing colorful and revealing silk blouses and skirts—coming from work, going to dinner, taking a shortcut home, or avoiding a crowded tram. In some ways, Prague now seemed like a city of tourists and few surprises compared with this tiny, rough-cut gem that rarely got a second look from anyone on his way to Vienna or Budapest.

My room was an open flat on Panska, a former bishop's residence above a fifteenth-century chapel in what might once have been a cloister. The chapel remained under renovation. The building was nearly complete as a new Jesuit residence. I had a writing desk, a bed, and a nightstand. I lacked only hot water, as it was the last thing the builders were connecting, and I was the first one ever to stay in this room. I went five days without bathing until I couldn't stand myself (though no one else seemed to mind). I discovered a tub in another wing of the residence, turned on the spigot, and the water came out hot enough to make tea. That night I returned, locked the door, and bathed for one luxurious hour. The next day the minister saw to it that my own bathroom had hot water.

Although I said I had come here with the purpose of learning the language and seeing Eastern Catholics on their own turf, I slowly realized that what I wanted to do was some anthropological "deep hanging out." More than that, though. I was looking for the validation of this life that I'd found when I journeyed "east" with my father into the churches and mining towns of Pennsylvania. I came hoping to find some of that same enthusiasm as I now approached ordination to the priesthood, something I could point to and say, "That's it."

My knowledge of Russian allowed me to pick up Slovak grammar as though it were second nature to me. All I had to do was study vocabulary and practice sentence formation. I enrolled in a Slovak course at Comenius University, tested into the third out of four levels, and sat for five days a week under a waterfall of language instruction entirely in Slovak. I was one in a class of six.

A week into my stay, Father Holub, the minister in the community, asked me if I'd be interested in visiting a part of the city few non-

Slovaks ever see. An old Jesuit who had lived alone in an apartment on the outskirts of town, and acted secretly as a priest during Communism, had died in his sleep that week. The landlady found him when, for the first time in fifty years, he hadn't stirred by five o'clock in the morning in his one-room, second-floor flat.

Seven of us (I was the odd one out) drove in an old panel truck to a suburb northeast of the city, though I lost my bearings and couldn't say exactly where we were. When we got out, the neighborhood reminded me of a place in Moscow where I had gone with Richard to visit a family that had reached out to Caritas. The same stale smell of diesel seemed to have replaced oxygen in the air. Auto mechanics kept a shop in the front yard of the building next to the priest's. Two men watched us as we piled out of the van—one sitting and drinking a beer at 11:00 in the morning, the other turning away from an engine dangling precariously on a tripod—to consider who might have come here in such numbers. They turned back to their nonlabor when the old woman came out to greet us. She gave Father Holub a kiss on the cheek and began to cry once again for the loss of the old priest who, when he wasn't sneaking out somewhere to say Mass, had worked here in obscurity, studying Italian, Polish, and English, reading Teilhard de Chardin and books on the Catechism, and otherwise filling his solitude with prayer.

Inside the flat, a learned man's life was frozen in time, right down to the dentures and reading glasses resting on the top of a chest of drawers. His personal items would be distributed to friends. The Jesuits were there to collect his books for their growing library. As we worked, our own sweat and the dust motes that lifted into the air from shelves and bindings made the fusty room smell like a standoff between tenacity and resignation. It was a rancid smell of perspiration that comes from an all-meat diet. In a few hours we loaded the van and left.

The following weekend, as though every priest who died in this country would be replaced by three, I went to two ordination liturgies (the first Mass a new priest says), one of twin brothers, the other of an older man who, after years of manual labor, had returned to school in the hope (with what time he had left) of becoming a Jesuit.

The Saba brothers came from Handlová, which a recent census determined had the highest percentage of atheists in Slovakia. Handlová is a town in the mountains to the northeast of Nitra. The spire of the church rises above broad green fir trees in the village center. On the day its sons returned as priests, the church was filled to capacity, making either a joke or a lie of the people's statistical lack of faith. I was pulled into the choir loft to sing and didn't protest. It struck me then, and throughout my stay in Slovakia, that the Slovaks have a reverence for music that rivals the more visible musical fame of the Czechs and the Viennese. Whether or not they were atheists, music must have been the one thing during Communism that offered the possibility of transcendence and the celebration of difference, in the way that composers, musicians, and vocalists know what it is to feel one note against another.

The other liturgy was in the northern town of Kežmarok, near the city of Poprad in the High Tatras. The mountains were still snow-capped in June, their sheer summits rising well above the tree line. One of the Jesuits pointed out the unmistakable Kriváň peak to me as we drove. "There's your mountain," he said. I knew that *krivý* meant "crooked." The Kriváň is "curved." But I didn't know that it's the centerpiece of Slovakia's High Tatras.

Mass was in a village church that could barely hold fifty people. Most of the worshipers stood outside and listened to the liturgy as it poured through loudspeakers set up for the occasion. Ján, the new priest, had some sort of handicap or injury that required him to walk with a cane. He had a disposition, though, that seemed to be a cross between grief and what the Russians call *nechayannaya radost*, "unexpected joy." What else surprised me about this village was the number of Slovak Roma who had showed up for the Mass. I had seen gypsies from a distance two years ago. In the East, most Slovaks speak of them disparagingly or dismiss them. In Kežmarok, though, they seemed as eager to welcome and celebrate with "our priest" as Ján's immediate and extended family. They carried with them their own unexpected joy. After the liturgy, several approached Ján for his blessing, and he embraced them all.

When we returned that evening, after detours to drop off Jesuits in Ružomberok, Nitra, and Trnava, Bratislava already felt like home. My summer began to cohere to its own quotidian rhythms. When I wasn't in class, reading in the library upstairs in the institute, or at table in the Jesuit Residence, I ventured out on my own to concerts, cafés, curious neighborhoods, once a small dinner party held by a couple from the American embassy, where we discussed Rebecca West and the Balkans (I loved that modernist's classic travel narrative *Black Lamb and Gray Falcon*, and could find few people who had read it), and Vienna, where I had to go one weekend in order not to overstay my thirty-day passport stamp. When all was quiet, I sat on a quayside bench overlooking the Danube River, watching the cruise boats navigate the swift current and listening to Radio Devin on an FM transistor I had brought with me in hopes of training my ear to the uniquely long accented vowels that make Slovak the most melodic of the otherwise hard Slavic languages.

Toward the end of July, I was invited to go with a group of music students from the choir at St. Ignatius Church to a forest park outside of Bratislava. No reason. It was a beautiful Sunday. One of the younger priests overheard the invitation and said I shouldn't miss it. "Your Slovak is quite good now, Andrew. And these young people are as curious about you as you are about them. Go. It will be good for all of you." So eight of us got on a bus that dropped us off at the gates of what looked like the entrance to a state park, where we strolled for the afternoon, stopping to kick a soccer ball, test swings that were too small for us, and indulge in flavored ice.

And we talked, for hours, occasionally in a few words of English, but mostly in patient Slovak. I *had* learned that much. What did they want to know? What is New York like? Why are Americans fat? (In response to which I pointed out three large young Slovak men, one wearing a New York Giants shirt.) Why did I want to come to Slovakia? And, finally, What made me decide to become a Jesuit?

This last question was asked by a lynx-eyed young woman named Andrea, who clung to the arm of her boyfriend, Jaro, with an affection that made me, and I'm certain a few other men, jealous. The question should be a matter of finding the right vocabulary, I thought. I can say this, and I can say it in Slovak. But when the words I managed to utter—"God," "faith," "searching"—sounded too empty or adrift from the real narrative, I stared blankly at her and said, *"Ne viem."* "I don't know."

What I didn't know, then, was that Jaro was listening patiently to my silence. "I understand," he said, as though I had in fact explained to everyone's satisfaction, and in Slovak, why it was I had become a Jesuit, and why I wanted yet to be a priest.

At first I didn't hear him, so I just smiled and nodded, as though we were both assenting to the theological mystery of it all.

"I mean that I was a Jesuit, too," he said.

I looked at him with surprise, then over at Andrea. "You were?"

"He left in his philosophy studies," Andrea said. "A year ago." Jaro seemed bashful, yet proud that his girlfriend should answer for him.

I was thrown into the same power of questioning that the others had felt toward me, the mix of curiosity and incredulity. He could see it coming. "So why did you leave?" I asked.

He gave a short laugh, suddenly handsome and commanding as he said with a clarity he couldn't have practiced, "I didn't want to be a priest."

"A priest? Or a Jesuit?" I asked.

"It becomes the same life. You should know that. I loved the studies, I loved the community of men, but I couldn't love it all the time, and I didn't want to." Then he said in controlled and correct English, "Many people in Catholic countries think that religious life is the top of a great mountain. We are called to climb, and so we climb. If we leave, it's as though we have fallen. I didn't want to stop believing. I just didn't want to work as a priest. And, Andrew, I didn't fall. I go to church. I sing in the choir. I've gone back to school. I'm happy." He took Andrea's hand. "Who knows what's next?"

And I felt humbled for what I had questioned and tested in my own vocation. I once had his clarity, the resolve and desire to say, I will *do* this. And I wanted it again.

One week before I had to return to the United States, I traveled back to Eastern Slovakia with a fellow Jesuit scholastic of the Eastern Rite named Vasil. The trip was a long one. Slovakia is a small but decentralized country. We went first by train to Poprad in the north, then transferred to a local connection for Stará Ľubovňa. As we left the station in the first of two small cars, I realized we were surrounded by a family of Roma who had settled peacefully into the slow rocking of the World War II–era car. An old man drooped with sleep while the woman I guessed was his wife peeled an apple. A young mother with dark, windburned skin and almond eyes (she couldn't have been more than sixteen) held an infant to her naked breast. The child fed voraciously, and drops of milk spotted the girl's floral print dress. She never looked away from the face of her baby, as though there was no one else in the world. I was mesmerized by her beauty and her composure. Two children stood on the seats and stared out of the windows. They were pointing and speaking rapidly in a language I couldn't understand. So I looked in the same direction and saw a red fox running through the newly mown farmlands along with the train. It kept up with us for about twenty or thirty yards, then fell behind as we pulled away.

Vasil watched me watching them and seemed irritated by both the breast-feeding mother and the animated children. "They are gypsies," he said to me in English, "you know?" He giggled nervously. "They'll get off at the next stop. Don't fall asleep."

From Stará Ľubovňa we took the bus to Prešov for an ordination liturgy it seemed the entire city had been talking about at the Greek Catholic Cathedral of St. John the Baptist. This was the home of the Rusyns in Slovakia, the "tribe" my father's father had come from. The Catholic seminary and cathedral in which the ordination was being held were given to the Orthodox during Communism, then returned to the Catholic Rusyns in 1990. (When I'd been here in 1994, it was all under construction.) When the Orthodox left, Vasil said, having heard over and over again the story that has now become legend, they took everything that wasn't nailed or bolted down, including the copper wiring in the walls. As soon as we arrived and Vasil greeted the rector of the community, we were asked to be acolytes.

The ceremony was an exhausting affair for which we were required to stand most of the time. By the end of it, I had to urinate so badly I nearly passed out. But I had a glimpse of the sublime and in-effable that emissaries of Prince Vladimir of Kiev were said to have experienced listening to this same liturgy at Hagia Sophia in tenth-century Constantinople. Those who heard the strains of the choir didn't know if they were in heaven or on earth. Is that what this life is going to be? I thought to myself as I watched the two *ordinandi* lie down prostrate before the bishop of Prešov: beautiful and painful? Then I looked to the right of them and saw a young woman in the front pew with (I guessed) her father and mother. She had those pre-cipitously high cheekbones of every girl in Slovakia, full black hair tied back to accent them, and sloe eyes. She was crying. Vasil noticed her, too, gave me a nudge, said in a whisper, "That's his wife," and pointed to one of the new priests on the floor. While the other man had chosen to remain celibate, this one had decided to marry before he got ordained a Catholic priest, as one may do in the East.

That week, my last in Slovakia, I had heard the Divine Liturgy in Bratislava, Prešov, Stará Ľubovňa, and Litmanova, in a cathedral, a city church, and two small village chapels the names of which I never recorded, and sung in a language most Eastern Catholics would never hear in their lifetimes. I couldn't say that these sounds had become part of my prayer, but they were beautiful and tenacious enough to become part of my memory. Yet I had to accept that, while it was the Jesuits who had brought these voices to me, it was becoming increas-ingly clear that this direction, this theology, was considered an exoti-cism, "smells and bells," and if I wanted to be taken seriously in my own province I had better leave them right here, in the country that was no more exotic to me than Scranton, Pennsylvania.

Slovakia would never be a place I'd be sent to as a Jesuit. I knew that. The country had plenty of priests, and the numbers were grow-ing. In the United States, the numbers were dropping like lemmings into the sea. I wasn't sure I'd get a chance to study, even peripherally, the Eastern Rites for theology, and so wouldn't be ordained for a mission among Rusyns here or in the States. There were schools, parishes, and retreat houses in my own province that needed men far more desperately. *"Dveri, dveri, premudrostiju vonmim."* "The doors, the doors, in wisdom let us be attentive," the priest calls on the people attending the Divine Liturgy before the consecration of the "holy gifts for holy people." However beautiful and soulful it all sounded and felt, however widely it had opened me up to a corner of my faith that would have remained shut had I not been attentive and tried those doors, it would forever remain far from me.

Perhaps there's another story about Slovakia I'll need to tell for myself one day. As a Jesuit, though, I decided that I had come this far so that I could say goodbye, and then *go forth in peace*. From the East, that is, but not yet from the notion that I had been called to be a priest. One added a spiritual dimension of discovery to my life, the other was meant to be the basis on which that life would be defined.

Vasil had become a difficult traveling companion, severe and unpredictable in his mood swings. Peas in a tribal pod, we were, but he and I parted ways in Košice, the second-largest city in Slovakia, a few miles north of the Hungarian border. I got on a train for Bratislava. Vasil returned to Stará Ľubovňa. And two days later, August 5, 1996, I left Slovakia, writing in my journal that "in Kuty, near the Maly Tatras, I smelled autumn and felt the change and transition of travel upon me, the crossing of a border. Not this month, perhaps not this year (I am looking forward to another semester). But soon. Like that faint odor of woodsmoke in the air."

Advancing to a stage of formation in the Jesuits requires a vetting that's done through what are called *informationes*. The provincial sends around to various members of the province questionnaires about the scholastic: "What's your assessment of the candidate up to this point?" "Is he a good Jesuit?" "Does he live the vows?" "Should he be, in your opinion, allowed to move to the next stage of formation in the Order?" If I was considered a nonconformist among the Jesuits, a "fringer," I was one who also tried to make others on the fringe feel welcome, a team player even if I asked what the game was before participating, a contemplative in action who veered more to the contemplative than to the active. But my superiors and contemporaries alike seemed to understand and accept these honest quirks. There was no reason to suspect that I wouldn't be given the green light to begin my studies for ordination.

I remember reading once that afterthought is the writer's blessing, and curse. After my first year at Le Moyne, the editor of *America* magazine wanted to know if I would like to move to New York for my second year of regency and work on staff. It was a generous and tempting offer, but when I discussed it with the formation assistant, we both decided that another year of teaching and living in the same community would be good for me. I wanted to return to the classroom with what I'd learned the year before, so I stayed in Syracuse.

That fall a priest came to the community to replace a Jesuit who had gone to teach elsewhere. He was in his fifties, average height and build, hirsute and owlish. He was known as something of a scholar and, more important, would have a say as a *formator* in the final decision for or against my moving on to theology. In spite of the marked difference in age between us, he sidled up to me right away, clearly wanting to make some friends there in the North Country. I understood the feeling and so obliged when he was looking for someone to join him for a movie, a pint, or a day out at Cazenovia. Something about his attention, though, always made me feel a little uneasy, as though I had seen it somewhere before.

One day he asked if I would give him a ride to the airport. When we were walking down the stairs to the cars, I mentioned something about the irony of having a fleet of them. Believing, I guess, that humor signaled camaraderie, he opened the door to the garage with a gesture to go ahead and then patted me on the ass as I walked by.

I was stunned but silent. It was a short drive across town. I dropped him off and asked another Jesuit when I got home if he could make the return run in a few days' time. Later I decided the incident was probably something he already regretted.

Still, I remembered the words of a psychologist who gave a group of us new regents a crash course in managing our lives outside the classroom. "Make a note of anything strange, or anything that makes you uncomfortable, and *always* tell someone else about it." So I mentioned this to my spiritual director, who told me to tell the assistant, and to keep him apprised. I did both. Life went on.

You're wondering, no doubt, how naïve I could have been to believe that life in a climate like this could "go on," as though these things happened all the time. Regardless of bad press and blatant misrepresentations of religious life, though, they don't. After having lived in Jesuit communities around the world, I was shocked by this anomaly but led to believe I had handled it as well as anyone might. Nothing untoward. Misplaced enthusiasm. And as I look back, I realize that this wasn't the case of an older gay man seeking the affections of a younger man. It was the result of what happens when any man—long past the midway point in his journey—has never faced the fact that we may stand to lose more than we could ever possibly gain.

The homosexual male is a fact of life in every religious order. By that I don't mean that men are having sex with men because they're all thrown together into a place of "silence," or that the real problems of pedophilia are rooted in a gay priesthood. These are unfortunate caricatures and prejudices. More realistically, the gay Catholic priests and seminarians whom I've known have found, in addition to their desire to preach the Gospel and serve a community of believers, a natural affinity to religious life. They mourn the sacrifice of physical intimacy as much as any heterosexual man. But their gain is a spiritual *and* emotional intimacy among other men, which is, not surprisingly, going to be stronger than a heterosexual male finds in that same environment, or I should say stronger than what I found myself capable of.

While seminaries and religious orders are certainly not meant to be places of active homosexuality, they are by design homo-*social* communities. Men live their lives with other men. The difference is the commitment of vows, which direct men not to one another but to work and prayer, "in friendship and communion with *all*." In the psychology of loss, one might argue that gay men seem well suited for religious life. The Catholic Catechism states, "Homosexual persons are called to chastity." And what is a man with religious vows called to if not to that? When the "act" of sex is sublimated through prayer and living the vows (something many men, gay and straight, find fulfilling), sexuality shouldn't keep a person from pursuing this path toward what the Catechism also insists is the desire of all persons: Christian perfection. Only a man who knows himself can accept with equanimity and humility the fact of what is lost and what is gained in life. So I believed then, and so I believe now. The Church shouldn't be asking of her priests, "Are you a heterosexual, or are you a homosexual?" The Church should be asking, "Do you know yourself well enough to live these vows?" That's, in the end, what I had to ask myself.

Two weeks later I was standing at the mailboxes reading a letter.

"Anything good?" I heard a confident voice say as it literally sneaked up from behind. I could smell coffee on the breath, it was so close.

"Letter from home," I said. "Local stuff." I turned away and took a step to make it clear I didn't want to engage.

"Well, don't let them think you've gone to the missions," he said and, walking past, reached out a hand and slapped my backside.

I'm a man with a slow fuse. I consider and reconsider before I do something I might regret later, unless I can see my regret so clearly that its recurrence would be more of a curse than a blessing. I bounded up the stairs to his room, knocked on the door, and pushed it open. He was at his desk, reading glasses perched on his nose. "AJ, what's—"

And before he could finish I said, "If you ever touch me like that again, I will rip your fucking head off and *mail* it to the provincial." I was shaking as I spoke, but I forced myself to stand firm and not show any weakness.

"I'm sorry. I—"

"Just don't," I said, and left.

The next day I received a letter of apology ("I knew when I heard the knock that it was you, and that you were angry . . ."), and for the next couple of months he seemed repentant. I told the formation assistant about this second incident, though I realized much later that the assistant thought I was merely recounting for him, again, the first, and so he didn't seem to think anything was wrong, even wondering out loud why I should be concerned. My spiritual director said, "Be careful."

For the next few months I kept my distance. This behavior *was* unusual, and I didn't know at the time if it was I, personally, he'd taken a liking to or if he was helplessly awkward, clueless, and lonely. But distance is hard to maintain in a small community. Like when you are growing up in a big family, you learn acceptance; you can't avoid someone all the time. He had a say in my future, for chrissakes. If he was asking, I'd have to offer some form of forgiveness. Gradually my coldness thawed. Outwardly I was obliging, visibly friendly, and although this later came back to haunt me, I believed that he understood those unspoken, appropriate boundaries, as well as my justified anger. He wanted to learn how to cross-country ski and asked me to teach him. He began a policy of taking every scholastic in the community out to dinner for a check-in. When he had an extra ticket to a Chekhov production in Syracuse, of course he asked the Russian speaker if I'd like to join him. And so I did, because there seemed to be no more weird, presumptive behavior about him, although it never occurred to me to ask why he had an extra ticket in the first place.

You see, the other fact of religious life is power. For all of the Christ-like humility with which we tried to live—and teach—there remained this real and unavoidable human will. It comes as a necessity within a hierarchy and is tempered by the personal insight of those to whom it's given. That's why it's given to so few. And, for better or for worse, power was given to that man that year, and there was nothing else I could do. How cowardly now to think that I played into the fact that I needed him not to be angry with me because I didn't want there to be any question about my suitability for ordination and further studies. So I forgave clueless bumblings, did my work, and bided my time before I could move on.

That June I attended a conference at Loyola Marymount University in Los Angeles. This same Jesuit said he would be visiting a fellow Jesuit out there at the same time and could, conveniently, pick me up at the airport. After a few days, I had planned to visit my sister, who was living in San Francisco. "I have to go to Santa Clara," he said. "We'll share the drive, and I'll drop you off at the airport rental car counter in San Francisco. It'll save you some money on your summer budget. Everyone'll be happy." By this time I was feeling about as spooked as I had been in the encounter with Beth. I thought of buying a train ticket and disappearing on my own, hoping that the assistant would understand when I told him why I had gone way over on my travel budget. But the assistant would more likely have wondered if I was paranoid and noted that the expensive last-minute ticket raised questions about poverty. Better to ask for forgiveness than to ask for permission, they say, but I did neither. This guy couldn't possibly be thinking of anything other than helping a scholastic out with a ride, I was sure.

And then that long trip north turned into a sickening mix of erratic driving, awkward silences, and self-centered questions about why I was increasingly distant and uncommunicative when all he wanted was to be friends. I had the excuse of a bug I had picked up at the conference, and so tried to sleep as much as I could, all the while promising myself that from the moment I got out of that car I would never second-guess my gut about anyone or anything again.

But when I landed back in the Bronx and settled into the role of summer minister for a small group of novices, I received e-mails asking me if I wanted to get together with some friends of his for a show in the city. "You'll like them. They're erudite." I passed on the invitation. I got a last-minute call to see if I wouldn't change my mind. Postcards arrived. "Why so distant? Let's have dinner sometime." I ignored them. When I saw my spiritual director at the end of July and told him how things had developed, he said, "Keep everything."

"But what should I *do*?"

"There's nothing you can do. He might be overly enthusiastic, but he's not doing anything wrong."

Jeff directed me on a province retreat that August in Upstate New York. Years ago I had thanked him for drawing me back into the community at Ciszek Hall. He said, "I felt as though I was being asked to fight for your vocation while you were off fighting other things."

"Not fighting," I said. "Finding. And it was a search I'd gladly do all over again." Then I settled into my usual patterns of prayer on retreat, hours marking off the day as I went "to be with the Lord," surrounded in silence by one hundred other New York Jesuits.

Until, right in the middle of those eight days, a letter arrived for me. I wondered if there was some emergency at home. No one gets mail on retreat. There was no return address, only this note inside, written on a small card: "I hear you're going to visit your parents after the eight-day. Stop in Syracuse and we can patch things up over dinner."

Intrusions that are little more than one person's blindness to another's reality I can accept. I'd certainly be in need of forgiveness if I thought back on when I'd been guilty of such myself. But the time of retreat is sacred time and sacred space. "Don't fuck with the Long Retreat." This intrusion was insolence and selfishness, the presumption that something was so desperately wrong in my nonengagement that not even another Jesuit had the patience to wait. It nearly made me sick. I took the letter to Jeff and explained to him, then, what had been happening over the course of the year.

"I know what it's like to want to be friends with someone so badly you're worried he won't feel the same," I said while Jeff read, "but this *insistence* has gone too far. Why would anyone think that this constitutes friendship?"

Jeff handed the off-white card and envelope back to me and said, "You have to put a stop to it. Lay down some boundaries. You could have someone talk to him, or you could confront him directly."

"I've tried telling the provincial and the formation assistant. They think I'm overreacting. And confronting him directly is precisely what he's looking for. Contact. I won't do that." I wanted to be left alone, I said, especially on this pivotal retreat. I would be moving in a month to theology studies, where I'd begin my final stage toward being ordained a priest in the Society of Jesus. And yet here I was, thrown into some cat-and-mouse game with another Jesuit? "Who does he think he is?" I blurted out in my frustration.

"Maybe he doesn't know," Jeff said. Then, "I think you should write a letter. Make it clear and concise. Nothing sociable or extraneous. Tell him his behavior has become inappropriate. Given these actions, you no longer consider him a friend. Any further contact would be overstepping reasonable boundaries."

And that's what I did, in those same words.

L eafy Brattle Street seemed another world to me altogether as I cycled in the direction of Radcliffe College and on to the small campus of Weston Jesuit School of Theology, the last stage of Jesuit formation before I was—God and the provincial willing—ordained a priest. I locked my bike up in front of the library (a good bike I bought before I left Syracuse) and went early into St. John's Chapel, where the president and faculty of Weston would welcome us with a Mass.

In the fall of 1997, I was one of a hundred other Jesuits living and studying in this community of graduate students and theologians, but I walked into the chapel alone.

Weston shares a campus with the Episcopal Divinity School, and so St. John's is set out like an Anglican church. The seats and pews face not the front but the aisle, like a choir. I sat down in the middle, toward the wall, where I could hide my backpack, and lowered my head in my hands to rest. I was sighing a long and exhausted sigh for having finally gotten to where I was at that moment, the kind of sigh Augustine says in a sermon somewhere is the most articulate form of prayer, when the sound of heels on the chapel's wooden floor made me look up. I saw a young woman with the confident bearing of a dancer wearing a cornflower blue summer dress enter with two other students I knew weren't Jesuits. They took their seats across from me, and I watched them as they settled. Then I put my head back into my hands.

After Mass that same woman joined our orientation group of four because no one else had shown up from hers. We went around the table and introduced ourselves, then listened to a monologue masked as a presentation on the mission, classes, faculty, and larger community of Weston Jesuit. At the end I collected a stack of papers and folders, filled out registration forms, took one more cookie, and got up to leave.

"So where did you say you were from?" she asked me as the rest of the table was dispersing. Her name was Amelia. Like Earhart. I repeated it in my head after she had introduced herself to our group so that I wouldn't forget.

"Do you mean from most recently, or from originally?"

"Start with most recently." She pulled her straight brown hair back into a ponytail. She had gotten some sun. Her nose and cheeks were freckled.

"Syracuse, New York."

"And?"

"Dallas, Pennsylvania. It's a small town near Wilkes-Barre."

"That's near . . . ?"

"It doesn't matter. No one ever cares. You?"

"What, care about Pennsylvania? Or where am I from?"

"Where are you from?"

She laughed, exuberant and flirtatious. "You're the one who started it," she said. "Fort Lauderdale, Florida, by way of London, England. But I've been living in Boston for the past four years."

"England must have been a long time ago." There was no trace of an accent. "What were you doing here in Boston? Working?"

"I was at Harvard, studying sociology. I did my senior thesis on religion and Generation X, and my adviser told me I should apply to Weston for graduate school. So here I am. I guess you could say I'm a Catholic who knows the answers to the big questions but who hasn't yet questioned the questions."

"I was wondering why someone would want to do a theology degree if he . . . or she didn't have to."

She looked puzzled. "*Have* to?"

"I mean, I want to, but not like you do." I pointed to my name tag and the SJ.

"And that stands for . . . ?"

"Society of Jesus. I'm a Jesuit."

"Ah!" she said. "Where's your collar?"

"I'm not a priest yet. But that's why I was sent here. Besides, if I were a priest, I wouldn't necessarily be wearing a collar. Not in school anyway. I thought you were a Catholic."

She blushed. "I am, but you don't get too many guys walking around Harvard telling people they're studying to be priests."

"There are a few," I said. "But they don't wear their collars either, and they avoid women who are smarter than they are."

We stopped at the bike rack. She made fun of the fact that I used two locks and carried my bike seat in my backpack. "There are so few reasons why Cambridge isn't perfect," I said.

"I prefer my in-line skates. Do you skate? We should go sometime." I told her that I did, and that I would like that.

She waited as I put the locks into my bag and then said, "Well, I guess I should go."

I knew I'd see her again, but I didn't want her to go . . . yet. I'd had this feeling before, the pull of trying to save a conversation, trying to let it linger a few minutes more.

"Do you like chocolate?" I asked. I took a bar out of my side pocket.

"Thanks." She broke off a piece. Then she looked at me and cocked her head, as though calculating. "I could really like someone who carries a stash of chocolate around with him," she said.

I brushed it off but thought to myself, Careful, AJ. Feelings get complicated. Indifference is the Jesuit way. I got on my bike, cinched up my helmet, and said, "See you around."

There were two options for Jesuit theology studies in the United States: Cambridge and Berkeley. I was told Weston in Cambridge would be best for me. In a talk with the provincial, I broached the topic of studying in Europe to keep up with my languages. I was one of two men going out to theology in the province, and he said, "How would it look if I didn't send someone to Weston?" I don't know, I thought to myself. Like we were Jesuits who sent men where they were needed? But I didn't say anything. I had already said goodbye to my connection with the East and so had no compelling reason to be anywhere other than where the provincial said I should be. "Obey like a staff in the hands of your superior," Ignatius says.

Theology studies were different from philosophy in this one way: Theology is the point at which the Jesuit scholastic has gone from the stage of belief to witness. From duty to love. Closer to ordination, we were closer to a deeper commitment to the Order. The request to study theology is a request to embrace priesthood and the Jesuits as a way of life.

And for the next few months, Cambridge became a good new home to me. We lived in stately old Victorians at enviable addresses on streets like Avon, Kirkland, and Oxford, usually no more than eight or ten of us to a house. Each house appointed a "coordinator" from among its members (the grown-up beadle) and managed its own expenses—bills, shopping, automobile upkeep—based on budgetary needs. We maintained contact as a larger community on a weekly basis during liturgy, and socially on scheduled feast days. Keeping all of us together was the local superior, more of a spiritual leader to us than a disciplinarian *formator*.

I lived, appropriately, in a house on the fringe of the Jesuits' Cambridge diaspora, all the way down Brattle on Lexington Avenue. We were (in our ongoing stages of formation) one newly appointed Jesuit professor, two newly ordained priests, two graduate students (soon to be priests), and three theologians, including me. We came from Boston, New York, Baltimore, Detroit, Germany, Spain, Ecuador, and South Korea. In a spirit that mirrored the Jesuit community I had been a part of in Hunts Point, our lives found that quotidian balance between the work of the "apostolate" (which consisted as much of shopping, cleaning, and watching the Red Sox as reading the Church Fathers and writing exegesis papers on St. John's Gospel) and the community's need for prayer. Out of habit, I shaped my life around the liturgy that we held in an upper room each day at 5:15 p.m. Sometimes two of us, sometimes all eight. And that, too, spilled out into our meals, our conversations, and our unspoken reasons for why we had come here to live and study as religious men.

The work of being a theology student, though, was our primary mission. Now that we were trained in the foundations of philosophy, our classes were in Scripture, church history, systematics, traditions of spirituality, the sacraments, Canon Law, moral theology, and Catholic social teaching, courses required for our ordination as priestly ministers. Theology studies were, in a sense, preparation for a professional life, similar to law or medicine. But the beauty of Cambridge was that we were also free to cross-register for electives at any theological school in the Greater Boston area: Harvard, Andover Newton, St. John's Seminary, Boston College, Boston University, Episcopal Divinity. It was as though the ghost of William James hovered over the town, watching us in our varieties of religious experience, stroking his beard and saying, "Yes, yes, that's it." For me, those first three months felt like water on a sponge.

Father Stanley Marrow, SJ, one of Weston's Jesuit professors in Scripture, used to say that we studied theology to do as little harm as possible. Stanley was a refined, willfully eccentric scholar whose old-world training in philosophy, theology, and Semitic languages always seemed to clash with what he perceived of as popular culture's reinvention of Christianity and a democratic Jesus. "Jesus was utterly alone at Calvary," he reminded us in one of his more famous declarations. "Of the disciples, he lost twelve out of twelve. They would not have elected him president of a janitors' union."

There in William James's Cambridge, Stanley served as pragmatist and sobering prophet to anyone who believed he or she was destined to do something great for God in the world. "In ministry," he would announce tangentially but appropriately in a class on the New Testament, "the proper criterion is service, not the mutuality of compliments." We knew what he meant. We were faced with it each time we went from our studies to work again in hospitals, prisons, schools, universities, and parishes. Regardless of where we would find our ministry in the Church as priests, chaplains, or administrators—ordained or lay, Catholic or Protestant—we had to avoid the sin of our own idolatry.

The sin of Satan, Adam, and those in the desert who couldn't wait for Moses. We were studying not so that we might become gods but so that we might see and act as examples of how God *is* fully among us. We didn't *need* to be priests. Our part of the bargain was to love *because* we were loved first by that God who we believed created and redeemed all. What is rare, and takes courage, is being ready to accept—to *know*—love when it stands before us with nowhere else to go, waiting for you, me, anyone to respond. But among all of Stanley's reaching aphorisms, I remember most clearly this one, announced like some intimate aside in a lecture hall full of graduate students grappling with the obscurity and stark clarity of the Gospel of St. John: "To let another love you is to admit your need."

I saw Amelia regularly at Weston. Because the school was small, I saw everyone regularly, my fellow Jesuits as well as other students. It was impossible not to. But for her I seemed to search without even realizing it, and I found there levity and seriousness, a winsome spirit and grace. She could engage you fully—concerned squint to the eyes, furrowed brow—when she sensed an issue at hand was not to be taken lightly. And she could, at the same time, throw back her head and laugh when she seemed too happy to contain herself. She appeared to me—in a word—beautiful.

And that's why I remember so well the day Stanley Marrow shattered the dead bolt that had been thrown across the door of what I believed up until that point was my call to religious life, something more akin to a duty I felt bound to out of respect for those who had formed me, rather than witnessing love and admitting my need.

Amelia and I were walking toward the Charles River after a long study session in the library. We were talking about our dream jobs, and I told her that I had just left mine.

"College professor? Isn't there something else?" she said.

"I mean laboring somehow with words and ideas. Maybe Le Moyne wasn't exactly my dream job, but it felt like a good start. I got in the habit of sitting down to write."

"Writing I can see. But all you need is a room for that."

"And time."

We had stopped on Weeks Footbridge, lit up from both sides. "I'm curious," she said. "You don't say that as though it has anything to do with being a Jesuit or a priest. Why this path if it's not, I don't know, what you dream of for your life?"

I thought of Andrea's question in Slovakia. This time, language was not an obstacle. I stopped, stared down at the inky Charles, took a breath, and said nothing. There had been reasons in the past—good ones, and right ones—but I realized they had neither accompanied me nor given way to new reasons that were also good and right. "Honestly?" I said. "I'm not sure I can say anymore."

None of this was coming out of the blue. While I embraced the final stage of my training with a peace among the other peripheral trials, I had done nothing to resist my desire to spend as much time with Amelia as she was willing to spend with me. I never disappeared physically from the community, though I think my brothers knew (especially in my house at Lexington Avenue) that my heart, if not my mind, was gradually moving elsewhere. And yet, Amelia and I were careful to respect what boundaries defined who we both were at Weston. While I made my own gestures of friendship—a smooth stone from the shore at Hull that fit snugly in the palm, the Fagles translation of Homer's *Odyssey*, a loaf of bread from a batch I had baked for the house one afternoon—we maintained a practiced caution. Caution, but with an affection that was clearly deepening.

"I think I never believed that anyone could love me without one day walking away," I said, looking into the water. And that was true. "Not because of any great trauma. I guess because of those collective moments we've all had. After enough time, priesthood seemed like the best guarantee." Then I turned to her. "That I'd belong somewhere, to someone. And that someone would be God. Love would be my love for Christ. You have to admit, it's a pull that's pretty compelling."

She knew, she who as a young woman wondered, too, about what it meant to "love Christ." That was partly the attraction to theology. Partly. She said, "That's hard. Hard *to* admit. But I guess in some ways it's a fear we've all got, that no one can love us like we need."

Maybe it was her willingness to listen. Maybe it was the fact that she was so cute, with her silky ponytail, green eyes, and wide grin. I began to test caution and let myself feel a desire I had for so long pushed down inside, *that feeling of having been handed something I was certain I'd lost forever, a loss of my own making.* I took it to prayer every day: Had I ever let anyone love me, admitting my own need? And when I felt as though I was incapable of not saying it any longer, I heard from her those words, at once human and *theo logos.*

It was on the shore of Halcyon Lake in Mount Auburn Cemetery, a place more Arcadian than funereal that seems by design to have stopped time in the middle of nineteenth-century, antebellum America. We had gone there for a walk one day, looking for the graves of Henry Wadsworth Longfellow and Amy Lowell, for no reason other than to have an excuse to walk through those grounds together on a late autumn afternoon. Sitting down on a stone bench, as though our prior conversation on Weeks Bridge had happened minutes earlier, I asked, "What is this we're feeling? Is it love?" I hadn't considered the fact that she might not be in love with me. For some reason I just believed.

She breathed out with that prayerlike sigh. "It is," she said. "At least for me."

We watched swans float like white schooners across the lake.

"But what does that mean?" I asked her, my own brow furrowed now with concern. "Look at the opposite directions we have to go in when we walk outside those gates. Where to then? I'll be eight years a Jesuit soon. That's a long time. Is it over now?"

"I don't know," she said. "But it has to be worth finding out, doesn't it?"

"So, do we go our separate ways from here?"

"No." She got up and walked underneath a nearby willow tree, to think or gain distance, I wasn't sure. "Just because things get complicated doesn't mean we can't remain friends. How could we possibly pretend at this school that someone else doesn't exist?"

I felt the same but said, "That's not as easy as it sounds. In my experience, the life becomes all or nothing."

"I don't know what 'all or nothing' means. But in my experience, friendship comes first. And we were friends first, remember? I don't want to *not* see you, Andrew," she said, her tone plaintive now, as though it were prayer. "What kinds of vows are you keeping if they're keeping you from that?"

Back in September of that year, I had received another letter with no return address. The card inside announced a subscription to *Poetry* magazine, along with a note that said "Happy Birthday."

A week after my walk through Mount Auburn Cemetery with Amelia, the formation assistant came to Weston for a visit. Before we sat down for what I wanted to be a discussion about theology, priesthood, and the fact of love, not necessarily in that order, I told him about the subscription gift I'd received when I moved to Cambridge, putting it in the context of behavior over the summer and the letter I'd finally been forced to write from the confines of retreat in August. Most of my anger and fear had dissipated since then, but not my disgust. "Can't you make him stop?" I asked.

The assistant suggested that the gift was sent before I had written my letter, and that I was overreacting. "The man seems to mean well," he said. "I wonder, AJ, if he doesn't think he could be some kind of mentor to you."

I scoffed loudly at how absurd that sounded. "Sure. Whatever you say. I can see he's got a lot to teach a guy."

"He's a brother Jesuit, AJ. You're too hard on people, expecting them to live up to your ideal. It's going to make your life difficult, you know."

"You don't see it, do you? I'm not here to serve his whims. That's not what obedience is supposed to mean." The conversation went nowhere after that. Pro forma questions and answers about studies and my local apostolate, which I hadn't lined up yet, and I left without discussing the things that mattered.

But I didn't stay silent about any of this. I had another good Jesuit spiritual director at Weston. Kevin Burke was from a sheep-ranching family in Wyoming. He dressed in a suit and tie like every other East Coast professional but had a slight cowboy twang to his voice, which most of the men from the Missouri Province never lost. He was a popular professor of systematic theology and seemed to love his role and the responsibilities of being a priest.

"Maybe what the assistant wants you to do is rise above this," he said one day, challenging me to see beyond my indignation even as he shared my exasperation when I related to him all that had been happening. I told him I felt as though my faith not in God but in those superiors who were supposedly guiding me in my discernment had died. "And when it's all dead, your faith in every superior," he said, "where will you go? Will you stay? Will it be any better elsewhere?" All questions I took daily, weekly, monthly to my prayer. At least there was prayer, and now some of the simplest and oldest prayers I had ever summoned: *O Lord, please . . .*

Kevin had an explorer's imagination. His thoughts seemed to progress by way not of seamless connections but of seismic escarpments. The images and metaphors he chose were of heights, plateaus, and abysses, and the emotional as well as physical labor it took to abide in these shifting landscapes. I wasn't sure I understood it then, but he seemed to think the strata of fear, anger, belief, and trust that lifted and grated against me like tectonic plates that year were beautiful battles to be waging, should I want to emerge in some way as a man of God. When I said once that I wished I could have some peace in which to make a proper discernment, he said, "No you don't! We make our decisions along the way. We don't *git* to stop!" He spoke like that, explosive, engaged, as though it was a privilege for him to be in your presence. "Who does? Not the guy driving the street cleaner. Why should we?" God and good discernment brought me here, Kevin also reminded me. And of all the things we talked about that year, those words—as they always had—brought me the closest I could get to a kind of peace.

Especially when I brought up with Kevin the eye of my spiritual maelstrom: Amelia. I said, "How can it be love if we only met a few months ago? It's not like I've never been friends with an attractive woman before."

But Kevin was undaunted. "You can't separate these out, AJ—priesthood, the Jesuits, love—regardless of how straightforward you want it to be. Be angry with your assistant, or this guy who seems blind to everyone but himself. That's all the stuff of moving on in this life. But if you're going to be honest, be honest about the fact that you're in love. *That's* from God. And I don't mean falling in love with Amelia. You wouldn't have gotten this far if you weren't in love with the actual journey. Complicated? Hell yes! But you know? Pure and simple, too. My daddy used to say that faith's a matter of saying 'I'll stay,' or 'I'll go,' like those two boys in the Bible whose father asks them to go out and work in the vineyard. What are *you* going to do?"

In December I received a short letter from Syracuse. No return address. It said, "You didn't have to tell the assistant. But just to show you, I've enclosed a copy of the canceled subscription to *Poetry*. By the way, do you get much chance to read any fiction outside of studies? I recommend *Cold Mountain*." I filed it away with all the other letters and messages he had sent.

Papers were due over the next few weeks, and everyone, it seemed, was making plans to get away for the winter break. Amelia was working part-time at Widener Library. I hunkered down into my own end-of-semester work, intentionally creating distance so that some kind of resolution would force itself, a path of least resistance that would take care of things by way of inaction.

What I hadn't expected was the complete inability to remain inactive, as though in fact the Jesuits had done their job of teaching discernment well. "Love ought to manifest itself in deeds rather than in words," Ignatius writes. Papers or no papers, community or no community, I wanted to see Amelia and so went by Widener on a Saturday afternoon when I knew she was getting off work. I wanted to test the presence, or absence, of that love and didn't know how to go about it other than to move in its direction.

From a distance I caught a glimpse of her talking—animated and happy—with a friend of hers from Harvard, a guy on the soccer team, and I felt a stab of jealousy. I approached after he left, and we said hello awkwardly. I asked if she was busy that afternoon. I had a Christmas present for her. She told me she was free but she had to drop her books at home first.

"I'll walk with you," I said.

In the hallway outside her apartment, she had left a bag of some other things I had given to her along with the book and stone; my old fleece, which I had lent her, was on top. She looked down, and back at me almost defiantly. "You weren't supposed to see that. I was going to give them to the Salvation Army."

"Why?" The bag looked like some waif huddled on her doorstep, denied entrance into a world of warmth and safety it once knew.

She let go of the key in the door. "You never called, you stopped waiting for me in the library, and you wouldn't even look at me in Mass." All true. "So," she said, "I figured you had decided it was over. What could I do? I'm . . . I don't want it to hurt so much." Tears came to the corners of her eyes. "I see these things, I think of you, and it hurts."

"Please don't give them away," I said, but it felt as though I had already lost something, *a loss of my own making.*

She turned the key finally, opened the door, reached down, swooped up the bag, and said, "Sometimes I don't know what to do."

"*Most* times I don't know what to do."

We went to Casablanca Restaurant for a coffee. The gift I'd bought for her was an icon of Our Lady of the Tender Kisses, which I'd found at Holy Transfiguration Monastery in Brookline. It seemed right, this rare subject matter for the iconographer, yet still a thing of imperfect perfection and beauty. You'll say that I knew exactly what I was doing that day. And I will tell you now that I did, for in no way could that gift—the hope of some tender kiss—belie intention.

The gray December afternoon became a dark winter evening, and we got up to leave. She was flying to Florida in the morning to spend the holidays with her mother. In another week I'd be in Boulder, Colorado, skiing with a friend from St. John's College who lived and worked out there (I couldn't spend that Christmas with my parents in Pennsylvania. What would we talk about? What would I tell them? That next year at this time I might not be a Jesuit? "What'll you *do*?"

they'd ask. Good question. What *am* I going to do?). Somehow the western mountains seemed an appropriate retreat from all this. And yet I almost couldn't bear to watch her walk back through Harvard Square, turning once to watch me watching her. I was afraid that when she stepped out of sight I'd never lay eyes on Amelia, like Earhart, again.

On the last day of 1997, I was back in Cambridge at our nearly empty house on Lexington Avenue. Only Ivan from Ecuador and Damien from Korea were around. A chance to catch up on pleasure reading, I thought, or give an entire day over to writing.

The night before I had gone to see the movie *Good Will Hunting* by myself. The Harvard scenes made me think of Amelia, so before I settled into anything on New Year's Eve, at around midday I decided to call over to her apartment to leave a "Happy 1998" message on her answering machine, and tell her to go see the film before the reading period for exams started. The phone rang twice, and she answered.

"Amelia?" I said. "What are you doing back?"

"Andrew!" It was the voice and spirit I had missed. "I told you I'd be back today. You never remember anything," she said, teasing. "I took an early flight from Fort Lauderdale this morning. Just walked in the door."

I told her about my trip, Michael and I skiing almost every day, eating, talking, catching up. He had been a good friend during my year in Santa Fe, and I had seen him only a few times since then. She was impressed that we went to Mass on Christmas Eve and a yoga studio on Christmas Day. It was Michael's idea. He isn't a Catholic, but he had a great respect for the path I was on, and the crossroads at which I told him I stood.

There was a lull then in our conversation, until she asked, "What are you doing today?"

I told her that I was essentially alone in the house, not having been invited to the international students' New Year's Eve dinner. I was going to have a glass of wine and go to sleep early. "That's always the best way to welcome the New Year."

"Well, no one's around here either. A friend of mine from the Philippines and I were going to cook and then watch the fireworks at the band shell on the Charles. You're welcome to join us if you'd like."

Without caution or indifference, only the desire to be with her, I said, "I'd like that."

She made a chicken risotto for the three of us that night, and I brought over the wine I was going to drink by myself. It was too cold to go down to the river after all, so the three of us watched a televised celebration of one year passing into the next (as though no other strike of a clock at midnight on any other day of the year holds any significance), and then Amelia and I walked Lia home.

It was snowing, a hard and steady snow that had already left six inches on the ground. The two of us, alone now, strolled over to the river and Weeks Bridge, lit up and silent while the rest of Cambridge erupted with isolated pockets of shouts in the post-midnight revelry all around. Then we turned back in the direction of Amelia's apartment.

"Why don't you come up for a cup of tea?" she said as we lingered outside on the sidewalk. "It won't matter now what time you get home, will it?"

We climbed the stairs, and I followed her back into the kitchen, where we had just had dinner like old friends accustomed to new directions. We talked about the near-perfect beauty freshly fallen snow can give a place, and the quiet that comes with such beauty, especially at night. And then we didn't say much of anything. Except when I stood to go. She asked me if I would stay for a while longer, and we fell asleep curled into each other on her single bed, chaste in body if not in intention, our kisses tender, our touches pure, wanting in our need only to feel the skin, breath, and heartbeat of another.

I woke at 4:00 a.m. (her clock on the nightstand said) and startled at the surroundings of a strange room. I watched the snowfall drift against the closed bedroom window and accumulate in tiny piles outside on the ledge. "I should go," I whispered into her shoulder. "It's a long walk home if I want to get there before morning."

I made a show at breakfast in my house with Ivan and Damien, showered, slept a few hours more, and then walked the two miles back to Amelia's. In her kitchen once again, our long morning felt already like a time not hours but years in the past. There was no avoiding the conversation that had to come, and so, in the daylight, we tried to say as much, gathering up what belief and trust we could find and might lay claim to as two people wanting to know what it meant to say they knew love.

"You're supposed to want to stay when you come to theology," I said, as though we had been having an ongoing conversation for some time now, when in fact we'd sat close to each other in near silence. "And here I am, some might say looking for a reason to leave. Your question, remember? *Why a priest?* I've not been able to shake it. Why am I living this rather than some other life?" *This* sounded false somehow, as though I could no longer say that I lived *this Jesuit* life. There was no avoiding the guilt.

Amelia tilted her head to the left, an unconscious mannerism she has when she becomes serious and thoughtful. "It doesn't seem so irrelevant to me, to be making a decision like this in the middle of studying theology."

"You mean, wondering what God wants, or what we want God to want for us?"

"Is there a difference? Maybe you're looking at it all too cynically." I smiled as if to say, "Me? Cynical?" "I mean, it's bigger than we are," she said. "Bigger than the Jesuits, from what little I know. I don't understand completely what's expected of you every day, but I think Stanley's right. You can't know what God wants of you unless you know what it is to respond. You can't love until you know what it is to *be* loved. We all have that need."

Before she could say anything more, I said, "Well, God is love," with a hint of that cynicism. "That's why I'm in the Jesuits. Guaranteed. And look at where that's gotten me."

"Where has it gotten you? You're not in jail. We haven't done anything stupid. You're a young man studying theology in a religious order, wondering if he wants to be ordained a priest, as he once did. And I'm a woman wondering who that man is. Isn't this the right time for both of us to be asking what or who loves us, and why?"

I had the feeling, then, that I was leaning over the edge of a cliff.

But no anxiety or fear arose. Rather, I felt the resignation that some path or road had brought me to this, and a way beyond would soon be clear. I said, "Last year, when I came over to Widener to give you the icon, I was torn between believing I had to say goodbye to you forever and this need never to let you go."

She reddened and was quiet for a moment, studying tiles on the kitchen floor. "Please don't," she said, looking up. "Say goodbye, that is."

I shook my head, wanting to say, "Don't worry, I won't," but instead I said, "If I don't decide what to do, someone in the Jesuits is going to decide for me. It has to be about whether I want to live as a Jesuit or not. Stay if it's right, leave if it isn't. I owe it to myself, to them, and to you."

Before the spring semester got fully under way, I made a trip to New York to see the provincial so that I could lay out the situation in front of him, ask for his help in gaining some equilibrium, and then hope to make a good discernment. The year before I went to theology I'd heard a Jesuit speak at a province gathering about his own vocational crisis during studies. He had fallen in love, too, "pure and simple," and been faced with the decision of whether to remain in the Order and be ordained a priest or leave. He took it to prayer. He tried to work it out in a balance of pros and cons. He spoke to friends, his father, wanting someone, anyone, to tell him what to do. "Finally," he said, "I went to talk to the provincial, to level with him, pour out my heart. Of all the vows, the one I realized I had taken for granted was obedience." Father Provincial embraced him, said that he understood the difficulty, wanted him to make the right decision, and then asked, as he was leaving his office: "How are you fixed for cash?"

"I knew then," that Jesuit said, "I would stay."

My hope was that my provincial would say, "Look, don't worry about the priest in Syracuse anymore. I'll take care of that. Do what God and your heart are telling you to do with respect to Amelia. Pray and make a good discernment. It's all anyone can ask for. By the way, how are you fixed for cash?"

The provincial agreed to see me, along with the formation assistant, though I felt an impatience in him as we all sat down, as though he wanted this meeting to be over quickly. I stuck to my plan, narrated the events of the past year, unwanted affection from one side, *wanted* affection from another. "The unwanted affection hasn't been easy for me," I said. "It's hard to be at prayer about this when things are skewed between love and a kind of lunacy on the part of one of my brothers."

What I found was that neither the provincial nor his assistant had heard the whole story about my time in Syracuse, and after. Selective information had been passed along, largely in the belief that I had made the situation more of an issue than it ought to be. Again, in their assessment, I was overreacting out of some deeper reason that made me culpable. They seemed to think that I had angered a fellow Jesuit, who meant well, with my continual animosity toward him, and that there was "nothing wrong with a little pat on the backside."

"We've taken this very seriously," the provincial said, "asked around, interviewed people, and no one sees any untoward behavior. Let it go, Andrew. What's more important is that you sort out what being a priest and a Jesuit means to you. We can delay ordination if you need some time. Nothing's written in stone. Maybe put you back into a regency situation. Let's give it this semester and see what happens. We'll talk again in April."

I thanked them and took the train back to Boston.

Obedience. From the Latin *ob-audientia*. It means not to be compliant with a rule, as we take it narrowly to mean, but *to listen*, to put your ear to, understanding that it is at heart a desire to hear the voice of God. Chastity, in the end, was the most difficult vow for me to live as a religious. But obedience was the most terrifying, because while it offered a peaceful freedom that came as a result of a faithful and radical trust, it came, too, at a cost as great as, if not greater than, the one that chastity exacted. Done well, and with the heart, mind, and ear directed toward God, obedience could be a healthy tempering of the self and an effective way to live a good spiritual life. But if the one to whom you had vowed obedience didn't seem to know enough to *listen*, then the result, for the rest of your days, could feel like an enslavement, or the greatest loss imaginable, the death of God, the end of the self as a life snuffed out, making whatever vow of poverty or chastity one had been faithful to as empty as if it had been broken daily. "But you were in love," you'll say, "pure and simple," as though my quarrel with my superiors was just a cover. And because I found out what it meant to be loved in my hour of deepest need, I'll tell you again that you are right. But then, I didn't want to be breaking vows I had taken, though my heart was already elsewhere. So I did what the Jesuits had taught me to do when it was God whom I needed the most: I turned to prayer in a place of retreat.

There is a candle before me and behind that an icon of Christ All-Merciful I found in another room down the hall. It's painted not well but simply. Up close, the parts of composition fragment and lose their place. The eyes are two-dimensional. The hands are fat and poorly traced, in both figure and pigment. It's a Christ robed in humanity. All the better that the candle should make the imperfections shine.

Some people say we never actually change ourselves or our directions in life. Rather, we come to a realization of what's always been there. But I was trying to be a man of the *Exercises*, a man "created to praise, reverence, and serve God," and I believed (I still do) that by examining our will and keeping it oriented, we move toward the right path, "our desire and choice . . . the end for which we are created." That's why I went to the Campion Renewal Center in Weston, Massachusetts, during our mid-semester break of that year to make an early eight-day retreat. Time to head back out into the wilderness. Another Chama. Another Sinai. Another year and return to the foundations of the *Exercises*. Like every desert, too hot in the day, too cold at night. Never water when you need it, only when you least expect it. Rather than waiting for when the desert called me, though, I went out to meet it, seeking its solace, not knowing where it would take me this time.

The Campion Renewal Center is a grand and ascetic former seminary in the Massachusetts woods outside of Boston that, like Jogues Retreat House in Wernersville, once housed hundreds of young Jesuit scholastics studying to be priests. Now it's divided symmetrically between a spirituality center for lay Catholics and religious, and an infirmary for the old Jesuits of the New England Province. Tom, one of the guys in my house, dropped me off around lunchtime. The halls were nearly empty except for a small group of nuns on a Lenten reflection, their cars parked neatly in a pack across the road. I found my room and fell asleep on a narrow bed, missing out entirely on what food was being offered in the dining room. When I woke up, I went for a walk to orient myself. That's when I found the icon.

My director, it turned out, was away for two days. I'd be on my own until he returned. I'd never met him, a soft-spoken New England Jesuit named Michael Fury. "Like the character in *The Dead*," I said when we talked on the phone. "Yes, although I hear more jokes about 'Father Furious' than I do references to Joyce, so thank you," he replied. He was the only staff member available that week for a last-minute directed retreat. No matter. I knew the drill and dropped effortlessly into the familiarity of silence.

Silence. It was like a welcomed friend, a principle and foundation all its own, and the house was flooded with it. I moved between the chapel and my room. Daytime, my thoughts and prayers directed toward the cross and corpus in front of me, *"Christ, what am I going to do?"* on my lips, which wasn't in any way meant to be a name taken in vain. Nighttime, my world reduced to the flawed icon that I propped up against the windowsill. When I glanced above it, I could see the lighted Prudential building in downtown Boston rising beyond the trees and hills, letting me know that the world was still out there.

The next day Kevin Burke came to say Mass for the nuns. Afterward, he asked me if I wanted to get dinner at a steak house in the town. We didn't talk about anything of importance. I supposed he was waiting for me to guide the conversation to some form of spiritual direction. I was happy just to forgo the wilted salad and dried baked ziti they were serving in the retreat center dining room. But Kevin's silence carried with it a message. In my journal that night I wrote:

KB is another one in a long line of great spiritual directors I've had in the Society. Yet, I sense that he wants me to stay, as though, if he could speak candidly, he would tell me that if I left I'd be making a big mistake. Would I? It's in his tone, the things he talks about, the thought he gives to everything addressed to me. Well, I suppose if I were he, I'd do the same. A mistake is what I'm trying hard not to make.

I kept my prayer periods anchored to the liturgy. And, as though a mirror of the First Week of the *Exercises*, it occurred to me suddenly, after thirty-four years, that the Mass, too, begins with the movement of recognizing sin—"in what I have done and in what I have failed to do"—then reorients us toward God. There was Pride, again, masked behind my righteousness but smoldering with the conviction that "it's got nothing to do with me." Good old-fashioned Sloth, what the theologians called *acedia*, was also finding its way into my crumbling fortress, threatening its weaker indifference. And there was the Lust that comes with loneliness, trying to confuse me by taking the place of love. Was there Envy? Of others' peacefulness. But most threatening was my own Wrath. Whereas before I had wondered, "Isn't this more a condemnation of myself?" Now I steamed, "God damn those who have driven me to this point!" Each deadly sin tied me down in its own delicate and powerful way. And yet, recognizing that seemed to both weaken and strengthen me. I found a priest on staff and went to confession, wondering if knowing failure wasn't in fact the same as knowing that you're loved, regardless.

Wrath is more powerful than I thought. Even when I write "the names" for the purpose of prayer, anger rises. "Let it go, Andrew." My director here has asked me to write down instead those things that give me joy, something I remember Gerry asking at the beginning of the Long Retreat. So I do that: good tea; enough snow to cross-country ski; the rise of a trout to a fly; every song on *The Ghost of Tom Joad*; Psalm 42; Amelia.

About her I've begun to realize that those moments we've spent together feel very similar to what I feel when I'm at prayer. And I find in all of this some peace. God's will is on the tip of everyone's tongue, it seems, and somewhere in the bottom of my heart. Isn't God's will mine, too, if it's good?

For the first three days it rained. A cold rain. But then it cleared and I began going outside to walk the extensive grounds. Although suburban Weston, Massachusetts, was fast encroaching, Campion kept its land to itself and offered a few miles of trails through fields, a pine forest, and around a small fishing pond. And still not a soul. I was lord of the manor and wondered what it would have been like to have been here fifty years ago with what must have seemed like countless men called to be priests, cassocks fluttering beneath their winter coats, rosaries, scapulars, and an entire bone shop of pieties hanging from them as they wandered over lawns and woods in a wholly other time. I wondered if their interior lives were any different from mine. But they weren't talking.

The night before, I had finally met my director, ten years a priest at the most. I knew nothing about the man, nor he about me, which at first felt uncomfortable but then appealing. It's the work of the Holy Spirit, I thought, so perhaps that's best.

I told him why this wasn't my ordinary annual eight-day retreat: questions about priesthood, love, Amelia, a Jesuit who sought to control me, the superiors who saw nothing wrong with that. The story, though, began to feel like ground gone over until what tracks may have been discernible were lost to mud. But how could he help me if I didn't give him a chance to listen? And so I laid out everything as best I could, not flinching at the complicated uncertainty of it all.

That was the first day, when he asked me to write about my joy. The next day he brought me back to the *Exercises*. "You're in a place similar to the Second Week," he said, concerned but without emotion. "In an odd, but probably understandable, twist of the *Exercises*, you've already made your decision to leave, haven't you? And now you're looking for confirmation, although it must seem as though you're beginning the election process all over again."

I ran my hand along my chin, rough with the beard stubble of four days, kept my gaze focused on a spot on the rug a few feet in front of me, then looked up and said, "That's right."

"Okay, so let this guide you." He remained unfazed, matter-of-fact, and compassionate, all in one breath. "Take this into your prayer. Use Psalm 139 if you think it'll be helpful. Where do you pray?" he asked. I told him. "Well, why don't you go into the infirmary tomorrow morning for 9:00 Mass with the fathers? They'll put you to work pushing wheelchairs." Good, I thought, I could stand to do a little work.

The next morning, an hour before the liturgy, the psalm floated about me like a voice: "Lord, you have probed me, you know me . . . My travels and my rest you mark; with all my ways you are familiar." That Lord did in fact know enough about me not to be anxious with where I was going. So why should I? Then, praying with the fathers—Jesuits of many years, wheeled in, hobbling in, or walking of their own accord to the celebration of the Eucharist, all with that burning desire to be with their Lord, who knew them—made it plain to me what I would be leaving. Not a life of poverty, chastity, and obedience in decline but a community of men who, at the beginning and at the end of the day, expressed a singular longing. It is and always has been a pilgrim's journey, right from the days of Ignatius and his first companions. If the world is our house, why should I fear or mistrust the reach of any man? If it is of God, it cannot be withstood. And yet can't I also express a singular longing for another person?

I took Father Fury's direction to heart. I began to say that I was leaving the Society of Jesus. In my prayer, I imagined saying it to others. At supper in the refectory one night, I told a fellow retreatant, "I came here looking for confirmation." Later, on a walk, I said to myself out loud in those woods, "This is what I have to do."

With that, though, I began to feel a tactile pain. The mistrust of my own certainty. I took this back to Father Fury, and he didn't seem surprised. "Good," he said. "But we know better than to get tossed back and forth by this." We. He put me among the men of the *Exercises*. "Which is the certainty you want to live with?"

I returned to the Meditation on the Two Standards and found that I was not, as a result, relegated to the side of the evil spirit for not choosing life with the Jesuits. I heard the voice of Jaro in Bratislava: "I didn't want to stop believing. I just didn't want to work as a priest." The Jesuits were one formation standing beneath the banner. "The path of leaving and the path of staying remain in the shadow of the cross," I wrote that night in my journal. "There's no escaping either, nor do I want to. And although I have begun to feel the weight of leaving, I know, too, that the heaviness of staying will bear down in its own time."

Luke 5:1–11 for my prayer today. I know it well. Always the call, like Peter and Andrew, to put out into deeper water, and consolation in the gentle command of Jesus: "Do not be afraid." I thought I would find myself begging Christ to show me something I'd missed, to keep me on this path I'd already started. But, a sinful man in the fishing boat of the earliest followers, I thought again of the decision before me and called out right there in the chapel: "Please! Don't call me to a life of unhappiness." I heard a voice I recognized, a voice from my prayer: *Do you think there are other boats in other parts of these waters, where the labor is as rich and the currents as deep?* There has to be. A disciple in another way, but a disciple still. *Well, put out into that deep.*

The ineffable Christ suddenly became effable. *Deus absconditus* stepping away from the cleft and into full view. This was the Christianity of my prayer, of my faith, with me at all times, as promised, even when, in his hiddenness, I wondered where he had gone. Words from a prayer I once prayed in the past rose to me in this place of emerging clarity: "It's failure I fear. Failing here by not knowing what to do." But the answer then, as now, had been in doing what I believed this God, this Christ, was calling me to do.

Then I lost track of the days. I found the seminary library in the attic, a tinderbox of wooden floors, shelves, old and out-of-print books from the nineteenth and early twentieth centuries, along with the standard classics. The windows were clean, and so in the daytime there was as much light in there as there was outside. At an empty table that should have sat ten, I reread chapters of *Confessions*, *The Seven Storey Mountain*, and that last, great "Conclusion" of Thoreau's *Walden*. It seemed that I was being drawn to conclusions. As I read Merton's final *Meditatio* again, after almost twenty years, his desire to separate himself from the world and remain forever within a community of prayerful men suddenly felt to me like an inverted confession when this passage lost its reference to who "they" were: "For I knew that it was only by leaving them that I could come to You: and that is why I have been so unhappy when You seemed to be condemning me to remain in them. Now my sorrow is over, and my joy is about to begin."

I worked on some poems, but nothing came of them. When I went outside, I rarely walked farther than the pond, sat on a bank on the opposite shore, and threw stones onto the ice. The warm weather was making the water cloudy as its surface slowly melted. And through all of this, hunkered down in a place that waited patiently for its own hearing, I missed Amelia.

Could I say that I was ever "called" to be a priest? I asked Father Fury this in one of our periods of direction, and he wondered what I meant by *called*.

"What others might say. If I entered the Jesuits to be a priest because I felt called to ordination, why this denial of that calling? Fear of sacrifice? Temptation? Loss of faith? If I was *called*, these shouldn't matter. If I wasn't, what was it all for?"

"What do you say?"

"I say I walked a long but worthy road that led to a place where I didn't belong."

"The Jesuits?"

"The Jesuits. I don't feel any resentment. I feel gratitude. The men I've known? More than gratitude. But I feel, too, as though I've gone as far as I can go with any desire."

He thought about this for some time and then said, "Whenever someone asks me when I got *the call*, I tell them that we're all called. They say, 'Yeah, but to the priesthood,' and I say again, 'We're all called.' And they think I'm being a smart-ass liberal Jesuit, and they go away unhappy. But it's true. We're all called. The Catechism says that the whole community of believers is consecrated to be a holy priesthood." I knew this from a class on the sacraments but couldn't see at the time how it pertained to me. "The many are the faithful who participate in the common priesthood," Father Fury went on. "The ordained participate in the ministerial priesthood. They differ, but you can't have one without the other. The proper priesthood to which anyone is called is the priesthood of Christ. So were you called? If you're sitting here listening to this, I'd say you were. And still are."

I had taken to rubbing my chin a lot. "That's a good lesson, but it doesn't tell me what I've done with eight years."

He didn't take this as badly as I had expected. "No, it doesn't. But let me ask you, what drove you to this life? What did you envision doing . . . as priest *or* Jesuit?"

"You know how many times I've heard that question? It's a little late now, don't you think?"

"Still a few days left to give me a good answer. What've you got to lose?"

While I was at Mass, reading in the old library, alone in front of the poorly rendered icon, the same answer came without any struggle to invoke it. Once upon a time, when I was a young man, what I wanted most was to be part of a community of believers. Spiritual, intellectual, literary, emotional. It hardly mattered how many or which one, as long as I had work to do and something to say. What mattered was the one that gave me an identity, that community all men go in search of. And to what end, this community? As a Catholic, I had always stared at a long tradition of questions that got answered on spiritual, intellectual, literary, and emotional journeys. Always one among the many, most of those writers felt as though they didn't fit but at least belonged to a *whole community of believers*, priestly, turning inward to ask their questions, outward with some semblance of an answer, inward when another question began tugging at them again.

When I became a Jesuit, on the Long Retreat of the *Spiritual Exercises*, this became a desire to serve God, to imitate Christ in a priestly order of men, a desire that remained so until I felt the loss not of God but of who I was as a man. And now one question concerned me, one I always figured I could find in God while I kept it at bay from my fellow men and women searchers: Love. Pure and simple. Not some diffuse and vague feeling of warmth. Rather, *this*: How should a man love well? Without a life in search of that, I decided, I would find nothing, in service of no one. I would be a driftless and emptied community of . . . what? Certainly not a believer. The great mystery of Christianity is that God loves us *first*. If I doubted the possibility not of loving but of being loved, then I doubted everything.

I could return to my house in Cambridge, settle back into studies, show my superiors that I had settled down in my heart, and go on to be ordained for whatever work the Society of Jesus saw fit for me to do. Or I could—in front of my God—say that I wanted to start over, to cross out of this land, and embrace whatever waited for me in a place I felt as though I had left a lifetime ago and no longer had any knowledge of. Yet one in which I was willing to risk love, as physical and beautiful as it is spiritual, and terrifying, too, in its own poverty, chastity, and obedience. I turned to Jeremiah then, and listened to the prophet of faithfulness. God calls us to faithfulness, whatever we do, regardless of what returns or departures we inevitably make in our lives; it is the faithfulness to continue.

The day before my retreat ended I remembered something one of the priests from Le Moyne had said to me about the morning of his ordination. "I was staying at Cornwall and had planned to drive down to the chapel at Fordham. As I was going over the Tappan Zee Bridge, right in the middle of the Hudson, I was suddenly overcome by a feeling of ambivalence and uncertainty. I thought, I can turn back right now, park the car, and walk away as easily as I could drive to the Bronx, where my life will change forever. My life had already changed forever," he said, "but I needed that feeling of spiritual . . . *fear* to remind me of the choice I had made. I was afraid, and for that reason I knew the discernment had been a good one. I knew I was in love with this life. So I always wait for that feeling of uncertainty now, that feeling of being in love, as though I'm about to drop off a bridge, before I know that I'm certain of what it is I'm doing. How do you think the prophets felt?"

And so with my answer there came—in two waves—first the calm of having put a past behind me, then the certainty of uncertainty. The second collapsed on me with the exhaustion that comes with knowing that a Herculean task of labor awaits. The voice of Don Gannon, from the first day of novitiate, echoed from out of that past: "That may mean a more difficult path."

I wasn't going to cut and run. I had exams and papers to finish. I wanted to talk to my brothers on Lexington Avenue, tell them about my decision before it had reached the rumor mill, because the eight of us got on well as a house. And there were others I wanted to contact, though not many: Jeff, Gerry, some of the guys at Le Moyne, and of course David. With David it would be hard, and not because I had failed to keep our brothers' pact. We had ceased to see each other for more than a few weeks at a time in any given year (which is why he appears less and less in the course of this narrative), but even that was forward-moving time, given our shared history. We picked up where we left off, and never retraced steps out of nostalgia, except when we'd talk about the Land Cruiser in Monte Cristi. It wasn't easy to get on without friends in this life. Now I would be leaving him as well to his own difficult path.

The formation assistant had to be first, though, because he was in charge of every step I ever took or would take as a Jesuit. He was the boss and would be until I received and signed my dismissal papers from the Vatican. And I had to tell my local superior, because he would be concerned with the ongoing life of the Weston community: Who lived in what house? Who was enrolled in course work? Were we living our vows and progressing toward ordination, or were we discerning how we might "follow the Lord on another path," as they used to say? This superior of the Weston Jesuit community, about whom I have written little, but to whom I am in debt for his kindness, said to me when we sat down to talk about my departure, "I'll be sorry to see you go, Andrew. I know what a tough decision this has been, but I watched you and I never doubted that you remained a man of prayer." Could he have known that these were words I had longed to hear? I thanked him, and as I got up to leave he asked me how I was fixed for cash. I told him that the formation assistant was sending me money for food and rent until I could get a job. "Let me know if I can help," he said.

After that, I would have to pack my things and move out of my room on Lexington Avenue and into a world I had lived on the poor fringe of. Who will be there to help me with this? I remember thinking, when I had a rare clear moment to think. And I realized that there was no guarantee that there'd be anyone at all. I hoped Amelia would be, and she had assured me, before I left on retreat, that she would. But we both knew, too, that this decision had to be first about the Jesuits: remain or leave. Now we would have to begin again at some beginning, one that required its own new world of work and prayer. I thought of one of Kevin Burke's Western stories of a rancher whose dog kept him from walking any farther on a night when a thick fog covered the range. In the morning, when the fog had cleared, he saw that he stood at the edge of a great cliff. I knew that fog, and I knew that cliff. And standing at the edge as clarity rose to me, I found myself amazed at how far I could suddenly see. A wilderness and a paradise spread out in every direction. So that's what the old man had been trying to teach me all those years. I remembered my father and mother then, as I sat alone and at prayer in the hushed bearing of the main house chapel, and I wept. It was they who would take this leaving the hardest.

At midnight on my last day of retreat I woke and made one final meditation on the path that lay before me. I held the proverbial Jesuit's skull in my hand and asked: If I were at the moment of my death, would I be happy with this choice? And sleep came with the peacefulness of that prayer.

The next morning, a balmy one in March, I walked out to the pond, which had nearly broken free from its ice. Sheets moved and shifted in the deep, but along the banks there was clear spring water. On the grass, frost was general, but it wouldn't last more than a few hours. Winter was over. And though I've never had any theological affinity with Thoreau's brand of Transcendentalism, I couldn't help but think of *Walden* and the lines he wrote about leaving a place not more than a few miles away from here. "I left the woods for as good a reason as I went there." But as I packed up my bag in the room that had served as my cloister for the past eight days, returned the icon of Christ All-Merciful to the study in which I had found it, and walked down the stairs of Campion Renewal Center, I didn't feel so much the leaving, in spite of the heaviness of loss in the Society I would soon have to face. I felt what I had felt seven years ago when I stood outside Jogues Retreat House in Wernersville, Pennsylvania, a day of similar melting ice and early spring, a day on which I descended stairs knowing what I had done and what I had yet to do: "I am changed," I said to myself and walked out the front door.

Tom was already waiting in the driveway. Patrick, the scholastic from Detroit, was with him. Dressed in jeans and flannel shirts, they looked like bookish hoodlums leaning against the maroon Dodge Aries K that served as the all-purpose vehicle we were apportioned for distances outside the Cambridge environs.

"So? How was it?" Tom asked. What else could he ask?

I said, "Traveling in twos. Sent on a mission to come and get me."

"I thought I'd tag along for the ride," Patrick said, opening up the trunk. It was good to see them both, and I felt a tinge of regret and sadness at the presence and generosity of these men, brothers in the Lord. "Throw your bag in here. There's not much room in that back-seat."

I put my old Lowe pack, the same pack I had been carrying around with me since novitiate, on top of the spare tire.

"That's all you've got?" Patrick asked, and I said it was.

"All right then. Let's go home."

EPILOGUE

You'll no doubt want to hear how I fared when I left. If there was fear and trembling. If love lasted. Well, as the old preachers used to say when they meant "This is so." What I feared most was the uncertainty, the sudden flash that maybe, in the end, there would be nothing out there for me after having lived eight years as a Jesuit, and yes, that made me tremble. But when it came time to move out of the community in Cambridge, I felt the once familiar, disorienting, and yet strangely welcome drift of having crossed a river that bends and flows in a direction as natural as it is unexpected. While I've been scared a few times since then, I've never been afraid that my decision to leave the Jesuits was the wrong one. It was a need—to let another love me—and every day I admit that need.

Here are the details I remember. It was a Monday in July. The superior at Weston let me borrow the community pickup truck. Ivan and Patrick from the house, Mike Taylor from Philosophy Studies at Fordham (who had come for the summer to study Greek at Harvard), and Amelia all helped me lug my bags and boxes of books across town into the small upstairs room I'd found for rent on Traymore Street. When that was done, everyone had somewhere else to go. But Amelia lingered. We made plans for dinner that night and parted. "Our first date," she said over her shoulder.

Something else, too, about that morning, something that assuaged the fear.

I should have started job hunting right away. A check for fifteen hundred dollars that the formation assistant had sent to my new address was all I had for rent, food, and moving expenses. But I went upstairs and sat down on my unpacked stuff, paralyzed by the fact that I had no *ordo* to shape the hours, the week, my life. Anyone walking into that room would have been unable to discern if I had just arrived or was about to leave. What hasn't changed? I thought. What do I already do? Where can I begin while I wait to make a new beginning?

It wasn't quite noon, so I biked over to St. Paul's, hoping that I might catch the 12:00 Mass. I was early and took a seat in the middle pew, not too close to the altar, not too far from the door. The priest emerged from the sacristy to place the gifts on the side table and look over the readings, and it struck me then that this was something I would never do, prepare to celebrate the liturgy as an ordained minister. And I felt an overwhelming sense of gratitude for the knowledge that *his* place was a place I'd never belong, but that I still had a place in our collective earthly pilgrimage. If I had found myself one day on that altar, serving out of some sense of duty not to resist the pressure of what I had already begun, would I have done that duty nevertheless? I can't say. I can say, though, that I accepted then what I believe has always been my call to remain at least (as others have) a good and faithful servant, because there's still work to do in this fold. Work and prayer.

I wonder if there will come a time when stories like mine—like those of Frank, Billy, and Chris; or Mike Taylor and Harlan Fails, who also in their own discernment left the Jesuits—might be a puzzle to someone looking back on religious life in the twentieth century. They may see Catholic priests given the choice to search for a spiritual and physical partnership in marriage that is as deep as the single-mindedness of the celibate, one vow as worthy of ministry as the other. Or, more radical still, they may hear a woman's voice uttering the Eucharistic prayer with sacred host elevated in the pinch of thumb and two fingers at the holy sacrifice of the Mass. Ask me now, and I will tell you that I would welcome these changes, which some Catholics pray fervently will never happen, while others wait patiently for the day. And yet, regardless of what might change or stay the same, I know there will always be religious—the Benedictine, the Trappist, the Jesuit—living their seemingly timeless vows of poverty, chastity, and obedience, in the world but not of it, just as there will be those of us who followed that path with a kind of restlessness that wouldn't let us rest there. I say I know because one common striving binds us: certain and searching remain the nature of our belief. From where I write now, a husband, a father, a man of prayer in the Church that still guides me, I live with that as my compass.

So let me end here with what I can only call my continuing.

Today, the twenty-eighth of August 2006, is the name day of our son, Cole Augustin, a tradition that my mother taught me to observe and that I will hand down to my children as well. The boy is a wonder to Amelia and me. Playful, trusting, with just a hint of benign mischief and a smile set on his face in which I see brief flashes of my father. He is beautiful, a gift undeserved. David McCallum, SJ, five years a priest and sixteen years later still my friend, came all the way from New York to baptize him at Holy Trinity Church in West London, which Amelia and I call home for now. And it occurs to me that there was a day this past month when I could say, finally, that I have been making my way on this leg of the journey longer than I made my way as a Jesuit. (Somehow the milestone escaped me.) If I'm certain of anything after all that time of searching, it is this: faith is not just the substance of things hoped for but what is given and what we receive, changed in the solitude and communion of a long retreat.

ACKNOWLEDGMENTS

I am most grateful to my agent, Betsy Lerner, for her unwavering belief in this work, right from the start. Paul Elie, my editor at Farrar, Straus and Giroux, pushed me to a place of deeper candor. His assistant, Cara Spitalewitz, led me patiently through the nuts and bolts of production. James Martin, SJ, and Lori Toppel read through and commented meticulously on the entire manuscript when I really needed their good ears and sharp eyes as writers. David McCallum, SJ, was (and remains) my wise Jesuit counsel on all matters personal, literary, and spiritual. Royal Hansen and Stein Wivestad gave me a great deal of feedback on an early draft of this story. And I owe a debt of gratitude to a number of people who have either read various sections of this book or helped me to track down and confirm (or deny) information: Jared Crawford, Harriet Davidson, Francis Evans, Susan Hamilton, Patricia Hampl, William Hogan, John T. Krivak, Matthew Krivak, David Lloyd, Paul Mariani, Jack Martin, Jeffrey Stachnick, and Jeffrey Trexler.

I want to single out my mother, Irene Krivak, and my late father, Thomas F. Krivak, for their own place in this writing endeavor. I am grateful to them not only for the many books they gave me the chance to read but for a faith that cannot be found in books.

There are a few editors I wish to thank for giving me writing jobs when I needed them most: Paul Baumann (*Commonweal*), Ben Birnbaum (*Boston College Magazine*), Robert Coles (*DoubleTake*), Nancy Newhouse (*New York Times,* Travel section), and Patrick Queen (*Columbia Magazine*).

ACKNOWLEDGMENTS

The Cambridge University Faculty of Divinity, Cambridge, England, let me use their library and resources as a visiting scholar during the 2004–2005 academic year, which was invaluable to my research. While I was there, Professor Denys Turner and Edward Morgan were helpful interlocutors. I am grateful, too, to Dr. Gordon Johnson, president of Wolfson College, Cambridge, for inviting me into the Wolfson community at a time when he could not have known how much it meant to me. I also read an early chapter of this book at a Wolfson College Small Talk Colloquium in the spring of 2004 and had, with the few good souls who turned up, an interesting discussion on the nature of religious narratives. And here in London, a special thanks to Marc Fox and Clara Kwan, who provided me with a computer to use when my older, shakier laptop gave up the ghost in the final stages of completing this manuscript.

Finally, this book would not have been written without the support, encouragement, and love of my wife, Amelia Dunlop. She asked me in the fall of 2000, the year we were married and after I had been telling her countless stories about "the Company" I kept in the Jesuits, to "tell me what it was like from the beginning." I wrote a hundred pages and gave them to her for Christmas. That was the start of this writer's journey, and since then, she's read every word.